Information Systems Foundations: Constructing and Criticising

Information Systems Foundations: Constructing and Criticising

Dennis N. Hart and Shirley D. Gregor (Editors)

ANU

THE AUSTRALIAN NATIONAL UNIVERSITY

E PRESS

Workshop Chair

Shirley D. Gregor *ANU*

Program Chairs

Dennis N. Hart *ANU*
Shirley D. Gregor *ANU*

Program Committee

Bob Colomb *University of Queensland*
Brian Corbitt *Deakin University*
Colin Freeman *ANU*
Chris Freyberg *Massey University*
Sigi Goode *ANU*
Peter Green *University of Queensland*
Juhani Iivari *University of Oulu*
Robert Johnston *University of Melbourne*
Eija Koskivaara *Turku University*
John Lamp *Deakin University*
Ed Lewis *Australian Defence Force Academy*
Nigel Martin *ANU*
Mike Metcalfe *University of South Australia*
Craig McDonald *University of Canberra*
Simon Milton *University of Melbourne*
Steven Pace *Central Queensland University*
Michael Rosemann *Queensland University of Technology*
Elizabeth Tansley *Central Queensland University*
Tim Turner *Australian Defence Force Academy*
Leoni Warne *Defence Science and Technology Organisation*

ANU
E PRESS

Published by ANU E Press
The Australian National University
Canberra ACT 0200, Australia
Email: anuepress@anu.edu.au
Web: http://epress.anu.edu.au

Cataloguing-in-Publication information is available from the National Library of Australia

ISBN 1 9209 4221 1

ISBN 1 9209 4220 3 (online)

Cover design by Brendon McKinley with logo by Michael Gregor
Authors' photographs on back cover: ANU Photography

Contents

List of figures

List of tables

Information systems foundations

This volume contains the papers presented at the Information Systems Foundations: Constructing and Criticising Workshop at The Australian National University from 16 to 17 July 2004.

The focus of the workshop was on the theoretical foundations of information systems and the practical implications of candidate bodies of theory both from within the discipline and in related areas. In particular, the central aims were to critically assess the current theoretical foundations of the discipline, to determine where these foundations might be lacking, to build on, extend or improve them where possible, and to draw out their implications for practice.

The workshop was the second in a biennial series focusing on the theoretical foundations of the discipline of information systems held at The Australian National University. We believe the first workshop in 2002 achieved its aim of presenting papers that were both thought provoking and stimulating and the second workshop sustained this tradition. Requests for the Proceedings of the 2002 Workshop continue, an indication that the work of our participants is valued. Both workshops have allowed discussion among delegates and social interaction in pleasant surroundings and a distinctive feature of the workshops has been the general spirit of enthusiasm and camaraderie that has pervaded both occasions.

It is probably fair to say that since our first workshop there has been an increasing emphasis in the information systems discipline on the nature and bounds of knowledge of the discipline and the nature of the artefacts with which it deals, in addition to the epistemological issues that have been a primary focus of attention for some time. Our workshop aims are congruent with this trend and through the focus on questions of fundamental theoretical importance, our authors should stimulate further debate to the benefit of theory and practice.

The papers contained here were accepted after a double-blind review process and we thank our program committee and reviewers for their assistance.

We also acknowledge and thank the sponsors of the workshop: the School of Business and Information Management and the National Institute for Economics and Business at The Australian National University. Thanks are also due to Dora Gava for assistance with the workshop organisation and to Sigi Goode who acted as webmaster.

David Kennedy of the Department of Communication, Information Technology and the Arts provided a thought-provoking keynote speech addressing the contributions of information technologies and systems nationally, which provided a good grounding for subsequent discussions.

We dedicate this volume to Kit Dampney, who died in March, 2004. Kit was the organiser of a previous Information Systems Foundation workshop at Macquarie University in 1999, which sowed the seeds for our current workshop series. Kit was genuinely esteemed in our community and his vitality and passion for his work and for communicating his ideas will be well remembered. His own work in mathematical category theory and information structures was significant. Janet Aisbett has written a moving tribute to Kit, which is available from the web site of the *Dampney Centre for IT Applications*, named in Kit's honour [1] .

---

[1] http://dcita.newcastle.edu.au/dcita_news3.htm

To conclude, we honour Kit Dampncy's memory and inspiration and thank our delegates and authors for their participation.

We look forward to another successful workshop in 2006.

Dennis Hart
Shirley Gregor

Part I. Foundations of information systems theory and research

1. The struggle towards an understanding of theory in information systems

Shirley Gregor, *School of Business and Information Management, The Australian National University*

Abstract

Information systems (IS) is a relatively new discipline with many researchers having their foundation studies in other disciplines. The IS discipline is moving towards some sense of its own identity and some agreement on what constitutes suitable foci of research. Coming from other fields of study, however, our researchers bring perspectives on particular modes of enquiry and methodological paradigms as well as perspectives on what is meant by 'theory'. The argument of this paper is that IS needs to critically examine the types of theorising relevant to its own discipline and recognise the unique nature of the theory that is needed. Perspectives found useful come from the philosophy of science (excluding positivism), interpretivism and Herbert Simon's depiction of the sciences of the artificial. It is shown how these perspectives can be melded, leading to a typology of interrelated theories that is unique to information systems.

Introduction

This paper is, logically, a precursor to an earlier paper that sets out the different interrelated types of theory that can be employed in information systems research, namely: (i) descriptive theory, (ii) theory for understanding, (iii) theory for predicting, (iv) theory for explanation and prediction, and (v) theory for design and action (Gregor, 2002). What that paper failed to do was show clearly why the distinctive nature of the information systems discipline requires a perspective on theorising all of its own. The aim of this current paper is to show clearly how ideas can be combined from some views of theory in supporting disciplinary areas to give a typology of theories that is appropriate for information systems research.

The information systems discipline is relatively new. Many researchers studied originally in disparate areas ranging from physics and chemistry to mathematics, psychology and sociology. It is perhaps natural that researchers will bring with them from these areas different views on the nature of theory, knowledge and epistemology. It is unfortunate, however, if we do not stop to think whether and how ideas from different disciplines apply in the information systems field. The argument in this paper is that information systems, being a field that requires knowledge pertaining to the world of physical systems, the world of human behaviour, and the world of designed artefacts, requires theorising that relates to all these types of knowledge and allows them to be addressed in an integrated manner. While ideas on the nature of theory can be taken from other disciplinary areas, this borrowing should not be done uncritically, but with an eye on the unique nature of information systems.

Information systems can be defined as:

the effective design, delivery, use and impact of information technology in organisations and society (Avison and Fitzgerald, 1995, p. xi).

Information systems is not another management field, like organisational behaviour (contrary to the view of Webster and Watson, 2002), neither is it about technology alone, like computer science. A characteristic that distinguishes information systems from these fields is that it concerns the use of artefacts in human-machine systems. Lee (2001, p iii) uses these words:

> research in the information systems field examines more than just the techno-logical system, or just the social system, or even the two side by side; in addi-tion, it investigates the phenomena that emerge when the two interact.

Thus, we have a discipline that is at the intersection of knowledge of the properties of physical objects (machines) and knowledge of human behaviour. Information systems can be seen to have commonalities with other design disciplines such as architecture or engineering, which also concern both people and artefacts, or with other applied discip-lines such as medicine, where the products of scientific knowledge (drugs, treatments) are used with people. Necessary knowledge for information systems encompasses the knowledge types found in the natural sciences (e.g. the properties of a communications medium), the social sciences (e.g. change management), mathematics (e.g. representational languages) and technology (e.g. design of an artefact).

Dictionary definitions show that the word 'theory' can take on many meanings, including: 'the general or abstract principles of a body of fact, a science, or an art', 'a belief, policy, or procedure proposed or followed as the basis of action', 'a plausible or scientifically acceptable general principle or body of principles offered to explain phenomena', 'a hypothesis assumed for the sake of argument or investigation' (Merriam-Webster, 2004).

In the remainder of the paper a number of different views of theory are given, choosing perspectives that are relevant to different facets of information systems work. Thus, perspectives are taken from the philosophy of science, encompassing both the natural and social sciences, and from theory of technology. Interpretivism and positivism are dealt with separately as they are so often referred to in information systems research, though usually in discussions of research methods rather than in terms of formulating theory. Positivism is presented first, basically to clarify some areas that are often confused and to argue that it is not a defensible position.

The aim in presenting these different views is to show how they can all (except positivism) be drawn upon to propose a 'theory of theories' in information systems that addresses the field's unique nature.

The lingering death of positivism

Positivism is a term used frequently in discussions of research in information systems, but rarely is it treated in depth or in terms of its historical development. Many philo-sophers of science regard positivism as defunct: 'Logical positivism, then, is dead, or as dead as a philosophical movement ever becomes' (Passmore, 1967). Why then is the term still used so uncritically in information systems? Positivism is discussed here in some detail to show the shortcomings detected by philosophers of science and to pave the way for less narrow views on theory from the philosophy of science.

Some sense of the historical development of positivist schools of thought is beneficial (see Godfrey-Smith, 2003; Magee, 1997). Comte (1864) is generally credited with the coining of the term 'positivism', using the word to contrast actual with imaginary, certainty with the undecided, the exact in contrast to the indefinite. Logical positivism as an extreme form of empiricism was developed in Europe after the First World War by what became known as the Vienna Circle, established by Moritz Schlick and Otto Neurath. It was formed in opposition to systems of philosophical thought that the logical positivists found pretentious, obscure, dogmatic and politically unattractive (such as Hegelian idealism). Logical positivism was a plea for Enlightenment values, in opposition to mysticism, romanticism and nationalism (Godfrey-Smith, 2003). A. J. Ayer, G. E. Moore and Bertrand Russell were responsible for the transposition of the ideas of logical positivism to England where they had a profound effect, with much of English philosophy retaining a strong empiricist emphasis ever since.

Many of the Vienna Circle were Jewish and had socialist leanings. They were persecuted to varying degrees by the Nazis, who made use of pro-German, anti-liberal philosophers, and who also tended to be obscure as well as anti-liberal. In contrast to the logical positivists, Martin Heidegger joined the Nazi party and remained a member throughout the Second World War. Some logical positivists – Carnap, Reichenbach, Hempel and Feigl – escaped to the United States where they were influential in philosophical development after the war. There was some softening and re-specification of the tenets of logical positivism and the later more moderate views are more usually called 'logical empiricism' (Godfrey-Smith, 2003).

At the base of logical positivism is the famous Verification Principle. This says that only assertions that are in principle verifiable by observation or experience can convey factual information and be meaningful. Assertions that have no imaginable method of verification must either be analytic (tautological) or meaningless (Magee, 1997). Thus, the two central ideas of logical positivism relate to language: the analytic-synthetic distinction and the verifiability theory of meaning. The first idea relates to the distinction between analytic statements, which are true in themselves (basically a tautology), and synthetic statements, which are true or false in relation to how the world is. The second idea is that experience is the only source of meaning and the only source of knowledge. Thus, if a sentence (in a theory, say) has no possible means of verification, it has no meaning. Scientific statements were to consist of verifiable, and hence meaningful, claims.

Karl Popper in his autobiography (Popper, 1986) takes the credit for 'killing' logical positivism as early as 1934 by pointing out some of its mistakes in *Logic der Forschung* (Popper, 1934), not published until 1959 in English as The *Logic of Scientific Discovery* (Popper, 1980). Popper was opposed to the concentration upon minutiae and especially upon the meaning of words by the logical positivists, and the avoidance of metaphysical problems. A difficulty with the Verification Principle is that it is neither analytic nor empirically verifiable itself and therefore, according to its own criterion, is meaningless. The Verification Principle has the effect of outlawing more or less the whole of metaphysical speculation in philosophy – everything apart from logic. Popper also showed that the Verification Principle eliminated almost the whole of science. An aim of science is the search for natural laws, which are unrestrictedly general statements about the world that are known to be invariantly true: for example, Boyle's Law, the law of gravity, or $E=mc^2$. Popper showed that these laws are not empirically verifiable, acknowledging that the English empiricist David Hume had made this observation two-and-a-half centuries before. The problem is that of induction: from no finite number of observations, however large, can any unrestrictedly general conclusion be drawn that would be defensible in logic. For example, we cannot prove 'all swans are black' no matter how many swans we observe.

The point of this discussion of positivism is that positivism is just one philosophical perspective on science, and a form that has largely been debunked. Focussing on positivism as being representative of views about theoretical formulation and epistemology in science obscures the rich value that can be found in many other writings in the philosophy of science, as discussed in the following section. The information systems literature provides many instances where 'positivism' is a label given to various, often conflicting, impressions of what scientific thought means. This habit is so widespread that no opprobrium should attach to the identification of particular instances. Positivism is characterised as being associated with naïve realism, a 'value-free' view of scientific enquiry, hypothetico-deductive methods, unilateral causal relationships or laws, statistical analysis and so on (see Orlowski and Baroudi, 1991). This depiction obviously does not match the original tenets of logical positivism, and neither is it compatible with the writings of prominent philosophers of science (see Nagel, 1979). Discussion of positivism is lingering on in information systems and our researchers are seemingly unaware that it is moribund. Orlowski and Baroudi (1991), for example, footnote the possibility that positivist dogma may be losing its currency among mainstream natural scientists, seemingly unaware of its recognised killing-off many years previously in what can only be regarded as very mainstream philosophy of science (Popper, 1936; Passmore, 1967).

The author believes that 'positivism' should no longer be even mentioned as a defensible position in discussions of theory or epistemology in information systems. If what is meant is a scientific perspective, then it is better to say so; to go directly to writings in the philosophy of science and to examine issues separately and carefully. The conclusion from this summary of positivism is that it is not a fruitful source of ideas on theorising in information systems.

A 'scientific' perspective

Unfortunately, if we turn to the philosophy of science for views on theory we still find disagreement on many important issues. Godfrey-Smith (2003) notes that there has been a state of fermentation in recent years concerning many problems: causality, the distinction between experimental laws and theories, induction, and the cognitive status of theories, to name just a few. Some of the views of prominent philosophers that appear especially relevant to at least some types of information systems theory are discussed here. Note, however, that the term 'post-positivist' is not appropriate for describing these views since some are pre-positivist (Hume, Locke, Kant) and some are anti-positivist (Popper).

Sir Karl Popper is a philosopher of science whose views appeal to many working scientists and who is regarded as a hero by many (Godfrey-Smith, 2003). Popper (1980, p. 59) gives this view of theory:

> Scientific theories are universal statements. Like all linguistic representations they are systems of signs or symbols. Theories are nets cast to catch what we call 'the world'; to rationalise, to explain and to master it. We endeavour to make the mesh ever finer and finer.

Popper sees theories as uncertain and as approximate representations of reality. His ontological position recognises theory as having an existence separate from the subjective understanding of individuals. Theory is an inhabitant of World 3, the objectively existing but abstract world of man-made entities – language, mathematics, knowledge, science, art, ethics, and institutions, for example. Other worlds are World 1, the objective world of material things, and World 2, the subjective world of mental states (Popper, 1986).

Popper saw the work of science as being to take a theory that is proposed, to deduce an observational prediction from it, and then to test the prediction. If the prediction fails, then we have refuted or falsified the theory. If the prediction is supported, then all we can say is that the theory has not been falsified – yet. This position is referred to as the 'hypothetico-deductive' model and is reasonably common among philosophers of science and practising scientists.

Popper was not much concerned about where theories come from in the first place, and was strongly opposed to the use of inductive methods in science; that is, in building or supporting a theory on the basis of a large number of observations of a certain kind. Popper has been criticised on these grounds and others have included, in the hypothetico-deductive model, a first stage in which observations are collected and a conjecture (a theory) is generated from these observations (Godfrey-Smith, 2003).

Space precludes a detailed treatment of many of the compelling issues that are discussed under the heading of the philosophy of science. In summary, views that appear useful in discussion of information system theory, which in synthesis can be referred to as a 'scientific perspective' of theory and theorising follow:

1. Theories, as systematic and responsibly supported explanations, are the aim of science. Such explanations may be offered for individual occurrences, for recurring processes or for invariable as well as statistical regularities. The explanations offered can rely on different ideas of causality and what constitutes an explanation (Nagel, 1979, p. 15).
2. Theorising, in part, involves the specification of universal statements in a form that enables them to be tested against observations of what occurs in the real world (Popper, 1980).
3. Some propose a distinction between experimental laws and theories, though the distinction is not clear-cut (Nagel, 1979). Experimental laws, such as the gas laws, which relate pressure, temperature and volume in invariant relationships, refer to 'observable' entities in at least a loose sense of the word. Theories, on the other hand, tend to offer a more comprehensive interrelated set of explanations and include terms like 'molecule' or 'gene' which are less readily directly observable, relying on assumptions for their definition. This point is interesting because the experimental laws, which may result from close observation and description of nature, and not necessarily impute causality, may give rise to a broader scientific theory. For example, an experimental law arising from observation, such as 'All platypuses suckle their young', can be eventually fitted into a theory about the nature of mammals.
4. It is expected that theories and laws in the social sciences, for a number of reasons, will be pervasively generalised in statistical terms (e.g. 'most rural Americans belong to some religious organisation'). Compared with the natural sciences, theories in the social sciences will have narrower scope, or lower-order generality (Nagel, 1979). This observation is not intended pejoratively as social scientists can still manage to advance explanations for a large variety of social phenomena.
5. Dubin (1978) gives a very detailed treatment of how theories can be specified in the social sciences, which is in accord with the scientific perspective described here. He describes how theory can be used for both understanding and prediction, and how ideally it should deal with both process and outcomes.
6. The development of theory or conjectures in the first place can occur in many ways: as a result of observations of what occurs in the real world (Nagel, 1979; Godfrey-Smith, 2003) or from insights, imagination, problems or feelings (Popper, 1980).

7. Scientific theory often, but not always, involves the use of mathematical tools and logic, both for specifying and testing theory (Godfrey-Smith, 2003).

8. Epistemologically, knowledge for the building and testing of theories, can be gained both empirically (the 'empiricist' tradition of Locke and Hume) and from thinking (the 'rationalist' view of Descartes and Leibniz). Kant (1781) developed this intermediate position: that thinking involves a subtle interaction between experiences and pre-existing mental structures that we use to make sense of experience, and others, including Schopenhauer and Popper, have followed in this tradition.

9. Naïve realism is not necessarily a part of a scientific perspective, and neither is a theory-neutral view of observations of the real world (see Godfrey-Smith, 2003 for a 'scientific realist' view).

This scientific view of theorising has been little recognised in information systems research, usually because writers in the field confuse scientific views with positivism. Researchers who use Dubin's principles for the formulation of theory are implicitly following a scientific-like prescription (e.g. Weber, 1997).

An exception in information systems is Lee (1989), who explicitly describes a scientific methodology for case studies and provides a description of the scientific method that is largely congruent with the perspective given above. A second exception is Cushing (1990), who describes the role of frameworks, paradigms and scientific research in management information systems in similar terms, and suggests that frameworks are a precursor to the development of theory with generalisations and laws. Otherwise, the richness of the discussions in the philosophy of science on the nature of theory has been little recognised in information systems as a source for our perspective on theory.

From this discussion of scientific views of theory, we can draw several useful ideas for information systems. Observation of phenomena can precede analysis and description (Type I and Type II theory) and description of regularities (predictive Type III theory). Scientific-type laws that allow both prediction and understanding can also be searched for, but as they will have aspects of human social behaviour included, they are likely to be cast in a probabilistic form (Type IV theory below). Insights for a new theory can come from almost anywhere.

Interpretivism and constructivism

Intrepretivism and constructivism are related approaches to research that are characteristic of particular philosophical world views. Schwandt (1994) describes these terms as sensitising concepts that steer researchers towards a particular outlook:

> Proponents of these persuasions share the goal of understanding the complex world of lived experience from the point of view of those who live it. This goal is variously spoken of as an abiding concern for the life world, for the emic point of view, for understanding meaning, for grasping the actor's definition of a situation, for Verstehen. The world of lived reality and situation-specific meanings that constitute the general object of investigation is thought to be constructed by social actors (p. 118).

Many of the ideas in these approaches stem from the German intellectual tradition of hermeneutics and the *Verstehen* tradition in sociology, from phenomenology, and from critiques of positivism in the social sciences. Interpretivists reject the notions of theory-neutral observations and the idea of universal laws as in science. Theory in this paradigm takes on a different perspective:

> Knowledge consists of those constructions about which there is a relative consensus (or at least some movement towards consensus) among those competent (and in the case of more arcane material, trusted) to interpret the substance of the construction. Multiple 'knowledges' can coexist when equally competent (or trusted) interpreters disagree (Guba and Lincoln, 1994, p. 113).

The emergence of interpretivism in information system research is described by Walsham (1995). Walsham saw interpretivism as gaining ground at that point against a predominantly positivist research tradition in information systems. Klein and Myers (1999) consider that theory plays a crucial role in interpretive research in information systems. Theory is used as a 'sensitising device' to view the world in a certain way. Particular observations can be related to abstract categories and to ideas and concepts that apply to multiple situations, implying some generalisability. The types of theory that information systems researchers are likely to reference are social theories such as structuration theory or actor-network theory.

The interpretivist paradigm leads to a view of theory which is theory for understanding (Type III), theory that possibly does not have strong predictive power and is of limited generality.

The technological perspective

Information systems involve the use of information technology and so we would like theory that can deal with technologies. Recognition that theory might relate to technology is rather uncommon and it might even be that there is definite prejudice against it. This view may go back a long way. O'Hear (1989, p. 216) says the ancient Greeks tended to despise the merely mechanistic or banausic. Popper saw the worship of science and technology as instruments for control over nature as shallow and worrying because of our ignorance of the effects our interventions might have. Nevertheless, the development of science and the development of technology have gone on hand-in-hand. For example, the start of the scientific revolution 'coincided' with the (mid-16th century) development of the telescope and the microscope (Gribbin, 2002, xix)

The classic work that treats technology or artefact design as a special prescriptive type of theory is Herbert Simon's *The Sciences of the Artificial* (1996), first published in 1969. Simon (1996, p. xii) notes that in an earlier edition of his work he described a central problem that had occupied him for many years:

> How could one construct an empirical theory?

> I thought I began to see in the problem of artificiality an explanation of the difficulty that has been experienced in filling engineering and other professions with empirical and theoretical substance distinct from the substance of their supporting sciences. Engineering, medicine, business, architecture and painting are concerned not with the necessary but with the contingent – not with how things are but with how they might be – in short, with design.

Simon contrasts design science with natural science, which is concerned with knowledge about natural objects and phenomena. Design science must take account of natural science since an artefact is a meeting-place or interface between the inner environment of the artefact and the outer environment in which it performs, both of which operate in accordance with natural laws. Simon discussed design science in the contexts of economics, the psychology of cognition, and planning and engineering design, but not information systems. It has taken some time for Simon's ideas to filter through to information systems and they are still not unequivocally accepted in this discipline.

Weber (1987), for example, recognised difficulties with design work in information systems. He saw the 'lure of design and construction' as a factor inhibiting the progress of information systems as a discipline and called for theory that gave information systems a paradigmatic base.

In 1992, Simon's ideas were adopted and applied to consideration of information systems design theory by Walls et al. (1992). Recently the ideas of these authors have enjoyed some currency, as shown in the specification of a design theory for knowledge management systems by Markus, Majchrzak and Gasser (2002). The explication of information systems design theory by Walls et al. (1992) is probably the most complete and thorough to date. Since 1992, there have been varying and rather scattered approaches to the problem and articulation of design theory in information systems and allied fields. March and Smith (1995) and Hevner et al. (2004) followed Simon's ideas closely, but with an important difference. They saw design science products as comprised of four types: constructs, models, methods, and implementations, but excluded theories. Jarvinen (2001) expresses similar views.

More recently, Iivari (2003) argued that determining the distinctive identity of information systems relies on the recognition that our knowledge and theory is concerned with the developing and building of information system artefacts.

Thus, these considerations provide a justification for a fifth type of theory of interest to information systems researchers: theory for design and action (Type V).

A typology of theory for information systems

The perspectives presented above provide justification for distinguishing five different interrelated types of theory that are relevant to information systems research (see Figure 1.1). Each type is described more fully in Gregor, (2002).

Figure 1.1. Interrelationships among theory types.

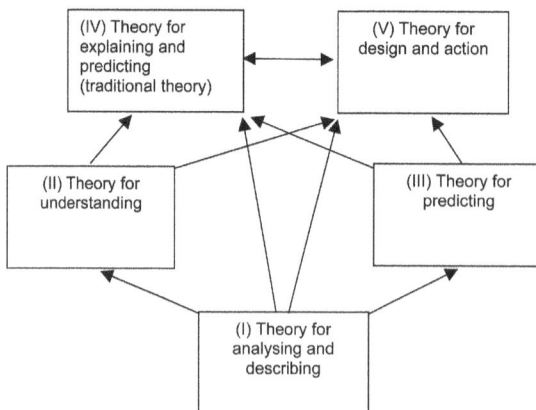

Type I. Theory for analysing and describing

Descriptive theory says 'what is' and is the basis for all other types of theory. Description and specification of constructs in theories of this type are needed (Dubin, 1978), as are descriptive frameworks that specify and classify the phenomena of interest in a theoretical domain (Cushing, 1990).

Type II. Theory for understanding

This type of theory says how and why something occurred. Theory from interpretive approaches can be used as sensitising devices that allow greater insights into familiar situations (Klein and Myers, 1999). Conjectures can be drawn on the basis of a number of limited observations that are used as a basis for hypothesis formation and theory building.

Type III. Theory for predicting

Predictive theories say what will be, given the presence of certain conditions. These theories give predictive power without necessarily having explanatory power (Dubin, 1978). Again, knowledge of this type, such as statistical regularities, can yield hypotheses for theory building.

Type IV. Theory for explaining and predicting

This type of theory says what is, how, why, and what will be. It is the type of theory commonly specified in the 'scientific' perspective (Dubin, 1978).

Type V. Theory for design and action

Design theory is the prescriptive type of theory that gives principles for the construction of a tool or artefact to meet a set of meta-requirements (Hevner et al., 2004; Iivari, 2003; Simon, 1996). Design theory is informed by, and can inform, theory for explaining and predicting.

Concluding remarks

The purpose of this paper is to show that the distinctive nature of information systems research, being concerned conjointly with the study of artefacts and human behaviour, requires a meta-understanding of theory that draws on work from the philosophy of science (both natural and social) in addition to work on the sciences of the artificial. Some of the misunderstandings surrounding the concept of positivism also need to be exposed and removed, so that full value can be gained from readings in the philosophy of science, which underpins notions of theorising. The outcome is that five interrelated forms of theory can be distinguished, all of which are needed for information systems research. Acknowledging the contribution that each type of theory can make will allow work in information systems to proceed in a more integrated manner.

2. Information systems theory as cultural capital: an argument for the development of 'grand' theory

Douglas Hamilton, *School of Information Management and Systems, Monash University, Victoria*

Abstract

Bourdieu's concepts of social fields and social power provide a theoretical basis for the view that the IS field is engaged in an ongoing struggle with other disciplines for academic prestige and support. While IS has produced a considerable amount of high quality theory and research, it is by no means clear that this is understood either by the academy or by the general public. The issue has become problematic to the extent that IS now faces something of a public identity crisis. It is claimed that broad or 'grand' theories play valuable roles as items of cultural capital for other disciplines, and that an IS theory of this type would help to address the visibility problem. It is further proposed that an opportunity to develop such a theory is currently available, and that IS academics are ideally placed to interpret phenomena generated by the spread of standardised IS concepts throughout the business world.

Introduction

The proposal in this paper is that the development of a prestigious grand theory in the information systems (IS) field is possible, opportune, and would be of considerable benefit to the field. 'Prestigious' is taken in this context to mean achieving a degree of renown, ideally with the public at large, but at least within the academy. While significant benefits could derive from the application of such a theory in research and practice, its primary value to the discipline would be as a resource contributing to its public image. An influential theory is a statement that its originating discipline is a source of marketable ideas, and worthy therefore of interest and respect.

The theoretical grounding for the paper is derived primarily from Bourdieu's concepts of social power and social fields (Bourdieu, 1980; Bourdieu and Wacquant, 1992; Swartz, 1997). On this, the IS field –comprising an array of academics, professionals, and institutions – is conceptualised as engaged in a more or less continuous struggle for relative power and status with other disciplines. The assets supporting or enabling participation in such struggles include both economic and cultural capital, where cultural capital is the combination of ideas, knowledge and research that are seen as intrinsically linked to the field, and which form the basis for its academic and community standing (Bourdieu, 1980). Major theories are, in this perspective, items of symbolic capital that have value as the end products of significant intellectual efforts.

While popular theory is always likely to be of benefit to a discipline (Abbott, 1988), such a development would be particularly opportune within the IS field at a time when talk of disciplinary crisis is in the air (Markus, 1999; Khazanchi and Munkvold, 2000; Benbasat and Zmud, 2003; Hirschheim and Klein, 2003). In relating the development of theory to the issue of disciplinary success, the argument is that the visibility and prestige of other disciplines has been shown to depend partly on their capacity to engage the public's interest in their intellectual products (Abbott, 2001). 'The public' in this context can be construed in a number of ways, ranging from a general population concerned with a variety of social trends and issues, to academic authorities responsible for allocating funds and determining relative resourcing priorities (Slaughter and Leslie, 1997).

The term 'grand theory' is used here to refer to the type of overarching theory constituted by a set of umbrella concepts designed to explain a broad range of social phenomena, and robust enough to act as the conceptual framework for a variety of research programs dealing with empirical data. Examples from other disciplines would include Marxism (Marx, 1981), psychoanalysis (Freud, 1938) and rational choice (Coleman, 1990). It is notable that such theories do not need to be generally accepted as correct to have a public impact, as recurrent surges of interest in Margaret Mead's anthropological theories demonstrate (Freeman, 1997; Freeman, 2000).

The claim that theory can be valuable is not to say that a powerful theory can be developed on request. But the argument in this paper extends to the claim that there is at least one area of general interest that IS theorists are ideally placed to address. The types of phenomena of concern are discussed in detail later in the paper, but can be briefly outlined here. In broad terms, the view is that IS structures for dealing with some basic types of business transactions such as account payments are becoming highly standardised and pervasive in social life, and are beginning to reduce the number of possibilities for social change. A number of related trends are driving this development, including data sharing among organisations and government departments, inter-organisational systems based on generalised data and process definitions, the emergence of systems with some degree of social autonomy (automated teller machines provide a simple but representative example [Dos Santos and Peffers, 1995]), and the widespread adoption of high profile proprietary enterprise software packages from vendors such as SAP and Oracle (Davenport, 1998). This trend and its social effects do not appear to have received comprehensive theoretical treatment in the IS field or elsewhere; in IS because the extant theories of IS integration (Segars and Grover, 1996; Wyzalek, 2000) and competitive advantage (Kettinger et al., 1995) that deal with large-scale IS structures do not address wider social effects, and elsewhere because theorists in other fields have tended to gloss over IS realities in favour of highly generalised and bland assumptions about IT capabilities (e.g. Bogard, 1996).

The view that gave rise to the development of this paper is that the IS field has an urgent need to improve its public profile, and that theory development along the proposed lines can help to achieve this. The underlying assumption is that the field is in fact in a state of crisis (Hirschheim and Klein, 2003), and that this stems from a combination of lost visibility with an emerging identity problem (Benbasat and Zmud, 2003). The presumption here is that IS is a significant discipline that addresses a specific set of issues and interests using its own concepts and techniques (Hirschheim and Klein, 2003). The need is, however, to convince external parties that IS offers value that cannot be provided by other disciplines, and that it addresses a particular set of practical and theoretical issues better than any potential competitor could.

Information systems: fading into the background

Contemporary studies of academic life suggest that a strong profile within the academy is crucial to disciplinary success (Slaughter and Leslie, 1997; Aronowitz, 2000). If this view is correct, then it follows that recognition is even more important for a discipline like IS that is struggling for an identity distinct from computer science at one extreme, and business studies at the other. The assumption that the importance of recognition has actually increased recently is predicated on the view that the field is facing a long-term reduction in its funding (and hence a loss of economic capital) consequent on a decrease in the number of students enrolled and a loss of management faith in the discipline (Hirschheim and Klein, 2003). A more concentrated focus on the development of cultural capital, at least for the time being, would seem to be mandatory.

The question of visibility is seen here as the critical issue. While internal disputes about the nature of the discipline and the constitution of its 'core' (Benbasat and Zmud, 2003) can be taken as a sign of disciplinary vitality, uncertainty about disciplinary content can become a problem when it is coupled with a low external recognition factor (Avgerou et al., 1999, p. 136). One probable outcome is a decrease in the extent to which the general public will recognise IS either as an area of independent interest, or as a source of acceptable jobs for young people, including new graduates.

It is of course possible to identify quite a number of related areas where IS contributions are significant, including knowledge management, IT governance, IT management, e-business, e-government and many more (Baskerville and Myers, 2002). But it is also correct to say that these topics generally fall within academically contested areas, and that other disciplines are staking their claims to ownership of some of the key issues, usually by developing courses and units dealing with those topics. At the same time, traditional IS concerns with systems definition and building are increasingly being subsumed by analysts and consultants better described as working in applied business and economics than in IS. 'Green field' systems development, on which the discipline first built its foundations (Somogyi and Galliers, 1987), is becoming progressively less significant as the business environment moves ever closer to full automation, and the prevalence of proprietary software and packaged technical solutions increases (Gosain, 2004). The danger is that the building of systems will increasingly be regarded as a purely technical matter, and that the more interesting questions of systems meaning and social significance will be arrogated by other disciplines.

The view presented here is a pessimistic one with respect to the discipline's current standing, and it is therefore important to note alternative views. Perhaps the most positive perspective put forward in the last couple of years was in a major paper by Baskerville and Myers (2002), where the authors claim that IS has made the academic and intellectual strides necessary for the discipline to be seen as fully independent, and therefore able to take its place as a source of ideas for other disciplines. Accepted at face value, this claim would invalidate the argument presented in this paper. The following discussion therefore focuses on the key issues raised by the authors, with a view to identifying points of disagreement. It should be noted that there is no fundamental disagreement about the general value of IS work – the question of concern is whether high quality IS output is having, or more importantly will have in the future, any significance outside IS.

'Information systems as a reference discipline' – Baskerville and Myers

Baskerville and Myers make a case that the IS discipline is not only in good academic health, but also that it has reached a state of maturity: 'the IS discipline is no longer just emerging, but has fully emerged as a discipline in its own right' (Baskerville and Myers, 2002, p. 1). With maturity now achieved, it will become a source of ideas for other disciplines, in the same way that those disciplines have been a source of ideas for IS. As support for this, they point to the concern with rigour that has been a hallmark of IS research practice, the establishment of high quality journals, the emergence of IS 'bodies of knowledge', the development of IS literature, and the establishment of an 'excellent scholarly communication network' (Baskerville and Myers, 2002, pp. 3-5).

It would be possible to debate some of the issues the authors raise on a point-by-point basis. The bodies of knowledge they identify are, for instance, strongly oriented towards applications (and hence are appropriate to an applied discipline), whereas whatever references there are to abstract theory tend to be to speech act theory, socio-technical concepts, social construction, and other concepts that originate in other fields (Baskerville and Myers, 2002, p. 4). But while this is not just a minor concern, it is possible for the purposes of this paper to accept the authors' major statements as fact, and still to question how they should be interpreted.

One of Baskerville and Myers' key points is that papers originating in the IS field are now being cited in other disciplines, and they focus particularly on a widely admired paper by Markus on power and politics in the IT context (Markus, 1983). It is indisput-able that the paper is of exceptional quality and deservedly well known. But as Bask-erville and Myers acknowledge, it is also the case that the theories utilised in it were imported from other disciplines (Baskerville and Myers, 2002, p. 6), and not developed within IS. Further to this, Latour (1987) has demonstrated the existence of a snowball effect with citations, so that the chances of more citations increase with each new refer-ence. The fact that the Markus paper was published in 1983 therefore becomes relevant. A different interpretation of the citation evidence is that researchers are referencing a paper generally acknowledged to be of exemplary quality, but without concern for its disciplinary origins. What the evidence does not show is whether researchers in other disciplines are in fact staying alert for opportunities to cite new developments in IS theory and practice; as Baskerville and Myers concede, 'it is ... possible that some of these disciplines are themselves too inwardly focused and the "not invented here" syndrome will prevail' (Baskerville and Myers, 2002, p. 9).

While it is clear that the IS field has generated some extremely high-quality work and publications, this does not automatically translate into significant intellectual or academic influence. Avgerou notes that 'from the conventional academic perspective, IS has serious limitations ... it lacks the distinctiveness of theory and method that is usually associated with scientific disciplines ... [and] does not have a clear location on the map of academic disciplines' (Avgerou, 2000, p. 576). Although IS researchers continue to mine reference disciplines for useful concepts, there seems to be no evidence that IS ideas are being adopted in the same way within other disciplines. To take a specific example, Baskerville and Myers discuss business re-engineering as an area of attention in IS, yet while it is surely correct to say that IS researchers have 'studied [re-engineering] quite extensively' (Baskerville and Myers, 2002, p. 6), the idea originated as an organisational theory, and embeds no discernible theory of IS (Hammer and Champy, 1993).

To put the case in this way is not to dismiss the idea that IS could, and perhaps already should, be seen as a reference discipline. And, as the authors point out, there is surely no convincing reason to think that other disciplines are 'more foundational' than IS (Baskerville and Myers, 2002, p. 2). Nevertheless, in the absence of references to broad theories originating in the IS field, the widespread citation of some IS papers seems to imply a recognition of credible research rather than any acknowledgement of IS as an independently significant academic discipline. Overall, there seems little direct evidence to challenge the view that IS, to the extent it is understood and acknowledged as an in-dependent field at all, is generally seen as an applied discipline primarily concerned with finding solutions to technical problems.

A critical point is whether IS benefits from an extreme diversity of topics (Banville and Landry, 1989), so that the development of new conference tracks is therefore a sign of disciplinary health (Baskerville and Myers, 2002, p. 11). That view is questioned here on the grounds that the persistent search for new issues to explore requires a constant probing into contested academic territories, and is therefore counter-productive for the development of cumulative discipline-specific knowledge. While this trend reflects the vitality and excitement of working in a new field (Avgerou, 2000), it does not improve the discipline's chances of defining and sustaining a distinctive academic profile. Perhaps what the issue shows is the potential for the interests of individual academics to clash to some extent with those of the other field, and these are matters that cannot be resolved on principle.

A problem of visibility

The author's experience first as a practitioner of more than twenty-five years standing and then as an academic dealing with business people as well as students-to-be and their parents, is that the capacity of people outside the discipline to 'recognise' IS has been steadily decreasing for some years. Anecdotal evidence from other academics strongly supports this view. Students signing up for undergraduate courses appear to have little or no background on which to base their understanding of the topics IS addresses. Nor is it easy to identify promising career lines that are specific to IS, and it appears in this regard that the lack of any concept of the elite IS professional is a critical problem for the profession. While it was originally anticipated that CIO positions might fill this gap, it now seems that the vast majority of these positions require strictly management skills (Earl and Feeny, 1994).

One way to illustrate the visibility issue is to consider the IS field's poor performance during the Y2K crisis. While the media influence on the presentation of events was strong, it was notable that the public discussion was led by a small number of self-appointed experts, rather than professional bodies such as the ACS (Australian Computer Society), and that decisions on acceptable mitigation practice were taken by a range of commercial and governmental organisations apparently without formal input from IS bodies. One of the most frequently cited 'authorities' on Y2K was Dr Yardeni, an economist with Deutschbank, whose perceived expertise was related to the presentation of a variety of estimates on the likelihood of various types of economic meltdown throughout the period of apparent crisis. His use of figures such as a '70%' probability of a Y2K-triggered recession (Dr Yardeni, quoted in Anon., 1998) revived memories of the economist who claimed high status as an authority on the grounds that he had successfully predicted 11 of the last four recessions. What became evident throughout the course of the crisis was a lack of IS theories and frameworks on which to base an assessment of the impact of minor changes to internal data and process structures. IS was effectively relegated to the role of providing low-level technical solutions rather than explanatory insights.

A number of papers in recent years have expressed concerns with IS and its directions (e.g. Benbasat and Zmud, 2003; Hirschheim and Klein, 2003; Weber, 2003; Lee et al., 2002; Lucas, 1999; Markus, 1999; Paton, 1997). Whether explicitly or implicitly, they share a concern with the visibility of the discipline, and a worry that its very real achievements may be lost in something of an IS diaspora, as topics, researchers and findings become spread as the fragments of a once coherent discipline. Two leading theorists state, for instance: 'we feel that some underlying structural patterns in IS are in definite need of attention because they could portend trouble in the longer run (possibly even in the shorter run)' (Hirschheim and Klein, 2003, p. 239). This is, if anything, a mild conclusion, given that they also comment that the field is in 'a state of fragmentation, and [suffers from] a number of significant communication gaps' (Hirschheim and Klein, 2003, p. 241). Their paper notes other issues including a major 'disconnect' between IS and organisational management. They highlight management's willingness to set IT issues aside as being peripheral to organisational interests, and suggest that this must be a serious concern for the discipline (Hirschheim and Klein, 2003, p. 251). A further claim is that management sees IS research directions as problematic, and as 'devoid of any practical relevance' (Hirschheim and Klein, 2003, p. 253).

The most frequent reaction to the perceived problems has been to suggest that IS needs to focus on identifying and consolidating its core body (or bodies) of knowledge in the interests of establishing and maintaining field coherence (Benbasat and Zmud, 2003; Hirschheim and Klein, 2003). While it seems certain that this would generate considerable benefits within the field, this paper takes a different tack, arguing on Bourdieu's principles that IS needs to consider its relations with external parties as critical. What is required is an increase in visible cultural capital, in the form of concepts and ideas that relate directly to external interests. It is argued that theory development and research at the portfolio or organisational level, where IS structures shape and constrain organisational possibilities and are beginning to be influential in broader societal terms, is the most promising way to achieve this. Put in the broadest terms, the loss of IS visibility reflects a lack of significant cultural capital in the form of publicly accessible ideas; this can best be addressed through developments at the level of general theory.

The value of cultural capital

This section discusses Bourdieu's concepts of social fields and power, and their relevance to a consideration of theory development in general. The value of theory for the mobilisation and coordination of the intellectual resources within a field is highlighted, and illustrated with some brief examples from other disciplines.

Bourdieu's conception of social structures is a perspective in which social fields are seen as embedded within a broader field of power. Fields can themselves comprise sub-fields and so on, down to whatever level of analysis is selected (Swartz, 1997). In the construction developed in this paper, IS is a sub-field within the field of academic disciplines, themselves embedded within a yet-broader field of education. The endemic underlying struggle for power between individual disciplines is manifest in contemporary experience through competitions for prestige, for new and/or higher quality students, and for funding (Slaughter and Leslie, 1997).

The idea that academic disciplines are in competition with each other is certainly not new. But as tertiary education has come to be seen more as an economic rather than social issue, the issues of relative performance and standing within the academy have assumed far greater salience than previously (Slaughter and Leslie, 1997). Placed in this context, Bourdieuan theory implies that struggles for relative prestige are endemic and inevitable, and that the current focus on economic factors will tend to intensify the severity of the battles being waged. Though such struggles are not necessarily to the death, it is in his view inevitable that the advancement of a field must be at the expense of one or more others (Bourdieu, 1980).

Bourdieu's approach in this regard is consistent with other findings concerning recognition and the value of image. That a politician's image is at least as important as the policies he or she stands for has become a commonplace observation in political analysis (Pratkanis and Aronson, 2001). While this trend has been deprecated, it has nevertheless been accepted as a fact of political life, and attention has shifted towards trying to establish principles for the conduct of public debates that will ensure an image is reasonably commensurate with the underlying reality. It is in any case accepted that all political candidates, whatever moral stance they take toward image-making, must ensure that their public image is a positive one (Pratkanis and Aronson, 2001, p. 140).

While the effects of image on the reputation and visibility of an academic field are neither as obvious nor as immediate as in politics, its relevance is easy to show. A review of the literature concerning research methods reveals, for instance, that there is a well-defined hierarchy of disciplines based originally on their relative scientific 'purity' (Kline, 1995). In this the natural sciences rank above the social sciences, and physics ranks first among the natural sciences. This has led to a situation where the term 'physics envy' has been coined to describe the tendency for researchers in other disciplines to attempt to emulate physicists as closely as possible in their selection of research methods. The endless debates on whether qualitative methods should be deemed adequately rigorous are testament to the power of this particular piece of cultural capital (Sutton, 1997). The need for qualitative researchers to justify their approaches at the most basic level continues to contrast with the lack of such a requirement for quantitative researchers.

Changes in governmental and social perspectives on education have also had an effect in this context. Image becomes a critical issue when performance is judged on the power of the discipline to attract new students, to acquire funding from external sources, and to achieve research targets. All of these issues are affected by the strength and clarity of the discipline's public profile, which must be sufficiently recognisable to ensure that it is familiar to students, parents, investors, and research participants alike. Introna (2003, p. 236) comments in this regard that 'the status of IS as an academic discipline is … a political [question] from the start', and the effects of the political aspect seem indisputable. Academics choose appropriate research topics, seek funding in approved ways, and write appropriate types of research papers in accordance with the need to satisfy externally defined performance targets (Slaughter and Leslie, 1997).

Theory as symbolic capital

Factors inhibiting an interest in theory development abound. Theoretical papers are generally judged to be difficult to conceptualise, difficult to write, and difficult to have published (Hirschheim and Klein, 2003). The performance value placed on rigorous research, numbers of publications and the pursuit of funding are further disincentives, both for the individual academic and for the discipline as a whole. From this perspective, it could even be argued that the IS field has a motive to discourage its leading academics from participating in theory development.

Theory development is inherently an objective to which standard management criteria for evaluation are ill suited. Targets for volumes of publications, the amounts of research funding obtained, and the numbers of new students signed up for courses can be specified, their achievement monitored, and funding rewards calculated, an outcome that accords very well with the contemporary passion for quick evaluation (Laverty, 1996). The investment of time and effort in theory development is in contrast always risky; not only does the activity produce nothing measurable; it may not even generate a viable 'product' (Aronowitz, 2000). The time spent in the pursuit of theory could therefore be considered wasted from some perspectives.

Yet Bourdieu's analysis, considered in conjunction with circumstantial evidence from other fields such as physics and sociology, suggests that the development of grand theory can be invaluable, at least from the broader disciplinary perspective, and that information systems' 'acquisition' of an influential theory would add considerably to the discipline's symbolic capital. The phrase 'Einstein's theory of relativity' is an example of a phrase which states physics' claim to be a discipline of the utmost importance every time it is used. People with no understanding whatsoever of its theoretical content can instantly recognise the equation '$E=mc^2$', and interpret it as a description of the forces behind nuclear weapons (Bodanis, 2001). As disciplines jockey for power, influence, and particularly money, in the contemporary university, the theory of relativity is an invaluable symbolic asset; irrefutable evidence of physics' relevance, importance and intellectual gravitas.

It may be that physics is a questionable example, given its dominant position, though arguing so seems more a tribute to the effects of cultural capital than a reflection of something intrinsic to physics. It can, however, be shown that the same effects can be seen in other disciplines, and that they occur irrespective of whether or not the grand theory in question is assumed to be 'true' in some absolute sense. As indicated earlier, sociology has a high recognition factor stemming from debatable concepts such as Marxism, but perhaps psychology provides the best example of a powerful theory with no demonstrable scientific proof to sustain it. Many scientists are still outraged at the lack of evidence to prove that Freud's theories are 'correct' (Webster, 1996), yet psychoanalytical theory survives and thrives.

Finding a site for grand information systems theory

Is it reasonable to suggest that IS can be the site for development of a major social theory? In arguing that the attempt is warranted, two factors are considered. The first of these has already been discussed, and is that influential theories provide valuable and long-lived symbolic capital. The second, mentioned briefly earlier, is that there is a gap that IS can target by providing an analysis and explanation of the social effects of the IS constructs that are now helping to define social relationships. These constructs are the sets of standardised data and process definitions that are spreading through organisations by way of enterprise software packages, EDI-facilitated relationships, and data sharing agreements.

Existing portfolio-level theory

A further factor influencing the recommendation in this paper is the view that there is a weakness in existing portfolio-level IS theory that has contributed to management's loss of faith in IS. That the management of IT issues is important from a bottom line perspective (Luehrman, 1997) does not equate to an interest in the technology or its applications for their own sake. The ongoing commitment to IT outsourcing by organisations in both the business and government sectors, now extending to encompass the off-shore transfer of some functions, seems indicative of a general loss of belief that IT is strategically significant (Hirschheim and Klein, 2003; Stewart, 2003). As has been pointed out by various theorists (for instance Hendry, 1995; Harvey and Lusch, 1997), organisations do not generally outsource functions they perceive to be part of their strategic core.

IS has had theories that address the relationships between IS and organisational structures and strategies. The strategic IS planning literature was a vibrant one at a time when theories of competitive advantage (Porter and Millar, 1985; Kettinger et al., 1995) and of the benefits of IS integration (Segars and Grover, 1996) were in fashion. But the theories on which the publications in these areas were based ultimately failed to convince, and the number of papers being produced on portfolio-level theory has fallen drastically.

The problems these theories encountered are, however, useful to indicate in which directions the development of a general IS theory might go.

In broad terms, competitive advantage theory appears to have foundered on at least two related problems. These are the issues of imitation and structural change, which together refute the idea that IT applications can generally be considered to be reliable competitive instruments. What the available evidence shows is first that it is in most cases at least as good to be a fast IT imitator (i.e. to wait and copy a promising innovation, usually at a lower cost) than it is to be a first mover (Vitale, 1986; Clemons and Row, 1988), and second that IT innovations usually operate to effect structural industry change rather than entrench specific competitive edges (Copeland and McKenney, 1988; Kettinger et al., 1995; Clemons and Row, 1988). Both these findings have been available for some time, and have not been refuted.

The weaknesses of theories dealing with systems integration are less obvious in that they deal with ideal structures (Martin, 1990; Wyzalek, 2000), theorists have acknowledged the practical difficulties of achieving integration goals (Segars and Grover, 1996; Hamilton, 1999), and the integration of processing platforms is not only possible, but frequently very effective (Weill and Broadbent, 1998). The problem is not just that there is virtually no empirical support for the view that comprehensive IS integration is achievable (Segars and Grover, 1996; Goodhue et al., 1992; Allen and Boynton, 1991), but that consideration of the negative possibilities inherent in integration is not part of the theory. Yet evidence is available that integrated systems structures are relatively rigid and difficult to change in practice (Allen and Boynton, 1991) and that an organisation implementing such structures must lose some capacity for flexible response to change as a result. The issue of how to balance efficiency gains against losses of this type has been neither conceptualised nor researched.

Toward a structural theory of information systems

The problems with extant theory suggest some directions for the development of a robust portfolio-level theory of IS as it relates to organisational and societal structures. The finding that IS innovations change industry structures rather than entrench competitive advantages (Clemons and Row, 1988; Kettinger et al., 1995) is one possible starting point. A good IS theory (in contradistinction to competitive advantage theory, which was predominantly business-oriented) would deal with a range of social phenomena that so far lack a broad analytical explanation. Those phenomena include the increasing encroachment of standardised IS structures on social behaviour through the implementation of standardised data and process definitions in a range of systems. As standard IS structures become more widespread, so commercial and government organisations come to look more and more alike, at least in behavioural terms.

The agency-structure relationship has been a central concern in sociological theory for a long time. Are social structures 'real' when it is clear that they are constructions that must be affirmed by human agents acting with some degree of individual autonomy? Putative answers, all of interest, and all shedding light on complex social issues have come from theorists as diverse as Marx (1981), Giddens (1984), and Bourdieu (1980) among many others. But the point at issue here is that these theories do not deal with the impacts of structures reified in formal information systems. Such structures clearly allow for voluntarism in principle, as people may choose to ignore IS constraints, but they cannot then achieve their transactional goals. Yet active resistance to the influence of standardised structures clearly becomes more difficult the more widely adopted they are. IS structures are in this perspective more rigidly defined, and more formally constraining, than structures that depend on rules interpreted and enacted by people for their enforcement (Giddens, 1984).

An analysis of the possible social impacts of such structures would be the central concern for theory development in this area. While it is perhaps a little premature to identify the issues in advance of the theory, three possible areas of interest can be mentioned. These are, first, the likely lengthening of IS change cycles as the number of organisations dependent on the same standardised structures continues to increase. Second is the capacity for standardised structures to be used to create, intentionally or otherwise, people who are system 'outsiders' in some way (the history of Nazi Germany's use of IBM technology is an extreme but nevertheless instructive illustration of what was already possible in this regard fifty years ago [Black, 2001]). Third is the change in social risk relationships – while the adoption of standard IS structures reduces the number of possible points of failure or breakdown, it simultaneously raises the stakes for any breakdown that does occur.

As the Y2K experience demonstrated, IS structures have considerable inertia once installed, making them highly resistant to change; much more so than structures maintained by human behaviour. The argument in this paper is that the possibility of developing an explanatorily powerful theory linking IS with organisational and societal structures is therefore a real one, that IS is the discipline best placed to develop such a theory, and that for the reasons discussed earlier, this would have a range of benefits for the discipline as a whole.

Conclusions and recommendations

Bourdieu has made the theoretical claim that cultural capital is a source of social power, and that it is crucial in the battle for relative standing within the academy (Swartz, 1997). Theory is one form that cultural capital can take, and the ownership of interesting and controversial theories is one of the ways in which a field can support its claims for relevance, interest, and public endorsement. For a theory to generate that type of interest, however, it is important that it addresses issues of general rather than specialised concern.

It has been argued that an opportunity exists for IS academics to develop a broad theory linking IS structures to social relationships and behaviours. An influential theory would bring with it a variety of benefits for the field, including an increase in public visibility, new ideas for practitioners working at the portfolio level, and a set of framing concepts for researchers.

Two recommendations are made; the first for an empirical investigation into the issues surrounding disciplinary recognition, and the second for further theory-oriented research into the social implications of contemporary IS developments. It would be possible, but perhaps somewhat gratuitous, to recommend that 'somebody' take up the responsibility for developing a grand theory in IS; history shows that the time and effort required are such as to require a major personal commitment. There is also a risk involved, in that the resulting theory is just as likely (perhaps more likely) to be received with an outpouring of scorn and contumely (Fish, 1999, p. 117) than it is to be accepted with approbation.

An empirical investigation into the extent to which IS is a 'recognisable' discipline could, however, be expected to be both possible and useful. A survey-based approach, designed to investigate the extent to which samples of different populations are aware of IS, its topics of interest, and its particular perspectives, is one possibility. Populations of interest would include secondary-level students, parents of school-age children, tertiary-level students already enrolled, and academics in other disciplines. Depending on their nature, the findings from such a study would help either to confirm the existence of an IS identity problem, or to refute the idea that the discipline is facing a crisis.

The second recommendation is that detailed literature-based research into what is known about the 'hard-wiring' of societal structures be undertaken. Anthropologists (e.g. Wolf, 1999), sociologists (e.g. Foucault, 1972) and linguists (e.g. Chomsky, 1996) have all addressed the ways in which societies constrain their human constituents. A synthesis of this work would be a useful preliminary to introducing IS considerations, and addressing the fact that it is now possible for social controls to be exercised, and influence exerted, by IS that operate independently of people. Such systems are no longer 'representations' of more fundamental systems (Wand and Weber, 1995), but rather are independent entities with significant social autonomy.

The development of one or more general IS theories will not, of course, be a panacea for IS image problems, but it can contribute to their correction. General theory has played an important part in the advancement of other disciplines (Abbott, 1988), and could do the same for IS. It is not necessary for all, or even a significant proportion, of IS academics to be involved in this type of theory development, or to be interested in its implications. The issue is one of public perceptions, and promotion of the view that IS has relevance beyond its own borders.

3. The reality of information systems research

John Lamp, *School of Information Systems, Deakin University*
Simon Milton, *Department of Information Systems, University of Melbourne*

Abstract

The examination of a practical issue with a web site has led, in this paper, directly to the consideration of the need for, and an assessment of the impact of, an approach based on fundamental theories of 'what is', to examine what information systems research is and the relations of its component areas of endeavour. The paper presents an examination of the use of the philosophical field of ontologies, and specifically the use of the ontological approaches upon which to base categories of information systems research activities. This theoretical analysis is intended to be used as the basis from which to develop a methodology to undertake the development of the categorial scheme for the web site that initiated the research.

Introduction

Since 1995, one of the authors (JL) has been maintaining a resource on the World Wide Web with the basic aim of providing a central point from which academic authors publishing in the information systems domain can obtain useful information on the publications serving that domain (Lamp, 1995). The database now contains information on 349 journals, and was accessed over 7500 times in February 2004. As the number of journals included in the database increases, so also does the difficulty of accurately identifying journals relevant to a particular query from within the database. There is a basic searching facility that simply matches a search term to descriptive entries in the database but, in common with most text searches implemented on a relational database management system (DBMS), there is no facility for maintaining result sets and refining searches through the manipulation of result sets (Ramakrishnan and Gehrke, 2003).

A number of users have asked whether it would be possible to categorise the journals according to their subject area. This has led to a research project, the full scope of which has been reported elsewhere (Lamp and Milton, 2003), but a key part of which is the determination of relevant categorisation schemes for information systems research, and the relations between those categories. It has also raised important questions about the nature of the discipline of information systems, the journals themselves, the articles published in them, and the readers of those journals. A key finding of Lamp and Milton (2003) was the lack of widespread adoption of any categorial scheme over the domain of information systems research. This is in apparent contradiction with views expressed by information systems researchers, as researchers and as journal editors (Lamp, 2002), supporting the need for such a scheme.

We assert that the artefacts of research (i.e. journal articles and other publications) are real, having an existence outside the cognition of their authors and readers. The question then arises as to how we can categorise these objects.

The method of this paper is as follows:

1. First, we establish that the information systems research domain is diverse.
2. Second, we examine the applicability of philosophical ontology as a tool to explore the diverse categorisation of the reality of information systems research and its community; in particular, the nature of the real artefacts, how people relate to that reality, and to identify a philosophy upon which to build methods for analysis.

Characterising information systems research

There are a number of publications dealing with what *information systems* are, and what *information systems research* is. From these papers, a number of common findings emerge:

1. There is often debate on what information systems is (Ives, et al., 1980; Seddon, 1991; Shanks, et al., 1993; Parker, et al., 1994; Holsapple, et al., 1994);
2. Information systems (IS) has many foundation or reference disciplines (Keen, 1991; Seddon, 1991; Avison, 1993; Holsapple, et al., 1994; Parker, et al., 1994; Walczak, 1999; Galliers, 2004);
3. IS is located in different university faculties (Avison, 1993; Holsapple, et al., 1994);
4. IS is perceived as weak on theory (Keen, 1991; Avison, 1993; Straub, et al., 1994; Gregor, 2002);
5. IS is perceived as practice dominated (Hurt, et al., 1986; Keen, 1991; Avison, 1993, Shanks, et al., 1993);
6. IS uses many different research methodologies, models or frameworks (Ives, et al., 1980; Avison, 1993, Shanks, et al., 1993; Holsapple, et al., 1994; Parker, et al., 1994; Straub, et al., 1994; Baskerville and Wood-Harper, 1998; Fitzgerald and Howcroft, 1998; Galliers, 2004).

The authors clearly perceive that both the nature and scope of the information systems domain are diverse; the approaches to researching information systems are diverse; the approaches to teaching information systems are diverse and that there is a lack of any single clear theoretical basis for the study of information systems.

The information systems research literature is characterised by only token adoption of any form of subject categorisation, whether proposed as specific to the information systems discipline or imported, with or without adoption, from one of the reference disciplines (Lamp and Milton, 2003). The degree to which an information system is adopted by users has long been used as a determinant of success (DeLone and McLean, 1992) and, in like manner, the lack of adoption of existing categorisation schemes may be seen as an indication of the failure of those subject categorisation schemes.

All of the subject categorisation schemes that have been applied to the information systems domain have had simple hierarchical structures, enforcing a single view of information systems subject categorisation. It could be hypothesised that such a single structured subject categorisation scheme is inadequate to capture the diversity inherent in the information systems domain, resulting in the lack of significant uptake of any of these schemes.

How then can this diversity be expressed in a categorisation scheme? Systems theorists (Ackoff and Emery, 1972; Checkland, 1981; Churchman, 1979) have identified the need to account for diversity, whether expressed as perspectives or as world views, in the models they create. While these approaches reflect the diversity of perspectives in information systems, they deal with different units of analysis. Rather than examining a possibly hypothetical system and the processes and entities that exist in that system, we are examining things that exist in reality, and such a study has its roots in ontology.

Ontology

Within philosophy, ontology is the study of things that exist; the objects, properties, categories and relations that make up the world. A definition of ontology as it is conceived by philosophers is:

> ... the science of being in general, embracing such issues as the nature of existence and the categorial structure of reality. ... Different systems of ontology propose alternative categorial schemes. A categorial scheme typically exhibits a hierarchical structure, with 'being' or 'entity' as the topmost category, embracing everything that exists (Honderich, 1995).

This approach to the definition and use of ontology has also been successfully applied in information systems, for example in comparing and evaluating data modelling frameworks (Milton, 2000; Milton and Kazmierczak, 2004).

Philosophers distinguish between reference ontologies, which aim to determine the fundamental categories and categorial structures, and domain specific ontologies, where a particular reference ontology is applied to a certain problem domain. An analogy could be made between the way that ontologies and data models are conceptualised, as shown in Table 3.1.

Table 3.1. Ontologies and data models

Ontology	Data model
Reference ontology	Data modelling language
Domain specific ontologies	Data models
Specific reality	Database implementation of specific database instances

Reference ontologies

Reference ontologies, such as that of Bunge (1977; 1979), Chisholm (1996), Basic Formal Ontology (Smith, 1978; Smith and Mulligan, 1983) and DOLCE (Gangemi, et al., 2002) are concerned with the most general categories of what there is in the world. They deal with concepts such as *thing*, *individual* and *property*. In the analogy proposed in Table 3.1, data modelling languages such as entity-relationship modelling are proposed as analogous to reference ontologies.

Domain specific ontologies

At this level, particular reference ontologies are used to create a domain specific ontology directed towards an aspect of reality, in the way that particular data modelling languages are used to create data models of a particular project, such as a university student records system or a banking system. Early artificial intelligence (AI) focus was at this level.

Ontology and artificial intelligence

At this point we note that AI researchers have a particular view of ontology, referring to it as

> ... an engineering artefact, constituted by a specific vocabulary used to describe a certain reality, plus a set of explicit assumptions regarding the intended meaning of the vocabulary words (Guarino, 1998).

As previously mentioned, ontologies developed within the AI community are often directed to a specific domain of knowledge in a specific context, and are intended to be implemented or defined within a specific software artefact. Examples are KIF (Genesereth and Fikes, 1992), Ontolingua (Gruber, 1992; 1995), and OIL (Fensel, et al., 2000).

Recent work by AI researchers around the Semantic Web and the IEEE Standard Upper Ontology (IEEE, 2003), and DOLCE (Gangemi, et al., 2002) is encouraging in that they all recognise the central role of higher level ontologies in information systems.

It is the higher level reference ontologies and the basis for the selection of a particular reference ontology for the creation of a domain specific ontology, directed towards information systems research, that is the concern of this paper.

Approaches to categorisation

The history of ontology goes back over 2000 years to Aristotle and his Categories. The influence of his concept of hierarchical structures can be seen in many current categorisation schemes, ranging from the Linnaean schemes used in the life sciences to the various library categorisation schemes of Dewey and the Library of Congress. The history of the study of ontology has not been one of smooth progress with, for example, Kant (1787, p. 80) even rejecting ontology as a valid area of study. Kant's attitude was based on his belief that ontology was a synthetic *a priori* knowledge of things in general. Franz Brentano (1933, p. 81) asserts that Kant completely misunderstood Aristotle's theory of categories, approaching it without a sound understanding of Aristotle's point of view. Rather than an *a priori* assumption, as Kant believed, Aristotle's categories were based on empirical observations of being, of individuation and of collection into species.

Despite Brentano's rejection of Kant, some of his views regarding perception had similarities. Brentano's ontology is based on the investigation of two types of phenomena. First, he identifies our inner perceptions, facts about ourselves and our intentional activity. Second, the sensations we have of the external world: colour, sounds, smells are identified. In his comments on intentionality we begin to see a way of accommodating perceived diversity:

> However various our ideas of things may be, the differences of the ideas are not just a function of the differences of the objects of thought; they are also a function of what the object is thought of *as*. It is possible that the objects may differ and yet that one and the same idea may serve to present either one of them. And also conversely: one and the same object may be presented by two ideas which differ with respect to the object (Brentano, 1933, p. 40 [emphasis in original])

One of Brentano's students was Edmund Husserl, who continued investigations into the concept of intentionality. In the course of this he created phenomenology, the key idea of which is intentionality. Husserl identified problems with Brentano's approach when dealing with serious misperception and hallucinations. In these cases, what is the object? Husserl considered those features of consciousness that make it as if of an object. The collection of all these features he called the act's noema. The noema includes all the object's features, whether perceived or unperceived, including features we may take the object as having without having ever reflected or paid attention to those features. Because this is determined by perception you could, in a particular situation, see a man, but later realise it was a mannequin, with a corresponding shift of noema. An example closer to our research area might be Isaac Asimov's *The endochronic properties of resublimated thiotimoline* (1948). This is written using the structure and language of a chemistry research paper, but was a parody intended to entertain, and not a scientific work intended to establish and transmit cognitive results. Some members of the research community took the paper seriously until the ruse was revealed. In this way, perception is always fallible and noema must shift with reconsidered perceptions (Routledge, 2000, p. 369).

The results of information systems research are reported in the research literature. For this reason, and because the *Index of Information Systems Journals* can be considered a surrogate of information systems research literature when considering relevant search terms, examining and understanding what the research literature consists of is fundamental to understanding the domain of information systems research, and for discovering other dimensions of the literature which might be useful as search attributes. The philosophical approach reviewed thus far resulted in a seminal investigation of literary works.

The results of information systems research are reported in the research literature. For this reason, and because the *Index of Information Systems Journals* can be considered a surrogate of information systems research literature when considering relevant search terms, examining and understanding what the research literature consists of is fundamental to understanding the domain of information systems research, and for discovering other dimensions of the literature which might be useful as search attributes. The philosophical approach reviewed thus far resulted in a seminal investigation of literary works.

Approaches to the literary work of art

Roman Ingarden developed and applied Husslerian phenomenology to the examination of literary works, including scientific works as a borderline case. His two books *The literary work of art* (1965) and *The cognition of the literary work of art* (1968) provide a powerful framework of conceptual and methodological tools with which he characterised literary works. His work was comprehensive and addressed the entire range of literary works, from classic literature to, in his words, '… the serialised crime novel or a schoolboy's banal love poem' (Ingarden, 1965, p. 8). Fortunately for this study, he also explicitly included 'scientific works [which are] clearly distinguishable from the works of so-called belles-lettres … and yet frequently spoken of as having greater or lesser literary value or as being devoid of it' (Ingarden, 1965, p. 9).

Ingarden proposed that literary works have a number of strata and that it is the characteristics of and diversity between strata that generate a polyphonic character to the work. These strata were described by him as:

1. the stratum of *word sounds* and the *phonetic formations* of higher order built upon them;
2. the stratum of *meaning units* of various orders;
3. the stratum of *represented objectivities* and their vicissitudes; and
4. the stratum of manifold schematised *aspects* and aspect continua and series.

In addition, he identified a fifth characteristic as being significant – the order of sequence of the literary work. Key in the examination of the various strata is identifying the connections between them. A detailed description of these strata and their various connections and contributions to the literary work of art is beyond the scope of this paper. It is important to note, however, that Ingarden saw these aspects as being applicable to scientific works. He proposed that scientific work differed in some elements of individual strata and the roles of the strata. The differences result from the role of scientific works in establishing the cognitive results attained and transmitting them to other conscious subjects. Ingarden (1965, pp. 329-30; 1968, pp. 146-53) identified five differences:

1. Sentences that appear in a scientific work are almost exclusively *true judgments*. Such sentences may be true or false, but they lay claim to truthfulness; for example, a paper may report 'The management style of company A was undemocratic', which is a result perceived as true by the author of the paper, and yet a second researcher may report a different result.
2. The structure of a scientific work naturally consists of purely intentional sentence correlates (almost exclusively states of affairs) and represented objectivities. This means that intentions are directed through the represented or portrayed objectivities on to objects independent of the scientific work (e.g. the real world).
3. Scientific works may, at the stratum of phonetic formations and the stratum of units of meaning, contain aesthetic value qualities. This is not essential and may be re-garded as a dispensable luxury. The central purpose of a scientific work is cognitive exchange, and everything else must be subordinated to this central purpose. Ideally the portrayed objectivities are transparent to the reader and ontically independent objects are seen in the light of the meaning intention of the scientific work. For example, information technology is rich in accepted metaphor. The use of terms such as 'viruses', 'windows' and 'mice' in information technology literature assists in cognitive exchange.
4. Scientific works can contain, as a special stratum, manifolds of schematicised aspects held in readiness, provided the sentences refer to objects that can appear in mani-folds of aspects. If they exist, their role is to assist in the transmission of cognitive results. The presence of decorative moments is dispensable and may be a hindrance.
5. The possible manifestation of metaphysical qualities is essential only when a given metaphysical quality is itself a subject of the cognitive result that is achieved and transmitted, or at least contributes to its transmission. In this case, they are not contributing to the aesthetic value of the scientific work in the way that they con-tribute to a literary work. Scientific literature tends to stick to facts.

From this discussion we can conclude three important things:

1. the journals and their articles are real (part of reality);
2. the articles contain true judgments of the authors; and
3. independent objects mentioned in articles are also real but must be understood from the perspective of the author and the intentions revealed in the work.

The approach taken by Ingarden is applicable to scientific works, including works in the field of information systems. This leaves the question of what is an appropriate ref-erence ontology to provide a framework for linking the results of the analysis of the information systems literature – the real artefacts – with the perceptions and intentional acts of information systems researchers using these artefacts.

Providing for perspectives: identifying an appropriate reference ontology

We have established that journals and their contents are real and have an existence separate from readers and authors, and Ingarden has written extensively on the nature of written works of the type in which we are interested. We note that many see inform-ation systems as being a diverse community with many different perspectives and dis-agreements about categorisation. An appropriate comprehensive reference ontology that is consistent with these traits is needed to provide a framework within which the results of the study of information systems research literature can be presented.

A number of ontologies have been used to provide an understanding of information systems. A frequently used ontology is that of Mario Bunge (1977; 1979). Bunge's ontology is exact and well developed. It is characterised by an approach that considers the real world as known to science and proceeds in a clear and systematic way. Wand and Weber, alone and with others (e.g. Wand, 1996), have used this ontology in many studies of modelling information systems. However, it has been noted that Bunge's ontology is 'oriented towards the physical world and therefore does not provide for human perceptions and social context' (Wand 1996). Indeed, Bunge's ontology can be categorised as one consistent with the philosophical stream of naturalism wherein it is held 'that the best methods of inquiry in the social sciences or philosophy are ... those of the natural sciences'. Naturalism is ontologically supported by natural science in that it insists that natural science be used 'in recognising what is real' (Kim and Sosa, 1995) and that 'our ontology is constrained by the result that all physical bodies are composed entirely of particles' (Kim and Sosa, 1995). This position is also methodologically difficult to defend because 'intentional states ... are said to be attributable to individuals only relative to an observer [which is] inconsistent with the objectivity of the methods of natural science' (Winch, 1958, quoted in Kim and Sosa, 1995).

We have established that scientific works such as those in information systems report true judgments of people written with intentions revealed in the works and, furthermore, that people who come from diverse perspectives and with different intentional states read articles. Naturalism cannot help us, despite rightly being a philosophy committed to realism (the existence of a world separate from our thinking about it).

Another ontological position that seems to be more amenable to use in the area of human perceptions is common-sense realism. Commonsensism holds that we really know most, if not all, of those things which ordinary people claim to know. I know that there exists at present a living human body, which is my body. I know that the earth has existed for many years past. These are unambiguous expressions, the meaning of which is widely understood. It should be noted that there is also an 'entirely different question of whether we know what it means, in the sense that we are able to give a correct analysis of its meaning' (Moore, 1925). Commonsensism is not concerned with this latter question. The common-sense world is delineated by our beliefs about what happens in mesoscopic reality in most cases and most of the time (Smith, 1995).

This approach does not dismiss the view of the world based on physics. Various proposals have been made to accommodate the world of physics within common-sense realism. Proposed alternatives have included treating the common-sense world as truly autonomous and the world of physics as a cultural artefact. Smith (1995) proposes that there is an overlap between the common-sense world and the world of physics. Paradigm shifts in science impact on our common-sense understanding of the physical world. However, a common-sense ontology does not necessarily need to be rewritten in the wake of paradigm shifts, contrasting with a naturalist ontology such as Bunge's.

Common-sense realism holds that there is only one world towards which natural cognition relates, and that this world exists independently of our cognitive relations to it. It concedes that our natural cognitive experiences are in many cases unable to be verified, but points out that common sense is aware of error in cognitive efforts.

> The thesis that there is only one world towards which natural cognition relates must thus be understood as being compatible with the thesis that there are many different ways in which the world can appear to human subjects in different sorts of circumstances (Smith, 1995).

An ontology based on common-sense realism, which has received some attention in information systems, is that of Roderick Milton Chisholm (1996). His ontology is consistent with the brand of realism followed in this paper through Husserl, Ingarden, and Brentano. The ontology is robust, located in the common-sense realism school of thought, and deals with static and dynamic aspects. Importantly for the work proposed in this paper, Chisholm addresses the question of perception and the intentional point of view. He states:

> I assume that our perception of our own states of mind is a source of certainty and that the deliverances of external perception should be treated as innocent, epistemically, unless we have positive reason to call them into question (Chisholm, 1996: pp. 4-5).

Chisholm's ontology is also able to accommodate 'noema' through 'appearances' thus helping to explain how people (and groups of people) can have perspectives on reality that change over time and appear to be not quite what they really are:

> Our qualitative experiences – the sensing of appearances – is subjective in being dependent for its existence on the existence of the subject of experience (Chisholm, 1996, p. 113).

To present the full coverage of Chisholm's ontology is beyond the scope of this paper, but his emphasis on the 'primacy of the intentional' (Chisholm, 1996) suggests that his ontology may provide an appropriate framework for analysing the reality of information systems research. It may be possible to use this well-respected philosophical research to build a sensible categorisation scheme for information systems research, but the question remains of how this can be done.

Establishing and empirically validating ontological categories

Traditionally, ontological studies have been methodologically based on introspection and analysis of world models and abstract theories. Logic has also been used to analyse the ontological commitments in theories (Quine, 1953). Smith and Mark (1999) have reported on an experiment in the use of empirical methods, based on common-sense realism, to test aspects of an ontological theory of geographic objects. Much of the work done in categorisation is based on mathematical set theory. All objects within a set are equally representative members of a set, and it is absolutely definable as to whether an individual item is or is not a member of a set. In looking at geographical objects, this clarity is not evident. Many geographical terms such as pond, lake, sea or ocean more closely resemble ranges on a continuum rather than precisely definable items. Clearly these geographical objects do not satisfy the requirements of set theory. Equally, comparison of published papers in the field of information systems research with some of the categories proposed in schemes covering information systems research reveal a similar vagueness in distinguishing categories. For example, papers on *entity relationship modelling* might be categorised as *systems analysis and design* or as *database*, or might be thought to lie somewhere between the two, depending on the emphasis of the paper. In these cases we are dealing with categories that are the products of human cognition rather than products of mathematical propositions.

Rosch (1978) looked at the ability of people to differentiate between objects and to identify individual objects which fitted in specific categories better than other individuals, and found a great degree of agreement as to which were good and bad examples. Rather than discrete set-based categories, she described categories with a radial structure, with prototypical or central members surrounded by more or less typical members. This has similarities with the approach of Franz Brentano to mereology. The common-sense world is complex and is divided in different ways and at different levels. Mereology concerns the basic organising relationships of part to whole, part to part within a single whole, of identity, overlapping and discreteness.

Most of the work done by Rosch and other cognitive scientists is based on studies of entities of tabletop space such as tools, small pets or of abstract items such as colours and diseases. Smith and Mark (1999) were interested in determining whether these approaches could be applied to geographic categories. Their experimental framework consisted of two complementary phases: traditional ontological work (largely deductive, introspective and formal) and research with human subjects (empirical, inductive). The ontological theories were used as the starting points for the design of experimental protocols to test the degree of fit of the ontological theories. This data can then be used to refine the ontological theories to form the basis for further iterations.

Conclusions

We have established that the information systems research domain is diverse. We have also established that the approach of Roman Ingarden provides a suitable way to discover the nature of information systems literature – the real world artefacts of information systems research. His work plays a significant part in studies of fiction, plays and poetics. So far, to our knowledge, no exemplars of a research methodology applying his approaches to scientific works exist.

Roman Ingarden's philosophy is in harmony with common-sense realism such as that espoused by Roderick Milton Chisholm and Barry Smith. Common-sense realism provides for perspectival views capturing the diversity of the information systems research domain.

It is likely that this project will require the sort of empirical validation undertaken by Smith and Mark (1999). However, the real objects in their research were not based on intentional acts. Consequently, we believe that no method is directly applicable to undertake this empirical validation, and this remains an active line of enquiry.

The results of this investigation are promising in that a number of different studies, using a common philosophical approach, have been found. When these studies are taken together, they point towards a soundly based, novel methodology for developing a categorial scheme that can be applied in a domain characterised by diversity and, more specifically, diversity of intentionality.

4. Qualitative research in information systems: consideration of selected theories

M. Gordon Hunter, *Faculty of Management, The University of Lethbridge*

Abstract

Qualitative researchers attempt to document observed phenomena relative to the meanings attributed to the phenomena by research participants involved in the specific incident or situation. Relatively recently, the information systems research community has responded to the call for more of an emphasis on conducting qualitative research. This paper presents three theories, Grounded Theory, Personal Construct Theory, and Narrative Inquiry, which may be considered within the qualitative perspective. In response to concerns about bias and reliability in qualitative research, data gathering techniques are described including the RepGrid technique and the Long Interview technique.

Introduction

This paper presents a discussion about conducting information systems research while taking a qualitative perspective to carrying out investigations. Within this qualitative perspective, selected theories are presented, including Grounded Theory, Personal Construct Theory, and Narrative Inquiry. The discussion shows the relationship of these theories to conducting qualitative research in information systems. These theories, developed in other fields of research, may be employed to further contribute to our understanding of the information systems discipline.

The discussion here does not present a comparison of qualitative and quantitative perspectives, nor a combination known as mixed mode (Nicholls et al., 2001) or pluralistic (Mingers, 2001). Indeed, it is the author's contention that the research perspective, approach, and method should be determined as a consequence of deciding upon the objectives of the investigation. Thus, one particular perspective, approach, or method is neither better nor worse than another, just simply more or less appropriate within the specific circumstances and objectives of the research project.

The next section presents a definition of qualitative research and discusses why it is currently considered important as a perspective for conducting investigations in the information systems field. Following this discussion, the selected theories are outlined. The theories are subsequently further elucidated through the presentation and discussion of selected examples of published research that has employed these theories in the information systems subject area. Finally, conclusions that discuss how this perspective and these theories contribute to information systems theoretical foundations are presented.

Qualitative research perspective

Qualitative researchers attempt to make sense of, or provide an interpretation of, observed phenomena relative to meanings attributed to these phenomena by individuals involved in specific incidents or situations. Thus, qualitative researchers spend a lot of time in the field, working closely with research participants in their natural surroundings. The qualitative researcher and the research participant work together to document and develop interpretations of events or situations relative to a specific research question.

Some time ago it was suggested that the study of information systems '... will remain a doubtful science as long as it continues to strive to develop its stock of knowledge primarily through the practice of the so-called scientific method' (Klein and Lyytinen, 1985). These authors were suggesting that information systems researchers, in order to advance the discipline, should consider other research perspectives. It was further suggested '... that information systems epistemology draws heavily from the social sciences because information systems are fundamentally social rather than technical systems' (Hirschheim, 1992). This suggestion recommends that information systems researchers move closer to the qualitative research perspective. However, as a caution, Galliers (1992), through his revised taxonomy of information systems research, recommended that information systems researchers should not blindly adopt a specific research method. Indeed, the adopted research method should be based upon the research question(s) and the objective of the research project.

More recently the information systems research community has responded to the call for more of an emphasis on conducting qualitative research (Benbasat and Zmud, 1999). Trauth (2001) in a series of manuscripts presents a number of challenges and considerations when conducting qualitative information systems research. Trauth suggests 'A significant portion of established and emerging IS researchers are grappling with the issue of learning about new research methods even as they struggle to keep up with new information technologies. This is especially the case for qualitative methods' (Trauth, 2001). Lee (2001) provides further elucidation by suggesting that information systems research is more than the study of technology or behaviour. Lee suggests that information systems researchers must deal, '... with the phenomena that emerge when the technolog[ical] and the behavioral interact, much like different chemical elements reacting to one another when they form a compound' (Lee, 2001). Thus, there is a growing community of information systems researchers who are conducting investigations from a qualitative perspective. Members of this community consider information systems to be more social than technical. They are interested in investigating interpretations of phenomena. The next sections present some theories, which respond to and support a qualitative perspective. The discussion includes grounded theory, personal construct theory, and narrative inquiry. Table 4.1 provides an overview of the subsequent discussion.

Table 4.1. Qualitative theories

Theory	Approach	Technique
Grounded Theory	Discovery of theory;	Categories emerge from data;
	Data analysis	Property: attribute of a category
Personal Construct Theory	Personalised system for interpreting past experiences	Elicited using the RepGrid:
		Elements
		Constructs
		Elicitation
		Laddering
Narrative Inquiry	Recounting of personal experiences	Contextually rich (experienced first-hand)
		Temporally bounded (beginning, sequence of events, ending)
		Long interview technique (grand tour questions, planned prompts, floating prompts)

Grounded theory

Grounded theory is defined as the process for '… the discovery of theory from data systematically obtained from social research.' (Glaser and Strauss, 1967). As an approach to research, Grounded theory may be used in two ways. On one hand, it may be used as a research philosophy. Thus, the researcher approaches a research question with no *a priori* research framework or theoretical context. A research question, considered interesting, is posed and data are gathered relative to the question. Subsequent data analysis, as explained below, is employed to support the researcher's contention about how the data may be used to respond to the research question. On the other hand, grounded theory may be used as a technique for analysing data, which involves the process of constant comparison. The theory suggests that categories and properties are concepts that are identified by the researcher and evolve from the constant comparing of the data. A category emerges from the data and may stand by itself as a conceptual element. A property is an attribute of a category. For example, the category 'Communication' may have properties of 'written' and 'verbal'. The constant comparison process may support existing categories or generate new ones. As Glaser and Strauss (1967) put it: 'By comparing where the facts are similar or different, we can generate properties of categories that increase the categories' generality and explanatory power'.

The data analysis process involves three types of coding. First, 'open' coding involves assigning the data to categories that are identified from the data by the researcher. Second, 'axial' or 'theoretical' coding involves identifying relationships between the categories. These relationships support the identification of an overall theoretical framework. Third, 'selective' coding involves ensuring that all available data are associated with an emerging category and that core categories are identified to support the conceptualisation of the theoretical framework. Eventually, a situation of theoretical saturation is attained where no new categories or properties emerge from the gathering of further data.

Personal construct theory

Kelly (1955; 1963) developed personal construct theory based upon his work as a clinical psychologist to help assess his patients' interpersonal relationships. He determined that individuals would develop a personalised system for dealing with current or future situations that was based upon their own interpretations of their past experiences.

An individual's personal construct system may be documented using the technique known as the Role Construct Repertory Test, or RepGrid. '[RepGrids] … provide a way of doing research into problems … in a more precise, less biased, way than any other research method' (Stewart and Stewart, 1981). It is also suggested by these authors that the RepGrid technique '... enables one to interview someone in detail, extracting a good deal of information ... and to do this in such a way that input from the observer is reduced to zero' (Stewart and Stewart, 1981). The two main components of the RepGrid are elements and constructs. Elements are entities within the research domain upon which the research participant may be able to form an opinion. The constructs are the research participant's interpretation of the elements within the same research domain.

The RepGrid technique has been employed in research areas beyond those for which it was originally designed. It has been used for general problem construction and market research (Bannister and Mair, 1968; Corsini and Marsella, 1983; Eden and Jones, 1984; Eden and Wheaton, 1980; Fransella, 1981; Shaw, 1980) and for knowledge acquisition for expert systems (Botten et al., 1989; Latta and Swigger, 1992; Phythian and King, 1992). Also, the RepGrid technique has been employed in a series of information systems research projects (Hunter, 1993; Hunter and Beck, 1996; Hunter, 1997; Hunter and Beck, 2000). The research question related to determining how members of various groups construe the skills and personal characteristics of 'excellent' systems analysts. That is, the research attempted to document the personal construct system of research participants within the domain of discourse relating to their experiences working with systems analysts.

RepGrids were used during the interview process because they bring structure to the interview while allowing flexibility and reducing researcher bias. It was considered important to determine the interpretations of the research participants. Thus, it was necessary to adopt a tool that emphasised gathering data from the research participant while allowing the participant to determine the subject matter and content of the data. This aspect is one of the advantages of the RepGrid technique.

RepGrids generate a large amount of rich, in-depth, qualitative and narrative data relating to a research participant's explanation of an elicited construct. The documentation of the research participant's explanations as interview notes forms the basis of the research data. Detailed comments were recorded for each pole of the elicited construct. The researcher determined a system of hierarchies for each construct, which depicted the relationships, within the interview notes, between an elicited construct at the RepGrid level and a detailed action statement, at the interview note level. The interview notes were obtained via the technique of Laddering whereby the researcher probes further regarding the research participant's detailed interpretations of a general comment.

The initial project in this series was conducted in Canada. Subsequent replications were carried out in Singapore and again in Canada. This data supported comments regarding cross-cultural aspects of how the performance of 'excellent' systems analysts is interpreted. Hunter and his colleagues were able to determine, among a number of results, that information systems professionals perceived 'excellent' systems analysts as being process oriented, while business professionals viewed 'excellent' systems analysts as those who were able to deliver content. Further, in the cross-cultural replication, the Singapore research participants viewed 'excellent' systems analysts as experts, while the Canadian research participants regarded 'excellent' systems analysts as coaches.

Narrative inquiry

Narrative inquiry documents '... a segment of one's life that is of interest to the narrator and researcher' (Girden, 2001). It entails '... the symbolic presentation of a sequence of events connected by subject matter and related by time' (Scholes, 1981). The narrative inquiry approach facilitates documenting stories that are contextually rich and temporally bounded. The contextually rich concept suggests that those events, which are experienced first hand, are the ones that are most vividly remembered (Tulving, 1972). As Swap et al. (2001) suggest, employing an approach where research participants relate stories about their personal experiences '... would be more memorable, be given more weight, and be more likely to guide behaviour'. (Swap et al., 2001). The second concept, temporally bounded, suggests that narratives should have a beginning and an ending, along with a chronological description of intervening events. Research suggests that the sequential aspect of relating events contributes to the appropriateness of the narrative (Bruner, 1990; Czarniawska-Joerges, 1995; Vendelo, 1998).

Narrative inquiry has been employed to investigate behavioural science (Rappaport, 1993), fiction and film (Chatman, 1978), and strategic management (Barry and Elmes, 1997). It has been employed to investigate various aspects of information systems by Boland and Day (1989), and Hirschheim and Newman (1991). Further, Hunter and Tan (2001) employed narrative inquiry to identify the major career path impacts of information systems professionals. They interviewed a number of information systems professionals at various stages of their career to determine why these individuals changed jobs. In order to ground the discussion in the research participants' personal experiences, individual résumés were employed as the main instrument to guide the interview and to elicit the narratives. The résumé was employed to assist research participants to reflect upon their work experiences and report these experiences in a sequential account of events as they transpired throughout their careers. The résumé approach has been used previously in information systems research (Young, 2000). The résumé is readily available and an untapped source of data (Dex, 1991), as well as acting as a milestone reference to assist human memory recall (Baker, 1991). While the résumé was used to guide the interview, the next paragraph describes a generic technique upon which the interview was organised.

The long interview technique (McCracken, 1988) may be used in association with narrative inquiry. During the course of the interview research participants were asked to reflect upon past work experiences. Initially, 'grand tour' (McCracken, 1988) questions were asked. These questions are general in nature and non-directive in manner, allowing the research participant to specify much of the substance or perspective of the interview. With reference to the research participant's résumé, questions were asked that focused the discussion on activities of the current position, why the research participant found the current position attractive and why the research participant left a previous position. This process was followed in reverse chronological order, employing the research participant's résumé as a guide to sequential dates. The discussion continued through the dates until the time of initial entry into the information systems profession. Throughout this section of the interview, 'floating prompt' (McCracken, 1988) questions were asked. The nature of these questions depends upon the content of each interview and, generally, relate to the researcher's decision to pursue a thread of discussion in more detail. Specific, or 'planned prompt' (McCracken, 1988) questions were asked near the end of the interview in order to address issues gleaned from the literature or previous investigations.

The objective of this research project was to document the factors surrounding job changes among a number of information systems professionals at various stages of their careers. It was anticipated that analysis of the interview data would help to identify and categorise events surrounding career path changes and career advancement. The results of this research have provided a more thorough understanding of the events within an individual's career path, which have resulted in the research participant's current social positioning within the occupational community. Finally, trends have been identified that indicate the more beneficial aspects relating to career advancement for information systems professionals. Suggestions have been made for the information systems professional, the organisations that employ these individuals, and societies to which information systems professionals may belong.

Based upon the transcripts of the interviews, common themes were identified. These themes represented two common trends for the profession. First, the information systems professionals interviewed tended to associate more closely with the profession than with a specific organisation. Second, there was an increased desire to remain current with technology and to have experience with the leading edge technologies. Hunter and Tan (2001) were able to provide recommendations and suggest implications for various stakeholders, including information systems professionals, and organisations.

Conclusions

This paper has outlined a qualitative perspective to conducting research in information systems employing grounded theory, personal construct theory, and narrative inquiry. Some published research examples have been presented to support the description of the theories and to demonstrate their application to the information systems field.

A concern about conducting qualitative research relates to verification. In general, qualitative researchers tend to agree that replication is the best means to validate conclusions determined from qualitative research. Further concerns about verification relate to researcher bias, and reliability.

Qualitative researchers become closely involved in research situations and with research participants. There arises then a concern about researcher bias. Thus, in an interview, questions may be posed in a certain way, or certain aspects of the discussion may be pursued more or less intensively. Some researchers would consider this flexibility to be beneficial, allowing the researcher to obtain relevant data. However, as Reason and Rowan (1981) suggest, '… it is much better to be deeply interesting than accurately boring'. In the end, emphasis should be placed on the research method in order to counteract the potential introduction of bias.

When conducting qualitative research, it is incumbent upon the investigator to gather data in a systematic way in order to address the above concerns. The RepGrid technique has been shown (Stewart and Stewart, 1981) to be an acceptable method to document the personal constructs of research participants. Its use in the information systems field will support a response to the call for applied theories (Lee, 1999) and practical relevance (Benbasat and Zmud, 1999; Robey and Markus, 1998). The Long Interview technique (McCracken, 1988) supports an open unbiased investigation. It allows the researcher to document a research participant's interpretation of an event.

Finally, these techniques respond to the concern for qualitative researcher bias by allowing the research participants to determine the response and to provide their own comment elaboration. The techniques lend structure to the qualitative data gathering process while allowing flexibility in the research participants' responses. Incorporating these techniques will support the grounding of interview data within the environment as interpreted by the research participant.

Part II. Research methods, reference theories and information systems

5. The grounded theory method and case study data in IS research: issues and design

Walter D. Fernández, *School of Business and Information Management, The Australian National University*

Abstract

While social scientists have been using the grounded theory method for almost 40 years, the IS field has been a late adopter of the methodology. Thus, even as grounded theory's importance as an IS research method has increased over the last decade, many misconceptions and misunderstandings about the method and its use still exist in our community. This paper presents important aspects of the Glaserian approach to grounded theory studies. The account is based on a personal perspective acquired from both doing grounded theory research and reading the wide grounded theory literature. Readers will benefit by gaining a deeper understanding of the approach, including its nature and benefits as well as its risks and demands. The objective of this paper is to help novice IS researchers interested in theory-building studies to grasp the complexity and nature of the method.

Introduction

Martin and Turner (1986, p. 141) defined grounded theory as an 'inductive theory discovery methodology that allows the researcher to develop a theoretical account of the general features of the topic while simultaneously grounding the account in empirical observations of data.'[1] In grounded theory everything is integrated; it is an extensive and systematic general methodology (independent of research paradigm) where actions and concepts can be interrelated with other actions and concepts – in grounded theory nothing happens in a vacuum (Glaser, 1978; Glaser and Strauss, 1967).

The grounded theory method offers 'a logically consistent set of data collection and analysis procedures aimed to develop theory' (Charmaz, 2001 p. 245). These procedures allow the identification of patterns in data; by analysing these patterns researchers can derive theory that is empirically valid (Glaser and Strauss, 1967; Martin and Turner, 1986). This is so because 'the theory-building process is so intimately tied with evidence that it is very likely that the resultant theory will be consistent with empirical observation'(Eisenhardt, 1989).[2]

An excellent example of grounded theory in information systems research can be found in Orlikowski (1993), which won *MIS Quarterly's* Best Paper Award for 1993. Grounded theory allowed Orlikowski to focus on elements of context and process and on actions of important players associated with organisational change. This influential paper played an important role in making IS scholars aware of the usefulness of grounded theory for

---

[1] Grounded theory is also a deductive method.
[2] Grounded theory is (a) an approach consisting of methods and (b) a theory of research. In this paper, 'grounded theory' and 'grounded theory method' refer to grounded theory approach.

IS research. Since then, many IS researchers have successfully used and published grounded theory studies (e.g. Baskerville and Pries-Heje, 1999; Lehmann, 2001b; Maznevski and Chudoba, 2000; Trauth and Jessup, 2000; Urquhart, 1997; Urquhart, 1998; Urquhart, 1999; Urquhart, 2001).

While grounded theory studies still constitute a minority group in IS research (Lehmann, 2001b), the value of grounded theory has now become acknowledged within the IS field. This recognition reflects the tremendous progress of interpretive research from its insignificance in the 1980s (Orlikowski and Baroudi, 1991) to its current mainstream status in the IS community (Klein and Myers, 2001; Markus, 1997). However, the increased interest and adoption of the grounded theory method brings to the surface the issue of shortage of guidance on how to apply the method in IS studies. This paper contributes by providing an introduction to the method that focuses on (a) describing the use of the grounded theory method with case study data, (b) presenting a research model (c) discussing the critical characteristics of the grounded theory method, (d) discussing why grounded theory is appropriate for studies seeking both rigour and relevance, and (e) highlighting some risks and demands intrinsic to the method. Figure 5.1 illustrates the structure of the paper.

Figure 5.1. Thematic structure.

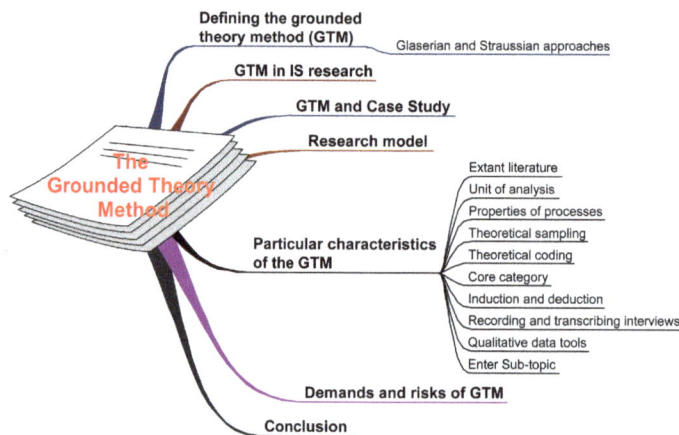

Background

The grounded theory method grew in importance and recognition over the years from the seminal work of Barney Glaser and Anselm Strauss (1967). These two sociologists come from different backgrounds and their collaborative work melds fundamental traditions in sociology (Glaser, 1978; Glaser, 1992; Glaser, 1998; Glaser and Strauss, 1967; Strauss, 1987; Strauss and Corbin, 1998).

On the one hand, Herbert Blumer, Evert Hughes and Robert Park trained Anselm Strauss in symbolic interaction at the University of Chicago's school of qualitative research, where Strauss was influenced by the pragmatist philosophical tradition (Charmaz, 2001; Glaser, 1998; Strauss and Corbin, 1998). On the other hand, Barney Glaser was trained in *quantitative* methodology and *qualitative mathematics* (a method in which mathematical expressions, such as those of statistical formulas, can be stated qualitatively) at Columbia University by Paul F. Lazarsfeld, an innovator of quantitative methods (Glaser, 1998; Strauss and Corbin, 1998). Glaser was also trained in theory construction by

Merton; particularly in theoretical coding, which Merton learned from Talcott Parsons and others (Glaser, 1998). Additionally, Glaser received training in explication of text at the University of Paris (Glaser, 1998).

The combination of the distinct backgrounds of Strauss and Glaser, while working together during the early 1960s, produced the *constant comparative method* later known as grounded theory (Glaser and Strauss, 1967). The founders of grounded theory continued to develop the method over the years independently of each other. Their separated paths led to what now is known as the 'Straussian' and 'Glaserian' versions of the grounded theory method (Stern, 1994).

Regardless of which specific grounded theory approach guides a particular study, there are important canons to follow for a study claiming the use of grounded theory. Dey (1999), based in Creswell (1998), produced a useful list of grounded theory tenets to introduce some of the basic beliefs behind grounded theory. Reflecting on these tenets, Urquhart (2001) emphasised two key beliefs of grounded theory: (a) the researcher has to set aside theoretical ideas; and, (b) the concepts are developed through constant comparison.

These two beliefs are fundamental building blocks of grounded theory. The first belief tells us that avoiding preconceptions is paramount in doing grounded theory. This point, which seems clear to the grounded theorist, usually puzzles the casual observer. How can a person put aside what she or he knows? The point made in the grounded theory literature is *not* that a clean slate is necessary or even desirable; the critical point here is that the research does not *start* with a theory to prove or disprove. With the Grounded Theory Method (GTM), when the researcher holds some deep-rooted beliefs, these can be captured as text and then analysed with other text as just another incident in the data (Glaser, 1978; Glaser and Strauss, 1967). The subsequent data analysis, through the constant comparison of incidents, will then falsify, confirm, or extend the applicability of the theory to the substantive area under study.

Furthermore, regardless of the particular approach one might adopt, without the concept of *constant comparison* grounded theory cannot be developed. Since its first publication in 1965, the constant comparative method has been a key concept in the development and understanding of grounded theory (Glaser, 2001)[3]. According to Glaser and Strauss (1967, pp.113-14), the constant comparative method facilitates the generation of complex 'theories of process, sequence, and change pertaining to organisations, positions, and social interaction [that] correspond closely to the data since the constant comparison forces the analyst to consider much diversity in the data.' This diversity is achieved by comparison between incidents and properties of a category, trying to observe as many underlying uniformities and diversities as possible.

The constant comparative method can be used to produce either conceptualisations or rich descriptive accounts. The conceptualisation versus description debate is at the heart of the difference between the Glaserian and Straussian approaches to grounded theory, which is discussed next.

The Glaserian and Straussian approaches

Methods evolve over time and often even their main exponents differ in their interpretation of the best way to evolve. This is indeed the case with grounded theory. The publication of 'Basics of qualitative research: grounded theory procedures and techniques'

---

[3]For a philosophical discussion on the constant comparative method see Glaser and Strauss (2001; 1967); for a procedural description see Glaser (1978; 1998).

by Strauss and Corbin (1990) and the highly critical public response from Glaser (1992) mark the emergence of an important schism in grounded theory, resulting in the 'Straussian' and 'Glaserian' models (Stern, 1994).

However, this paper does not aim to arbitrate on what Melia (1996) described as a war of words between friends. Indeed, I perceive both approaches as far more valuable contributions to qualitative researchers than the long epistemological discussions about them. Furthermore, many grounded theory IS researchers have already left this discussion behind and are concentrating on how the method can be improved, taught, and made more relevant to both academe and industry (among others, these include Cathy Urquhart, Hans Lehmann, David Douglas, Stefan Cronholm and Goran Goldkul).

Nonetheless, while accepting the validity of the two approaches, the discrepancies between them are substantial; especially in the use of Strauss and Corbin's 'axial coding' (Glaser, 1992; Kendall, 1999) and the form and nature of the theoretical outcome (Straussian full-description versus Glaserian abstract-conceptualisation). Consequently, researchers must opt for the approach more appropriate for their particular studies. My study followed the Glaserian approach because:

1. I was more interested in the conceptualisation offered by Glaser than on the full description of Strauss and Corbin. The Glaserian approach has a strong focus on abstract conceptualisations that are not concerned with people and time but tied to the substantive area of inquiry, which made it more useful to my study's particular goal; relevance to industry. In other words, a method focusing on conceptualisation offered a better probability of contributing to the experts in the substantive field; thus reducing the risk of telling the experts what they already knew.
2. The Straussian approach appears to be more useful for studies of individuals than studies involving organisational, political, and technical issues (Lehmann, 2001a, p. 9).
3. The preliminary literature review made me aware of practical problems reported by researchers in using the Straussian coding paradigm (e.g. Cronholm, 2002; Kendall, 1999; Sarker et al., 2000; Sarker et al., 2001; Urquhart, 2001).
4. The Glaserian approach is far less prescriptive and offers the flexibility of a number of potential coding paradigms, not just one.

In adopting a Glaserian approach I also selected the main methodological texts guiding the investigation. This was important to reduce both controversies and confusion (mine and my audience's). The main texts were:

1. *'The Discovery of Grounded Theory: Strategies for Qualitative Research'* (Glaser and Strauss, 1967),
2. *'Theoretical Sensitivity: Advances in the Methodology of Grounded Theory'* (Glaser, 1978), and
3. *'Doing Grounded Theory: Issues and Discussions'* (Glaser, 1998).

'The Grounded Theory Perspective: Conceptualisation Contrasted with Description' (Glaser, 2001) can also be consulted for a very extensive discussion contrasting the conceptualisation of grounded theory with the need for rich description of other qualitative data analysis methods.

Grounded theory and case study

While grounded theory is mainly used for qualitative research (Glaser, 2001), it is a general method of analysis that accepts qualitative, quantitative, and hybrid data collection from surveys, experiments, and case studies (Glaser, 1978). However, when combining methods like case study and grounded theory, utmost care must be exercised to ensure that the canons of case study research do not distort true emergence for theory generation (Glaser, 1998 pp. 40-2). For example, Yin (1994, p. 28) states 'theory development prior to the collection of any case study data is an essential step in doing case studies.' This statement, perfectly valid for some case study research, contravenes a key principle of grounded theory. Therefore, when combining case study and grounded theory, the researcher must clearly specify which methodology is driving the investigation.

I used grounded theory as the overarching methodology to study data from an exploratory case study and to drive data acquisition activities within and outside the case study. Yet, the reason for using the grounded theory approach was consistent with the three main reasons suggested by Benbasat et al. (1987) for using a case study strategy in IS research, namely:

1. The research can study IS in a natural setting, learn the state of the art, and generate theories from practice.
2. The researcher can answer the questions that lead to an understanding of the nature and complexity of the processes taking place.
3. It is an appropriate way to research a previously little studied area.

Additionally, as I had professional experience in the substantive area of my study, grounded theory was an appropriate approach because it provided a method to deal with my experience, controlling the risk of introducing bias into the study. This control is achieved by the constant comparative method, which forces researchers to state their assumptions and their own knowledge as data (in the form of memos or self-interviews) and to compare these data with other data from the study. The constant comparison of incidents then validates, modifies, or rejects the expert researchers' observations. Thus, for researchers with professional experience in the substantive field of their research, constant comparison is a valuable feature of the grounded theory method. To be sure, constant comparison *reduces*, but cannot completely eliminate, the risk of bias-induced distortions.

For these reasons, seeking to generate theory grounded in case study data was a particularly appropriate strategy for my research. Furthermore, this approach has been tested and detailed by Eisenhardt (1989) and it is one of the preferred ways of doing grounded theory in IS research (Lehmann, 2001b; Maznevski and Chudoba, 2000; Orlikowski, 1993; Urquhart, 2001). According to Eisenhardt (1989), using case data to build grounded theory has three major strengths:

1. Theory building from case studies is likely to produce novel theory; this is so because 'creative insight often arises from juxtaposition of contradictory or paradoxical evidence' (p. 546). The process of reconciling these accounts using the constant comparative method forces the analyst to a new gestalt, unfreezing thinking and producing 'theory with less researcher bias than theory built from incremental studies or armchair, axiomatic deduction' (p. 546).
2. The emergent theory 'is likely to be testable with constructs that can be readily measured and hypotheses that can be proven false' (p. 547). Due to the close connection between theory and data it is likely that the theory can be further tested and expanded by subsequent studies.
3. The 'resultant theory is likely to be empirically valid' (p. 547). This is so because a level of validation is performed implicitly by constant comparison, questioning

the data from the start of the process. 'This closeness can lead to an intimate sense of things' that 'often produces theory which closely mirrors reality' (p. 547).[4]

Recent evidence shows that the combination of case studies and grounded theory has been rewarding for IS researchers. For example, Lehmann (2001a, p. 87) claims that:

> Applying Grounded Theory to Case Study was very successful. It produced a prolific amount and yielded a great richness of information. ... The case settings, furthermore, contained more varied data than could be expected from individual, purely homocentric studies. Efficiency and abundance combined to make this method an exceedingly fruitful one.

According to Dr Anne Persson (Department of Computer Science, University of Skövde, Sweden), 'I have to say that the combination of case studies and [Grounded Theory] has been very rewarding. I seriously doubt that I would have achieved my goal without that combination' (personal correspondence, 13 Sept. 2001, 08:27:38). My experience with the method further attests to these expressions of satisfaction.

Walking the research model

I acknowledge upfront the difficulty in explaining simply and correctly a method that 'happens sequentially, subsequently, simultaneously, serendipitously and scheduled' (Glaser, 1998, p. 1). The spiral, and at times simultaneous, nature of grounded theory is a powerful and satisfying feature of the research method; it allows flexibility and continuous sharpening of emerging constructs via deep familiarisation with data, validation, and progressive expansion of knowledge and skills. This nature is represented in Lehmann's (2001) research model.

Lehmann (2001a) describes the grounded theory process as a spiral that starts by collecting 'slices of data' in a substantive area of enquiry, which are then codified and categorised in a continuous process that moves toward saturation and results in the theoretical densification of concepts represented by a substantive theory. Figure 5.2 represents this iterative process.

Figure 5.2. Grounded theory's building process (Lehmann 2001a).

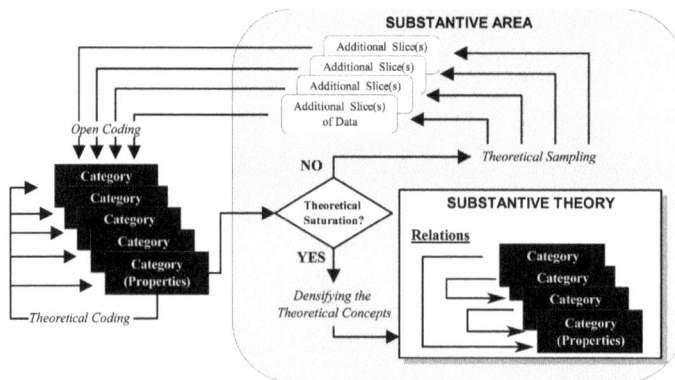

Although this model provides a good overview of the process of grounded theory, it fails to include the significant role of extant literature external to the substantive area in the formulation of the substantive theory, and the role of memos.

[4]These points are also in harmony with Yin's (1994) approach to case study.

To help explain the activities that developed the substantive theory in my study, I expanded Lehmann's (2001a) model, adding components from Eisenhardt's (1989) and from the Glaserian literature. By doing so, it is possible to present a picture (Figure 5.3) that includes the important role the literature played in my research and to acknowledge the key role of theoretical memos.

Figure 5.3. Expanded Lehmann's research model.

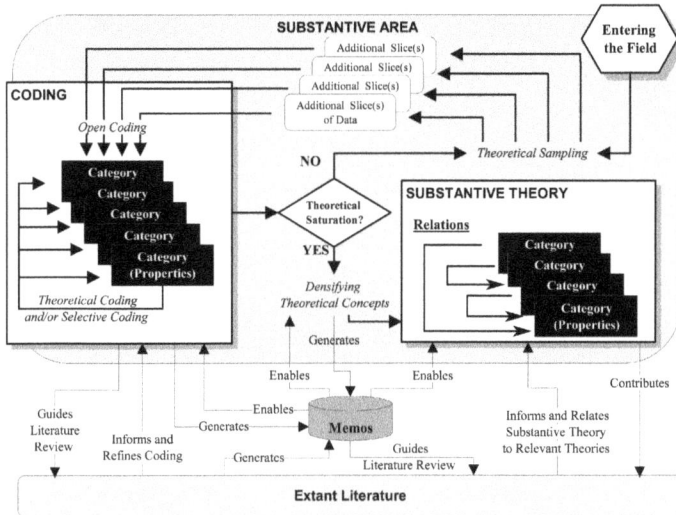

Entering the field is the first research action to be conducted in the context where the phenomenon is found. To enter the field I considered three important aspects:

1. First, following the grounded theory tradition, the study assumed that 'the problem' was to be discovered from accounts from people in the substantive area of enquiry. This contrasts with the need of other methods for precise research questions emerging from the literature review. The initial research question was as broad as possible and did not include *a priori* constructs or guiding theories. As I had a pre-research assumption regarding leadership as a main theme, this assumption was handled according to the method; that is, the researcher produced a 'slice of data' to be compared with others. However, this assumption was soon abandoned as a pattern different from the expected emerged.
2. Second, I had to address practical issues like crafting ethical protocols and obtaining approval, selecting the software and hardware required for interviewing and processing the data, producing transcription protocols, and training to administer leadership surveys.[5]
3. Third, entering the field included preparation work such as selecting an appropriate site, negotiating and obtaining access to the case, contacting participants and gaining their consent.

After entering the field, access was unrestricted and I became involved in *theoretical sampling*. Theoretical sampling was a data collection process that continued until the

[5]The surveys, MLQ and MLQTeam, were designed to measure the leadership style of the project manager and the project team. The purpose of the survey was twofold: (a) to measure a priori the leadership style of the team and of the project manager, based on a suspicion that leadership was a key issue; and (b) to have data from the survey to later compare with evidence from interviews if leadership emerged as a main concern (it did not). The surveys had the secondary goals of introducing the team to the research and to establish rapport. In this regard the exercise was successful.

very end of the research (including the write-up stage). This allowed me to take advantage of emergent themes, to acquire data continuously and to maximise observation opportunities.

All interviews were recorded in both digital and analogue forms. The tape recording was then transcribed and ATLAS.ti, a software application for qualitative data analysis, facilitated *open coding* and other coding activities.[6] Open coding involves 'running the data open'; that is, analysing the data to extract a set of categories and their properties. This is done by coding for as many categories as possible *without a preconceived set of codes* (Glaser, 1978). During open coding, I labelled the text of each interview, detecting new lines of enquiry, which guided subsequent data acquisition activity. Open coding generated 337 codes.

The writing of *theoretical memos* starts almost in parallel with open coding. Because memos are 'the theorising write up of ideas about codes and their relationships as they strike the analyst while coding' (Glaser, 1978, p. 83), memos are produced constantly in grounded theory, from the beginning of the analysis process until reaching closure, capturing the thoughts of analysts while they progress through the work. Memos raise the theoretical level via a continuous process of comparison and conceptualisation. They also provide freedom, flexibility, and enhance creativity (Glaser, 1978; Urquhart, 2001).

As codes and memos accumulated, I started to perceive relationships between them. This process, called *theoretical coding*, conceptualised the interrelation of substantive codes by generating hypotheses for integration into a theory. Therefore, theoretical codes emerged from open coding and theoretical memos, weaving a new story from the fragmentation of open coding (as suggested by Lehmann, 2001b). The grounded integration of concepts is a flexible activity that provides broad pictures and new perspectives. However flexible, theoretical codes *must* remain grounded on data, they cannot be empty abstractions. The concept of flexibility implies theoretical sensitivity to a number of possible coding paradigms, or coding families, consciously avoiding over-focusing on one possible explanation. Glaser (1978; 1998) provides a comprehensive (but not definitive) list of code families allowing for this flexibility.

The emergence of a pattern, in my study's case 'resolving conflicts', marks the beginning of *selective coding*. This process refers to delimiting the theory to one or two core variable(s) which act as a guide for further data collection and analysis (Glaser, 1978 p. 61-72). By doing so, the research focused on one of the several basic social processes or conditions that are present in the data. The delimitation of the analysis to those significant variables affecting the core variable contributes to parsimonious theory (Glaser and Strauss, 1967).

At this stage in the process, the role of the *extant literature* becomes very important because researchers need to acquire sensitivity and knowledge on grounded concepts. The literature is therefore read as a source of more data to be compared with existing grounded data. For example, in my study, readings about trust, shared mental models, conflict, psychological contracts, transaction cost economics, and organisational psychology raised the theoretical level and improved construct definitions (as suggested by Eisenhardt, [1989]). Most of these readings were outside the substantive area of research, yet they were made relevant by the actors' main concerns and the emerging theory.

---

[6] ATLAS.ti stands for 'Archiv fuer Technik, Lebenswelt und Alltagssprache' (archive for technology, the life environment and everyday language). The extension 'ti' stands for text interpretation. Technical University of Berlin's Project ATLAS (1989-1992) produced the first prototype of the software (source: http://www.atlasti.de/faq.shtml#acronym , accessed 20 October 2002).

The researcher achieves *theoretical saturation* when the main concern of the research can be accounted for, and further sampling fails to add significant value to the study through adding new categories or properties.

At this stage, when the theory becomes dense with concepts and enriched by relevant extant literature, the researcher has 'discovered' a *substantive theory*. Substantive theories are applicable to the particular area of empirical enquiry from which they emerged (Glaser and Strauss, 1967). They can be classified as 'middle-range' theories; that is, between 'minor working hypotheses' and 'grand theories' and they are relevant to the people concerned as well as being readily modifiable (Glaser and Strauss, 1967).

The objective of this section was to present an overview of the activities involved in this study. However, some concepts require further explanation, as discussed in the next section.

Particular characteristics of the method

While the grounded theory method has been in use for many years in the social sciences, it still has a minority status in IS research (Lehmann, 2001b). Thus, some critical and perhaps more obscure methodological aspects need to be discussed if one wants to dispel misconceptions. These characteristics are discussed next.

Role of the extant literature

As has already been mentioned, in grounded theory methodology the bulk of the literature review is conducted after the emergence of substantive theory. It is then, and not before, that data from the extant literature contributes to the study (Eisenhardt, 1989, p. 278; Urquhart, 2001, p. 366). The approach of reading the literature first with the objective of identifying gaps and relevant theories is opposite to the role that the literature has in grounded theory. Glaser (1998, p. 67) cannot be more specific in this regard:

> Grounded theory's very strong dicta are a) *do not do a literature review in the substantive area and related areas where the research is done,* and b) when the grounded theory is nearly completed during sorting and writing up, then the literature search in the substantive area can be accomplished and woven into the theory as more data for constant comparison (Glaser, 1998 p. 360:67).[7]

While uninformed observers of the grounded theory method may construe these dicta as a neglect of the literature (Glaser, 1998 p. 360), nothing can be farther from the truth. The purpose of the dicta above is to keep the researcher as free as possible of influences that could restrict the freedom required for theoretical discovery, not to ignore extant and relevant knowledge (Glaser, 1998). Adopting a grounded theory method commits the researcher to a rigorous and constant literature review process that occurs at two levels:

1. the researcher must be constantly reading in other substantive areas to increase their theoretical sensitivity, and
2. conceptual emergence forces the researcher to review convergent and diverging literature in the field related to the developing concept.

Because emerging theoretical construction drives the literature review, the extant literature is incorporated into the study as data. Therefore, most of the relevant reviewed literature will be presented, as it finds its way into, and becomes *integrated* with, the substantive theory. This closely reflects the nature of the method and the role and place

---

[7] Italic text in the original.

of the literature within it. Forcing a typical PhD dissertation's 'Chapter 2: Literature Review' would be incongruent with grounded theory and methodologically unsound, detracting from the true role of the literature in this type of research.

Unit of analysis

The *qualitative datum* is defined as a string of words capturing information about an incident; this incident (or unit of analysis) represents an instance of a concept coded and classified during the coding process (Van de Ven and Poole, 1989). The source of the datum may be a person, a group, a document, an observation, or extant literature.

Incidents are indicators of a concept. Figure 5.4 shows a model based on the constant comparison of indicators. In this model, the comparison of indicator to indicator generates a conceptual code first, and then indicators are compared to the newly emerged concept, further defining it. The constant comparison of indicators confronts the analyst with similarities, differences, and consistency of meaning, which result in the construction of a concept (or category) and its dimensions (Glaser, 1978).

Figure 5.4. The concept indicator model (Glaser 1978, p.62).

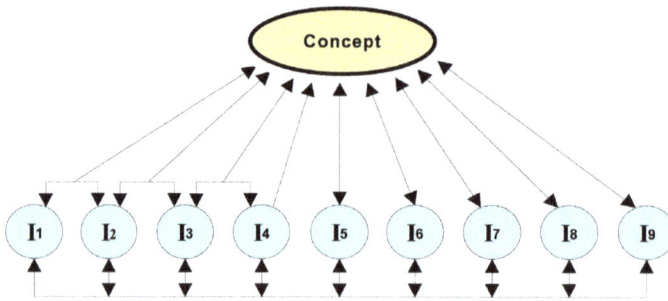

Incidents had many sources, from actors' accounts to field observations. However, interviews provided the study's most significant building block. These interviews focused on the client's core project team comprising the project manager and the associated team leaders, with multiple interviews over a period of time. The decision to include team members was based on the need to obtain a wide range of views from the people confronting the day-to-day issues and having similar (but not equal) level of responsibility in the IT project. This was important because:

> [g]rounded theory accounts for the action in a substantive area. In order to accomplish this goal grounded theory tries to understand the action in a substantive area from the point of view of the actors involved. This understanding revolves around the main concern of the participants whose behaviour continually resolves their concern. Their continual resolving is the core variable. It is the prime mover of most of the behaviour seen and talked about in a substantive area. It is what is going on! It emerges as the overriding pattern. (Glaser, 1998, p. 115)

Therefore, this study's focus on actions and accounts of actions is congruent with the assumptions of grounded theory. Furthermore, action occurs in a context and within a process enacted and constructed by the actors. Consequently, the study does not focus on properties of an actor or unit but on *properties of a process*. This is discussed next.

Focusing on properties of a process

My study centred on *properties of a process* not on properties of a unit (as a person, group, or organisation). Properties of a unit are more relevant to descriptive qualitative studies, while properties of a process are more relevant to studies aiming at theoretical conceptualisation (Glaser, 1978; Glaser, 2001; Glaser, 2002).

More specifically, the study's aim was to provide a theoretical conceptualisation of a basic social process (BSP). Basic social processes can be of two types: basic social psychological process (BSPP) and basic social structural process (BSSP). BSPPs refer to processes such as becoming (e.g. a nurse, a leader, a system) or inspiring (e.g. followers, peers) and are useful in understanding behaviours. BSSPs are concerned with social structures in a process such as centralisation, organisational growth, outsourcing, or recruiting procedures (Glaser, 1978).

BSPs are a type of core category (though not all core categories are BSPs) exhibiting the following characteristics (Glaser, 1978):

1. BSPs 'process out' at least two emergent stages that 'differentiate and account for variations in the problematic pattern of behaviour.'
2. BSPs may not be present in a grounded theory study (i.e. researchers may not have two or more stages in the central concept).
3. BSPs are ideally suited to qualitative studies where the analyst observes the evolution of a process over time (i.e. influencing outcomes in a project).
4. BSPs are labelled by a ground that reflects their evolving nature and a sense of motion (i.e. resolving, influencing, communicating, becoming).

As the second point above indicates, BSPs may or may not be present in a grounded theory study; their presence (or lack thereof) further guides the research design and execution. Therefore, understanding the distinction between doing unit or process based sociological analysis, is critical to the research design, regarding the particular demands they place on sampling, analysing and theorising (see Glaser, 1978, pp. 109-13, for a comprehensive listing of these differences).

Theoretical sampling

A basic question in case study research is concerned with the single-case versus multiple-case design of the study. In case study research, researchers determine *a priori* if the study is going to be single-case or multiple-case based, depending on the nature of the inquiry (Yin, 1994). Yet, under a grounded theory approach, that assumption could not have been made at the start of the research simply because at that stage it was unknown if the case would allow pattern detection and saturation. In grounded theory, sampling is driven by conceptual emergence and limited by theoretical saturation, *not* by design. As Glaser and Strauss (1967, p. 45) explain:

> Theoretical Sampling is the process of data collection for generating theory whereby the analyst jointly collects, codes, and analyses his data and decides what data to collect next and where to find them, in order to develop his theory as it emerges. This process of data collection is controlled by the emerging theory, whether substantive or formal.

Consequently, the selection of data sources is neither a random selection nor a totally *a priori* determination. For example, I decided *a priori* that a combination of data sources was most appropriate for this study. However, the specific details of what data was available and which datum was relevant depended on the emerging data.

Another critical *a priori* sampling decision was to control the variation by organisational delimitation while allowing for within-case diversity of access to multiple data sources. The sample was under the unifying influence of the cultural and organisational environment, which allowed controlling environmental variation while clarifying the domain of the research, as suggested by Pettigrew (1988).

One of the dangers in any type of research is to sample too superficially. To counteract this risk, the foundation case was selected because it provided the 'meatiest, most study-relevant sources' (a strategy recommended by Miles and Huberman [1994]). There were also opportunistic reasons to select the case. The selected project provided the best accessibility, as most people in the core project team were (usually) based in the same city in which I was located. This practical consideration was later proven critical as *in situ* observations gave me a better appreciation of what was going on and of what was important to the actors.[8]

As it happened, the single case was sufficient to provide enough data for the exploratory study, as Yin (1994) would perhaps have suggested. However, this was because the initial project resulted in a much richer source of data than first expected, with the project taking six times longer than expected to complete and presenting a substantial number of incidents for comparison and theory construction. While the argument presented by Yin (1994) for revelatory single case studies was *ad post* valid for my research, the validity of the single case study was based on the richness of the case. This richness allowed reaching conceptual saturation and thus permitted the closure of the grounded theory study, something I did not know *a priori*.

The core category: role and selection criteria

The objective of the research is to generate theory 'that accounts for the patterns of behaviour which is relevant and problematic for those involved' (Glaser, 1978, p. 93). To achieve this goal the analyst must discover the core category and delimit the investigation around it. The core category is the pivotal point for the theory; most other categories relate to it, and it accounts for most of the variation in pattern and behaviour. The core category 'has the prime function of integrating the theory and rendering the theory dense and saturated as the relationships increase' (Glaser, 1978, p. 93).

In my study, the core pattern was 'resolving conflicts', a basic process that engaged actors (people and organisations) in a series (pattern) of activities aimed at resolving incongruence and misunderstandings. Resolving conflicts is how managers of meta-teams (and the component teams) achieve project delivery. The core category in the resolving conflict pattern was 'trust,' which had a number of key interrelated categories that explained the core pattern.

Induction and deduction

According to Glaser (1998), the notion of induction versus deduction is often an over-simplification of complex patterns of thought present in grounded theory development. While grounded theory is classified as an inductive method (e.g. Glaser, 1978; Glaser and Strauss, 1967; Martin and Turner, 1986; Strauss and Corbin, 1998), theoretical sampling is a deductive activity grounded in inducted categories or hypotheses. This acts as a virtuous circle where '[d]eductions for theoretical sampling fosters better sources of data, therefore better grounded inductions' (Glaser, 1998, p. 43). The difference

---

[8] *In situ* observations were important. One can listen to historical accounts of disagreements; however, listening to the somewhat heated discussion between two parties with conflicting interests in real-time, as I did, gives the researcher yet another perspective to compare.

between an inductive and a deductive method relates to 'pacing'; if the researcher looks at data first and then forms the hypotheses (inductive), or if the researcher forms the hypotheses first by conjecture and then seeks research data to verify the deduction (deductive) (Glaser, 1998). This cycle of induction and deduction is represented in Figure 5.5.

Figure 5.5. The inductive-deductive cycle of the grounded theory method.

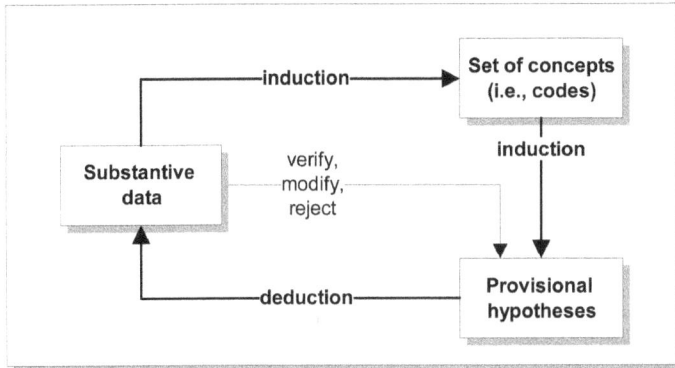

Two practical aspects of the research facilitated both induction and deduction activities, namely: (a) recording and transcribing interviews, and (b) using a qualitative data coding and analysis tool. These activities are discussed in the next two sections.

Recording and transcribing interviews

All interviews were recorded using analogue and digital technology. The analogue tape was then professionally transcribed and turned into analysable text. I used ATLAS.ti as the main tool to code and analyse the data and to collect memos. For example, while proceeding through open coding of a particular interview for the first time, I would load the primary document onto ATLAS.ti and simultaneously play the MP3 version of the interview on my computer. This had two effects: first, it improved recollection and mental activity (the interview was recreated with sound, not just words), which increased the production of memos. Second, it allowed the correction of transcription errors that can be very frequent due to the jargon used by actors.

Glaser does not encourage the use of tape recording (Glaser, 1998). He argues that recording is unnecessary because the researcher is after important concepts and patterns, not precise accounts as in other more descriptive methods. Therefore, for conceptualisation purposes the actual words are not as significant as they belong to one of many possible units in a process. Another perceived problem with recording is that it becomes time consuming and inefficient for this type of research. Interviews are often taken for transcription and then corrected, causing the analysis of many non-important parts. Glaser is very conscious of wasting time in what he considers superfluous activities.

However, I was convinced at the beginning of the study that recording the interviews was appropriate and necessary. Consequently, I decided to: (a) take a few notes during the interview; (b) do post-interview notes when required; and (c) record the interviews. This extra effort was justified as a risk mitigation strategy. By taking notes, I could then use these notes to record memos or to guide my next interview while the previous one was being transcribed. Furthermore, waiting for transcriptions was seldom necessary as I was able to control my pacing thanks to having open access to actors and data.

As Glaser predicted, the extra time involved in open coding full interviews, rather than coding just the important concepts, was substantial (ranging from 40 to 60 hours each for the first few one-hour interviews to eight to 20 hours each for the last few). However, this also allowed me to relive the interviews and the detailed analysis helped me to acquire a deeper understanding of the issues. This understanding facilitated the emergence by discovery of the core concept and made me, the researcher, more comfortable with the coding activity.

It is probable that without recording and coding literal transcriptions I could have saved some time; however, listening to the actors often triggered theoretical memos and facilitated the finding of relations – therefore, it was a productive activity, not a wasteful one. Moreover, listening and reading the interviews matched my cognitive style and therefore facilitated emergence.

While I found re-listening to the interviews and analysing the full text very rewarding and interesting, it must be recognised that Glaser is correct in his assertions – neither recording nor taking extensive notes are necessary activities for conceptualisation.

Nevertheless, not recording is too risky a strategy for a PhD student to follow. Above and beyond fulfilling the need for evidence in a PhD study by recording and transcribing interviews, researchers can revisit and re-code text as more evidence emerges and patterns are detected. The ability to have access to the full transcription and to replay the interview at any time is a distinct advantage, especially in studies of organisational cases that are conducted over a long period of time, at different points in the life cycle of the analysed phenomena. In any case, the iterative nature of grounded theory demands the constant comparison of incidents with already collected data. In doing this, previously undetected incidents are likely to emerge. These new incidents benefit the study and therefore justify the extra effort required to record, transcribe, and code potentially irrelevant data.

Using qualitative data coding tools in GTM research

Glaser (1998, pp. 185-6) also alerts against the 'technological traps' of data analysis tools such as NVivo or ATLAS.ti because they create unnecessary restrictions, inhibit the researcher's development of skills and impose time-consuming learning curves. Glaser perceives computing technology as an easy way out and as a hindrance rather than an aid to creativity. This is not my experience. Yet computing tools can be used in many ways and some of those ways will indeed have the negative consequences Glaser has mentioned.

Using ATLAS.ti in my study for open coding and memoing was a substantial advantage. It provided a fast way of checking and comparing incidents and the flexibility of exporting data to other tools as I perceived appropriate. The software's ability to collect memos allowed the efficient writing, analysis, and retrieval of memos at any time in the process. It is also true that ATLAS.ti was not everything I needed. I used additional techniques and tools: butcher's paper and a whiteboard to draw box diagrams representing the interrelation of emerging concepts; notepads and flowcharting software to draw many diagrams; a word processor to combine and analyse sets of incidents and memos; and mind-mapping software (MindManager) to organise ideas and themes.

Therefore, Glaser is correct in asserting that this is creative work, yet the generalisation that technology restricts creativity was falsified by this study's experience, as people familiar with computers do creative work with them and around them.[9] ATLAS.ti did not impose a significant learning curve; the software was found to be intuitive, the tutorials took a day to do – and after that I did not need to refer to the software manuals. Working with ATLAS.ti was not different from working on paper, yet retrieving and connecting concepts was extremely easy and efficient.

Finally, while ATLAS.ti has some automated coding facilities (i.e. coding all occurrences of a word or phrase), coding was done entirely manually, reading the text line by line while endeavouring to explain the incidents. Automatic coding is a disadvantage for the grounded theorist as it obscures the discovery of what is going on in the text; in this regard, Glaser's reservations are fully justified.

Demands and risks of grounded theory

Every methodology poses particular demands and grounded theory is not an exception. I strongly concur with the advice provided by Glaser (1978; 1998; 2001), based on his own experience and discussions with other grounded theorists, that the grounded theorist must:

1. tolerate confusion – there is no need to know *a priori* and no need to force the data;
2. tolerate regression – researchers might get briefly 'lost' before finding their way;
3. trust emerging data without worrying about justification – the data will provide the justification if the researcher adheres to the rigour of the method;
4. have someone to talk to – grounded theory demands moments of isolation to get deep in data analysis as well as moments of consultation and discussion;
5. be open to emerging evidence that may change the way the researcher thought about the subject matter, and be willing to act on the new evidence;
6. be able to conceptualise to derive theory from the data. This is perhaps the most important risk, as some people may experience difficulty conceptualising what is going on in the field; and
7. be creative in devising new ways of obtaining and handling data, combining the approaches of others, or using a tested approach in a different way.

Additionally, in adopting grounded theory methodology, the IS researcher has to confront two further risks. First, due to the minority status of grounded theory in IS research, it is likely that IS researchers, especially PhD candidates, will experience what Stern (1994), described as *Minus-mentoring* – that is, learning from books, employing grounded theory for the first time without the guidance of a supervisor with practical knowledge of the methodology. Minus-mentoring could result in methodologically unsound studies (Glaser, 1998; Stern, 1994). This has happened, for example, when studies claiming to be based on grounded theory have breached key tenets of the method (one of the main risks of using grounded theory within a second, overarching, methodology). However, *'Minus-mentees'* can reduce this risk by (a) networking with IS researchers conversant with the methodology; (b) reading the 'Grounded Theory Bibliography' (Urquhart, 2001); and (c) participating in relevant discussion groups (e.g. IFIP WG8.2, the Grounded Theory Institute).[10]

Second, grounded theory seems to be easier to use when the researcher is sensitive, through having professional experience or knowledge, to the field under study (Glaser,

---

[9] It has to be acknowledged that my familiarity with computers as work tools did make a difference in the usability of qualitative data analysis software. I would also suggest that the familiarity people in the IS area have with technology cannot be assumed in other areas of research, such as social sciences, where the bulk of grounded theory studies are conducted.
[10] Minus-mentoring was resolved in my case by the addition of an external supervisor with excellent practical experience on grounded theory (as well as following the strategies recommended here).

1978; Glaser, 1998; Glaser and Strauss, 1967). This sensitivity facilitates understanding or *'verstehen'* (Weber, 1968). My substantial experience as a senior practitioner in the field of IS project management was a distinct advantage in eliciting information from participants in the same field. This experience facilitated the understanding of some of the more subtle issues in the study.

There is also the risk of finding something that is not new. What if this has been done before? This appears to be more a natural fear than a probable risk. To be sure, it is possible to study some emerging organisational phenomena just to come up with a theory that already exists in the literature. Yet this is unlikely. If the study is conducted as the method indicates, diligent researchers should have included the relevant literature (convergent and divergent) and detected variations and particularities. As Thomas Kuhn (1962, p. 30) said: 'It is a truism that anything is similar to, and also different from, everything else'. A good grounded theory study should be able to point out similarities and differences, and to produce patterns that are particular to the substantive field of the research. Yet, as with any methodology, and indeed any human activity, there are no certainties.

Lastly, a grounded theory emerges through intensive intellectual action. Researchers need to interact with their data and while this interaction is often highly rewarding and satisfying, it is also extremely intensive, time- consuming and all absorbing, and the researcher must be persistent and resilient (as also attested by Urquhart, 2001).

Conclusion

The literature describes several virtues of the grounded theory method. Grounded theory allows researchers to deal effectively with the important issues of bias and preconceptions, and provides a systematic approach that takes into consideration extant theory but is not driven by it (Glaser and Strauss, 1967; Goleman, 1998; Sarker et al., 2001; Urquhart, 1997; Urquhart, 2001). Triangulation is embedded in the methodology (Glaser, 1978; Glaser, 1998; Glaser and Strauss, 1967). GTM values professional experience (Glaser, 1998; Urquhart, 2001). GTM can efficiently study emerging phenomena (Lehmann, 2001a; Urquhart, 2001; Van de Ven and Poole, 1989). GTM helps IT practitioners to better understand their own environment (Glaser, 1998; Martin and Turner, 1986). Furthermore, grounded theory can produce clear, logical and parsimonious theory that fulfils the canons of good science and simultaneously can be used in IS practice to explain and predict the phenomena in its environment. In other words, researchers can produce theory-building studies 'which are useful, relevant and up-to-date' (Partington, 2000).

To be relevant to practitioners' concerns, the theory needs to provide meaningful accounts for them. With the grounded theory methodology, researchers can significantly contribute by providing the knowledgeable person with theory grounded in their field of work (Glaser, 1978) that has been enriched by conceptualisation and extant literature from multiple sources (Eisenhardt, 1989; Glaser, 1998). By doing this, researchers can avoid stating the obvious to the expert and instead provide categories based on many indicators and showing ideas based on patterns. These conceptual ideas allow practitioners to transcend the limits of their own experience, adapting and applying the substantive theory to other situations.

Relevance for the grounded theorist means bringing tangible benefits to the experts. As Glaser said, when the field experts can understand and use a theory by themselves '… then our theories have earned their way. Much of the popularity of grounded theory to sociologists and layman alike, is that it deals with what is actually going on, not what ought to go on' (Glaser, 1978, p. 14).

Furthermore, research that focuses on actors' perspectives provides actors with oppor-tunities to articulate their thoughts about issues *they* consider important (Glaser, 1998). This articulation allows participants to reflect on empirically significant events (to them), gaining further understanding of past actions and acquiring new insights.[11]

I experienced a high level of participant cooperation while conducting my grounded theory study. This can be partly attributed to the open nature of the interviews, the focus on experiences *as perceived by the actors*, the method forcing me to act as a very active listener, and my being perceived as an 'insider' to whom the accounts did not require too much 'proper lining'.[12]

Consequently, I was intellectually stimulated by interacting with rich data, by the par-ticipants' positive attitude towards the research, and by a sense of contributing to a wider audience. This positive feedback helped to counteract the heavy demands grounded theory poses on researchers, as previously described. These demands are real; they should not be underestimated by those contemplating the adoption of the grounded theory method. But when these demands and risks are satisfactorily addressed, grounded theory offers a very strong methodological foundation for IS researchers wanting to engage in theory-building studies of emerging socio-technical phenomena.

[11]Incidents in which actors called me to 'run a few ideas through you' are evidence of this perception of value. They wanted to articulate their thoughts, and even when I kept a passive role in the conversation, only asking questions to clarify the problem, they felt that the conversation helped them.
[12]'Proper lining' is a term used by Glaser to describe the distortion often found when actors present aspects of their world (e.g. own person, group, organisation) to an outsider; this is caused by the actors' perception of what constitutes a 'proper view' of their world. Proper lining is a useful concept; when detected, it may tell us of an actors' perception (and importance of this perception) regarding how the external world should be looking into their context.

6. A hermeneutic analysis of the Denver International Airport Baggage Handling System

Stasys Lukaitis, *School of Information Systems, Deakin University*
Jacob Cybulski, *School of Information Systems, Deakin University*

Abstract

This paper attempts to demonstrate the principles of hermeneutics in an effort to understand factors affecting Information Systems (IS) projects. As hermeneutics provides a systematic method of interpreting text from multiple information sources, thus, Information Systems being prima facie defined and documented as text documents, are eminently suited for this mode of investigation. In this paper, we illustrate hermeneutics by analysing a sample case study document describing the well-known Denver International Airport (DIA) Automated Baggage Handling System project, which was extensively reported in the IS and management press and studied by Montealegre and his colleagues. As a result of the hermeneutic approach to the analysis of this document, a new 'flexibility' factor has been discovered to play an important, yet unreported, role in the DIA system demise. In the DIA case, the observed flexibility factor influenced the quality of the interaction between the actors, the prevailing environment and the information systems.

Introduction

Although there are several reports of information systems projects that have applied hermeneutics (Boland, 1991; Klein and Myers, 1999; Myers, 1994a), there are very few publications that explain the actual hermeneutic process taken by IS (and in fact, also non-IS) researchers. What this paper strives to do is close the methodological gap and to present one potential framework for the adoption of hermeneutics in the study of information systems.

In addition, hermeneutics is often viewed as an 'obscure' tool in the IS community because it is perhaps not particularly well understood. To that end, this research also focuses attention on making sense of hermeneutics and its philosophy.

Making sense of hermeneutics

The Oxford dictionary defines hermeneutics as 'of interpretation', taken from the original Greek *hermeneutikos* (Turner, 1987, p. 284). Hermeneutics has been well documented as a philosophy of enquiry, with its roots already evident in late antiquity where 'the Greeks, the Jews and the Christians had been reading and re-reading their vital texts, namely the Homeric epics, the Torah, Talmud and Midrashim, and the Holy Bible, respectively. In the process of their textual labour, these people revised their own idiosyncratic sets of rules for doing interpretation' (Demeterio, 2001).

Demeterio (2001) gives a useful definition of *hermeneutics* as 'a theory, methodology and praxis of interpretation that is geared towards the recapturing of meaning of a text, or a text-analogue, that is temporally or culturally distant, or obscured by ideology and false consciousness'.

Thus, the understanding that is sought is found within texts and text-analogues – records that have been created by authors. These records might be as prosaic as a report, or as interesting as a series of captured electronic mails (Lee, 1994), or even as a set of transcripts of interviews and case study notes (Montealegre and Keil, 2000; Montealegre et al., 1999). In any event, these documents purport to represent some sort of reality or truth.

This search for understanding is influenced by several interesting factors that rely on some assumptions that may or may not all be present and at work at any given time.

First, understanding can be viewed as an interpretive oscillation between several layers or perspectives. This is often referred to as the 'hermeneutic circle or cycle', where one examines a small fragment of knowledge and seeks to understand it, then looks at the 'whole' (whatever that means to the enquirer), and seeks understanding there as well – the smaller fragment being part of the whole, and the whole being composed of many smaller fragments. Understanding, then, is achieved when there is a consistency between the whole and all its component parts and vice versa. Or, as stated by Myers (1994b, p. 191): 'This hermeneutic process continues until the apparent absurdities, contradictions and oppositions in the organisation no longer appear strange, but make sense'.

Second, if understanding can be described as a stable oscillation between the parts of a whole and each individual part exhibiting consistency, then the very act of 'searching for understanding' would be the actual oscillation or (hermeneutic) cyclic action. As one searches for understanding, one acquires a small new piece of knowledge or a minor fact, seeks to understand this new piece in itself and also in the context of the already acquired knowledge and existing understanding of the whole.

Third, how does one know that understanding has been achieved? The repeated cycling between the parts and the whole will eventually yield consistency that is driven by the sum of knowledge or data in front of the researcher. Should that knowledge be incomplete, the researcher would actually have no way of knowing that fact. The only really useful test would be to introduce yet more data or facts and test by hermeneutically cycling through again. If the number of resulting cycles is sufficiently small, or even zero, then one could say that there is understanding, or as Myers (1994b, p. 191) would have simply said – it 'makes sense'.

But understanding and the processes of its acquisition must be something more than just the end product of a process. Kidder (1997, p. 1196) cites the seminal philosopher Hans-Georg Gadamer on understanding:

> If I am an English language speaker learning German, for example, I will very likely pursue a course of study in which I learn a linguistic apparatus that is neither spoken English nor spoken German. I will learn patterns of verb endings, noun cases, systems of adjective and noun agreement, and such – categories I may never have applied to language before, although I had been speaking language all my life. This apparatus is a third thing, a bridge to understanding a language that is not the same as understanding that language. When the

understanding actually occurs, I recognise it because suddenly the apparatus falls away and I simply speak German. So it is with hermeneutic: the interpretive process creates something that is neither my horizon nor the others. This third thing is a necessary medium; but it is just as necessary that this medium fall away. At this point in transcending the apparatus we can say that understanding occurs. There is still, however, the quality of a kind of third horizon here; one has not dissolved into the other culture; one has not erased one's own horizon; but one's horizon has become entwined with another in a unique instance of fusion.

So it can be reasonable to assume, then, that understanding comes from applying an apparatus (or tool) repeatedly over some data until the apparatus or tool becomes superfluous – that is to say, some understanding has been reached because the apparatus is no longer needed.

Using the Gadamerian analogy, successfully engaging in a conversation with a German would validate one's understanding of the newly learnt language – i.e. testing the understanding with new untried data. If the conversation is unsuccessful, by whatever criteria, then the apparatus is reapplied, learning restarted, and then another test is undertaken. This is the hermeneutic cycle in its simplest form. The act of understanding flows from understanding the whole to understanding all the little bits that make up the whole. Then when confronted by a new 'little bit' that purports to be part of the whole under consideration, if understanding has been achieved, then a consistency between the new knowledge and the context of the existing whole will be maintained without any conflict (Myers, 1994b, p. 191).

Practical hermeneutics

The apparatus that is so critical to achieving/acquiring understanding in Gadamer's case (see above) is specially designed to create a bridge between zero understanding and the final goal of complete understanding. The apparatus itself is specific to the task at hand. In the use of critical hermeneutics in the interpretation of texts (and text analogues), Harvey and Myers (1995, p. 20) quote Paul Ricoeur:

> In critical hermeneutics the interpreter constructs the context as another form of text, which can then, of itself, be critically analysed so that the meaning construction can be understood as an interpretive act. In this way, the hermeneutic interpreter is simply creating another text on a text, and this recursive creation is potentially infinite. Every meaning is constructed, even through the very constructive act of seeking to deconstruct, and the process whereby that textual interpretation occurs must be self-critically reflected upon. (Ricoeur, 1974)

This research will create, analyse and seek to understand these additional texts on the original texts under investigation.

There are already further issues to consider. There is a substantial cultural difference between an English-speaking Californian (say) and a German speaking Berliner. What if we are engaging with text rather than a person? What if the text was written 200 hundred years ago about things that were important at the time, but have become obscure in the 21st century?

This 'distance' between the hermeneutist (the enquirer) and the author (and text) under investigation is referred to as 'historicality' by researchers such as Myers (1994b, p. 189).

Critical hermeneutics does emphasise the fact that social reality is historically constituted. And one of the key differences between a purely interpretative approach and critical hermeneutics is that the researcher does not merely accept the self-understanding of participants, but seeks to critically evaluate the totality of understandings in a given situation.[1] The researcher analyses the participants' own understandings historically, and in terms of changing social structures. The hermeneutic-dialectic perspective, therefore, as an integrative approach, emphasises both the subjective meanings for individual actors and the social structures which condition and enable such meanings and are constituted by them.

This concept of historicality has also been called 'contextualisation' where Klein and Myers (1999, p. 73) refer to Gadamer's (1976, p. 133) observation: '… the hermeneutic task consists, not in covering up the tension between the text and present, but in consciously bringing it out'.

The distance of the investigators from the source text can be manifold. It might be due to one or any combination of:

1. *time :* the months or years or even millennia since the original text was written;
2. *language:* where the language of the text is no longer in day-to-day use or has been substantially modified;
3. *culture:* where the original text was created by an author within a cultural context alien to the investigator;
4. *intention:* where the original text's author set out intentionally to mislead, omit or twist events and facts to serve their own ends;
5. *social milieu:* where the prevailing social norms and accepted behaviours of that time and place of the text's creation have become forgotten or have changed.

It is the investigator's responsibility to acknowledge that they have a historicality factor to account for and that the text under investigation may well be a puzzle of many dimensions.

In addition to burdens that come with the text (historicality), there are burdens already surrounding the investigator – their prejudices that will colour their own interpretations of the text. These prejudices are actually 'pre-judgments', expectations of understanding. Butler (1998, p. 288) extends the notion of prejudice by including a reference to Heidegger's (1976) notion of 'tradition' and suggesting that prejudice is actually a combination of lived experiences, tradition and a sort of socialised comfort zone he refers to as 'das Man'. Butler (1998, p. 288) acknowledges the powerful influence exerted on individuals:

> According to Gadamer (1975), tradition influences a social actor's attitudes and behaviour through authority, and such authority is transmitted through time and history via cultural mechanisms. Heidegger (1976) argues that it is the quiet authority of das Man (roughly translated as 'the they' or 'the anyone') which provides reassurance in the face of existential turbulence. The state of being 'situated' or 'tuned' under the sway of das Man, (e.g. as operationalised through public opinion or group norms), provides one with familiar and comfortable surroundings; self-reflection precipitated by existential turbulence (a 'breakdown') shatters this tranquility and brings about an 'unhomliness' (Unheimlichkeit) of existence.

---

[1] This relates to our later issue on the actual nature of the dialectic whereby we must actively seek all the issues – both those that are in favour of the argument and those best ones that are against.

The suggestion espoused by Gadamer that prejudices are a natural attribute of individuals and should be accepted and dealt with has been thoroughly demonised by Wolin (2000, p. 45) although the basis for that vitriol is not the philosophical aspect.

Kidder (Kidder, 1997, p. 1194) on the other hand takes up the issue of the investigator's prejudice as being a useful starting point for the enquiry. He quotes from Augustine that one should 'identify the clear and obvious meanings first and then use this understanding to make sense of the more obscure and confusing passages' (Augustine, 427). Kidder (1997, p. 1194) goes on to state that 'what is clear and obvious to one in reading a text is likely to be a function of one's own cultural orientation and one's own prejudices rather than the function of some given accessibility of the text'. He goes on to say:

> So where does one begin? If one cannot begin with the obvious, are we to somehow begin with the obscure? The answer is that either option is more or less viable, but the crucial thing is that one avoids allowing the starting point to control the enquiry. False assumptions can be excellent roads to genuine understanding, but only if one is open, in the course of interpreting, to the clues that reveal the inadequacy of those assumptions and point the way to needed revisions. Thus hermeneutic properly manifests a circular or cyclic pattern in its unfolding: the progress of the enquiry returns one to the beginning, and the new beginning sets a new course of progress; the interpretation of parts yields a conception of the whole, but that conception brings new meaning to the parts, whose reinterpretation may again require reconception of the whole, and so on, in a circle that would be merely vicious were it not propelled by concrete and cumulative acts of genuine understanding (Dilthey, 1990; Schleiermacher, 1819) (Kidder, 1997, pp. 1194-5).

Critical hermeneutics is often called the hermeneutic-dialectic. There is the dictionary definition of 'dialectic': the art of investigating the truth of opinions, testing of truth by discussion, logical disputation (Turner, 1987, p. 284). The accepted usage of this term is taken from the original Socratic dialogues. Kidder's (1997, p. 1197) explanation of dialectic is eloquent:

> In an ideal Socratic dialogue, no one is in it to win the debate, but everyone is engaged together in the search for the very best arguments in support of whatever opinion is being considered, along with the very best objections that can be set against those arguments. If in the context of a Socratic dialectic, I propose an argument to which no one can respond with a substantial objection, it may fall to me to become the objector (and Socrates is often put into this situation, particularly with his younger interlocutors). If I discover that my objection is more reasonable than my argument then I do a virtuous thing, from the point of view of the dialectic, if I immediately abandon my original opinion and seek a new one. This sort of reasoning process, then, has everything to do with persuasion, but it is not one person persuading another to hold a particular opinion; it is rather a matter of putting persuasion into a larger context of enquiry and discovery, allowing the power of argument to sway oneself along with the others, and in a way that is open and deeply attuned to the reasoning on all sides of an issue.

In this paper a critical hermeneutic philosophy of enquiry will be brought to bear on the selected case study into Denver International Airport (DIA) Baggage Handling System (Montealegre et al., 1999, pp. 553-4) to develop better understanding of the event itself through the supporting documents under investigation. This case study is commonly used in information systems departments to teach issues related to project management, risk assessment, information systems strategy, etc. The case is so well known that numerous prejudices and preconceptions about the DIA project have become firmly established in the information systems community. By re-analysing the case using critical hermeneutics, we were hoping to reveal, to ourselves but also to our colleagues and our students, new horizons of understanding into the roots of the DIA project failure.

Research method

In this investigation, we initially reviewed the source document – BAE Automated Systems (A): Denver International Airport Baggage Handling System (Montealegre et al., 1999) and subsequently we performed its analysis focusing on the identification of actors, events, environmental factors and some of the authors' possible intentions in leading the readers to reach the specific conclusions in the case study. In the process in which we engaged, a number of iterations (cycles) through the document were made.

1. The first cycle was the preliminary reading and development of the first layer of document (and its case) understanding.
2. The second cycle identified all the principal actors described in the document. During this cycle, the deepening understanding of the case study was documented with each actor's insights. By actors we mean the people actively engaged in the phenomena described in the case study. Actors are instrumental in the outcomes of events, which are of special interests to the researchers studying information systems projects.
3. The third cycle looked at documenting everything that could be considered as background, or existing environment surrounding the events under investigation. Understanding of these existing environmental factors further reinforce (and in some cases negate) the researchers' understanding.
4. The fourth cycle examined the decisions that were made by actors within their respective environments, and the impact of these decisions. The actors' decisions indicate their intentions in influencing the events pertaining to the information systems development.

The cycles 1-4 were conducted by one of this article's authors and the process resulted in a very thorough factual horizon of the DIA case study understanding. Three additional text documents were created in the form of tables that summarised and cross-referenced the original case study.

The second author, at this point, joined in to provide a completely different view of the case, thus developing an alternate horizon, which complemented and in some cases contrasted the views and conceptions of the first investigator. The ensuing process of *collaborative hermeneutics*, as we call the use of multiple hermeneutic investigators, introduced into the study a richness of views and insights, which clashed, were deconstructed and eventually fused.

5. The fifth cycle introduces the second investigator's perspective of the events reported in the DIA's case study (Montealegre et al, 1999), to bring some new and independent insights. In contrast to the first investigator's approach, which was to immerse himself in the events surrounding the DIA case, the second investigator focused on the communicative intentions of the case study authors and on documenting his particular interpretations of each 'event' described. This approach brings in the dialectic perspective to this research by questioning the motivation, bias and prejudice of the case study authors.

6. Finally, another DIA centered document (Montealegre and Keil, 2000) was introduced and its contribution to the overall understanding then analysed. The analysis proceeds from the classical approach of Gadamer (1976) whereby the movement of understanding is from the particular to the whole then back again.

In the following sections, each of the cycles is described in some detail and examples from the DIA case study provided to illustrate the process.

First cycle

The researchers took the approach of reading the Denver International Airport Baggage Handling System document (Montealegre et al., 1999) 'quickly', as one would when trying to determine a document's suitability for a more intensive read. This initial reading created an immediate impression and started off the cycles of understanding.

It is at this early phase of understanding development that the value of critical hermeneutics emerges when considering the power and impact that 'simple' texts can have. Demeterio (2001) wrote about the potential impacts of text …

> … textuality can be infiltrated with power and forces that are formally considered extraneous to it and practically innocuous. Specifically, Marx argued that textuality can be warped by capitalist and class-based ideologies; Nietzsche, by cultural norms; and Freud, by the unconscious. These extraneous powers and forces are capable of penetrating deep into the text, by weaving into its linguistic fabric. Thus, even without the cultural and temporal distances that made romanticist hermeneutics anxious, or even without the differences of life-worlds that bothered both phenomenological and dialectical hermeneutics, there is no guarantee for the reader to be brought side by side with the truth/meaning of a text, because textuality can be veiled by ideology and false consciousness. The goal of this hermeneutic system is to diagnose the hidden pathology of texts and to free them from their ideological distortions.

In the DIA case study, the initial reading takes the reader into a summary of the case and also prepares the preliminary understanding.

The introduction to the case study commences with a summary of the project, describing it as being beset by risks: 'the scale of the large project size; the enormous complexity of the expanded system; the newness of the technology; the large number of resident entities to be served by the same system; the high degree of technical and project definition uncertainty; and the short time span for completion' (Montealegre et al., 1999, p. 546). The bylines at the head of the case study say that 'No airport in the world is as technologically advanced as the Denver International Airport ' (Montealegre et al., 1999), and then almost as an aside in the same headline of the case study – 'It's dramatic. If your bag [got] on the track, your bag [was] in pieces'.

So before even the preliminary reading has commenced, the reader has already scanned enough of the first page of this study and already the mindset has been seeded with notions of a highly complex project whose technological demands were so complex that it all went off the rails [sic]. The mind of an 'experienced reader'[2] is by now thinking about what classic project management problems could have led to this disaster.

The understanding that exists at this preliminary cycle is already deeply prejudiced and biased. Questions have already been (subconsciously) set into the researcher's mind

---

[2] The term 'experienced reader' is used to describe someone who is moderately well versed in project management methodologies and who has seen or read about enough project failures to know of standard failure patterns.

about what specific failure points will be identified and where blame might be allocated. After all, thinks one researcher, 'had appropriate project management controls been in place and effective, then this disaster simply would not have occurred'.

It is clear in hindsight that the power of the initial read (or should we say – scan) of the main document has set the mood for the interpretation of the remaining document. Thus, if the case study authors' original intent was to create a negative atmosphere leading to a classical investigation and identification of project management failure, then this was achieved before even the first page was turned.

An initial prejudice had now been set in place.

Second cycle

Here, the researchers sought to clearly document and identify each actor in the document, noting who they were, what their function/purpose was in the scheme of things, and what in particular they did that was of note. As a later exercise, we also mapped the number of times they were quoted/cited/mentioned in the document.

This second reading really focused on people and institutions. During this reading we highlighted individuals and organisations, then transcribed this data into a table. In this table we identified dates, who the actors were, and what, if anything, they did on their first appearance. Obviously some entries appear regularly throughout the paper so only their first appearance and what they did was noted. An example appears in Table 6.1.

What is notable in this second cycle is that the researchers decided to formally document all actors that could be identified and to note who they were and what they were involved in at first glance. This new text, a table of actors, is just our 'apparatus' as described by Gadamer (Kidder, 1997, p. 1196). It is an aid in the hermeneutic cycle. An interesting side effect of this process has been the disciplined examination of the original text from the viewpoint of documenting all identifiable actors.

The outcome of the development of the table of actors is a better understanding of the history of this project and how it came about, its political basis (the Mayoral elections), its economic basis (the importance of Denver as a hub), and a fair amount of negative references to BAE and the 'work ethic'.

A number of issues became evident and remained unresolved at this phase. Why were United Airlines clearly committed to the new airport and their own baggage handling system, while Continental seemed an almost disinterested party? Were the authors of the document trying to create an impression that the US airline industry was in disarray? If, as is implied in the document, it is a tradition in the USA that each airline looks after its own baggage handling system, why did DIA push for a single integrated automated baggage handling system?

Table 6.1. Actors (extract)

Ref	Who	When	Who is it?	What happened
Act01	BAE Automatic Systems Inc.	1992	Engineering consulting and manufacturing company based in Carrollton, Texas	Awarded contract
Act02	Shareholders	1994/05	Applied pressure on Denver Mayor Wellington Webb to intervene in project	
Act03	Denver business community	1994/05		Applied pressure on Denver Mayor Wellington Webb to intervene in project
Act04	Denver residents	1994/05		Applied pressure on Denver Mayor Wellington Webb to intervene in project
Act05	Federal Aviation Administration	1994/05		Applied pressure on Denver Mayor Wellington Webb to intervene in project
Act06	Tenant airlines	1994/05		Applied pressure on Denver Mayor Wellington Webb to intervene in project
Act07	Concessionaires	1994/05		Applied pressure on Denver Mayor Wellington Webb to intervene in project
Act08	Wellington Webb	1994/05	Denver Mayor	Called in German firm LogPlan to assess situation
Act09	Logplan	1994/07	German (consulting?) firm	Issued an 11-page report on the system
Act10	Gene Di Fonso	1983	BAE President	
Act11	Monte Pascoe	1983	Mayoral candidate and prominent Denver attorney	Brought airport issue in as an election issue
Act12	Dale Tooley	1983	Mayoral candidate	Unsuccessful
Act13	Frederico Pena	1983	Mayoral candidate	Successful mayoral candidate – agreed to commit to continued expansion of DIA
Act14	Colorado Forum	1983	Lobby group of 50 of Denver's senior executives	Urged the continuing commitment to the DIA
Act15	Local voters	1989/05	Denver and Adams counties	Voters supported the DIA by a margin of 62.7% for versus 37.3% against
Act16	Gail Edmond	1989/05	DIA Administrator	Claimed referenda passed on the basis of economic benefits, jobs etc.
Act17	Chamber of Commerce	1987	Their leadership	Promoting airport relocation
Act18	Frontier Airlines	1986		Bought by Texas Air

The understanding developed after this cycle has deepened considerably. It is evident that project controls and coordination were simply not in place, externally imposed deadlines and political imperatives were running roughshod over the management team, and interpersonal conflict was surfacing. The overall impression is one of chaos.

During the creation of this first derivative text document, the researchers became aware of deeper factors at work. It was clear that these extra things would reveal themselves further during the next few cycles. It was like a growing suspicion that there was definitely more to come.

Third cycle

Here the researchers read again through the document extracting and tabulating everything that could be construed as environmental facts. The definition of an environmental fact used when this table was constructed was 'any thing or context that would have influence on an actor when making their decisions or any thing or context that would force a decision to be made'. An example of this part of the analysis is provided in Table 6.2.

The result of this cycle enabled the researchers to develop the table of environmental factors that could be identified. It became abundantly clear that social, political and economic factors played an enormous part in this project.

Because of the detailed examination of the document, a number of hitherto seemingly insignificant factors emerged. For example, because of the hub nature of the old Stapleton Airport, a local storm could congest all air traffic across the United States since predictions about increases in travel demand for the local area appear to have been wrong. Moreover, this was a public works program and the local laws stated that there must be 30% of minority owned firms and 6% of firms owned by women participating in the project. And, curiously, the authors gave a detailed history of BAE, appearing to emphasise its list of failures (e.g. the San Francisco Airport baggage handling system) while still describing them as the pre-eminent baggage handling system developers.

During the creation of this second derivative text document we found ourselves constantly referring back to the first document as a reference. A feeling emerged that the environment in which this project was living was quite delicately balanced with considerable demands being made on the project by a variety of key stakeholders. What was becoming evident was that it appeared that each environmental factor was quite fixed and immovable.

Table 6.2. Environments (extract)

Env35	1992	The City did not get the airlines together to ask them what they wanted or what they needed to operate. The approach was more along the lines of 'we will build the apartment building, and then you come in and rent a set of rooms'.	Gene Di Fonso
Env36	1992	The direct relationship with BAE was delegated to Working Area 4, which also had responsiblity for building design efforts such as the people mover, airside concourse, passenger bridge, parking garage, etc.	
Env37	1992	BAE had to change its working structures to conform to DIA's project management structure	Gene Di Fonso
Env38	1992	At the time of BAE commencing work, substantial construction work had already been done necessitating in some instances to have the already completed work demolished.	
Env39	1992/05	Head of the DIA project team resigns.	Walter Slinger
Env40	1992/10	Chief engineer Walter Slinger dies.	Gail Edmond
Env41	1992/10	Gail Edmond takes over the job of chief engineer	
Env42	1992/10	City Council did not give Gail Edmond the same autonomy and power as Walter Slinger – they tied her hands and everybody knew it.	
Env43	1992/10	Just after Slinger's death, BAE employees' site-wide access deteriorated as their access was ignored or restricted.	
Env44	1992	City of Denver had denied BAE's original contract because it did not comply with minority employment requirements. BAE engaged outside contractors instead of their own employees.	
Env45	1992	The City of Denver was unable to supply clean power to the airport baggage handling system	
Env46	1992	The management team had no prior baggage handling competence or experience. They treated the baggage handling system as a public works project – like pouring concrete. Access was difficult with contractors out on their own – almost anarchy.	Gene Di Fonso
Env47	1992	BAE simply did not respond to the obvious incredible workload that they had. Their inexperience and project management vastly underestimated their task. Their work ethic was deplorable.	'Project Manager' from Stone and Webster, consultants to PMT.

The local laws about the desired mix of minority owned and female owned firms involved in public works contracts was flagged as being very inflexible given that BAE was forced to change its working structures to conform.

In addition, the researchers noted that the airport Chief Engineer, Walter Slinger, seemed to be something of a champion of the project and the one who was convinced by BAE that it was indeed possible. It seems that Slinger was also instrumental in making the actual construction work of the project operate – 'He had a lot of autonomy and could get things done'. The researchers have interpreted this statement as meaning that Slinger was able to make substantial decisions directly related to the project alone and without reference to higher authorities. This was changed when Slinger died and his job was taken over by Gail Edmond who was stripped of that autonomy by the Denver City Council and forced to validate all her decisions with them.

By this stage of the hermeneutic cycle, the researchers had created two new texts and were evaluating their contributions to the understanding of this case. It was becoming evident that the next text, to be developed during the fourth cycle, would reveal even more, and enable an even deeper understanding, of the whole from its component parts.

As a reflection it was at this point of the investigation, during the creation of this second derived text, that the first researcher suddenly realised how important Walter Slinger was to the whole project. The fact of his death, previously overlooked, now had a profound impact from this point onwards on the investigation. What was now becoming clearer was that Slinger's autonomy and flexibility died with him because Edmonds did not inherit these managerial freedoms.

Fourth cycle

This cycle examined the decisions identified in the case study document. Along with these decisions, the individuals making the decisions, the decisions themselves, and the outcomes were documented. Table 6.3 shows what the decision documentation table resulting from this cycle looks like. Surprisingly, the actual number of documented decisions by the case study's authors numbered only 23.

This hermeneutic cycle revealed quite forcibly that Denver started building the airport before any airline had officially committed to it. United, in fact, committed to the project in December 1992, at the same time as they commissioned BAE to build their own baggage handling system. It would appear that when both Continental and United committed to the project, there was sufficient flexibility available to make major construction changes to airport design.

Table 6.3. Decisions (extract)

Dec-11	1992	DIA decided to seek bids to build an airport-wide baggage system	DIA PMT	They contacted 16 companies and of the three who responded, none was considered suitable.
Dec-12	1992	DIA approaches BAE to bid directly for the airport-wide baggage system	DIA PMT	BAE developed a proposal for the most complex and innovative baggage handling system for the entire airport.
Dec-13	1992/04	BAE awarded contract for the building of an airport-wide baggage handling system	DIA PMT	$175.6 m contract signed. BAE required no changes in design, and that they would need unrestricted access to any place in the airport.
Dec-14	1992/08	United altered plans for a transfer system for bags changing planes	United Airlines	System redesign necessitated.
Dec-15	1992/09	Continental requested that an automated baggage sorter be added.	Continental	Implemented at a cost of $4.67 m.
Dec-16	1992/09	Addition of extra maintenance tracks for servicing of baggage carts	DIA PMT	Additional cost of $912 000.
Dec-17	1993/02	Projected opening of airport delayed from Oct. 1993 to December then later to March 9 1994	Mayor Webb	Panic set in.
Dec-18	1993/09	BAE loses maintenance contract for baggage handling system	DIA PMT	Industrial action by millwrights and electricians over BAE's proposal for a lower than union endorsed payment. BAE loses maintenance contract.
Dec-19	1993/09	Projected opening again delayed until May 15 1994	Mayor Webb	
Dec-20	1994/04	Reporters invited to witness the opening.	Mayor Webb	Disaster – everything broke.
Dec-21	1994/04	Opening delayed indefinitely.	Mayor Webb	Delay costs set at $330 000 per month.
Dec-22	1994/05	LogPlan engaged to review the baggage handling system and airport	Mayor Webb	LogPlan report recommended a backup system be implemented.
Dec-23	1994/08	Backup baggage handling system announced.	Mayor Webb	$50 m project.

This cycle also highlighted the communication gaps between the major stakeholders (DIA, Continental, and United), as well as the assumption made by DIA that each airline was responsible for its own baggage handling system. It is noted that United proceeded to take responsibility for its own system because '… They concluded that the schedule had gotten completely out of control from the standpoint of baggage, and they acted to serve their own needs' (Montealegre et al., 1999, pp. 553-4).

What had been revealed to the researchers by now was that there was a substantial change in the project environment with the death of the Chief Airport Engineer, Slinger, and the succession of Gail Edmond with the attendant loss of autonomy and flexibility and (evidently) project management skills that entailed.

Fifth cycle

In this fifth hermeneutic cycle, the second researcher developed another text based on the case study document and sought to interpret the text in terms of key stakeholders and the intentions of their communicative actions, and the opinions expressed by the authors. The researcher then included his interpretation of the case study authors' intentions and opinions.

Table 6.4, which we have titled 'flexibility factors', provides an extract of the stakeholder intentions, authors' opinions and researcher interpretations, developed during this cycle.

Table 6.4. Flexibility factors (extract)

Ref #	Intention of communicative action	Shareholder	Opinion	Phenomena	Researcher's interpretation/findings
M1	Background	United Airlines 1992	'integrated system would improve time efficiency, reduce close-out time for hub operations and decrease time-consuming manual baggae sorting and handling.'	Objectives	Operational efficiency is an important objective. However, efficiency alone cannot be driving large projects.
M2	Setting expectations	Author's hindsight	'There were, however, a number of risks inherent in the endeavour; the scale of the large project's size; the enormous complexity of the expanded system; the newness of the technology; the large number of resident entities to be served by the same system; the high degree of technical and project definition uncertainty; and the short time span for completion.'	Risks, scale, complexity, newness, granularity	Projects of huge size and complexity need well-tested methods. Novelty is usually incompatible with scale.
M3	Fact Setting expectations	Author's hindsight	'In August 1994, Mayor Webb approved the construction of a backup system. At the same time, he notified BAE of a $12 000-a-day penalty for not finishing the baggage system by DIA's original October 29 1993 completion date.'	Non-delivery, breakdown of communication, start of hostilities	Legal means such as penalties are not advisable in situations which require cooperation. Whenever there is still some chance of problem resolution, communication and negotiation should be used instead.
M4	Novelisation Setting expectations	Gene Di Fonso, President of BAE 1994	'He wondered whether he should just cancel the contract and cut his losses, or attempt to negotiate with the City the support required to finish the system as specified, despite the severe deterioration in communication and rising hostility.'	Rigidity, lack of communication, hostilities	Legal means such as penalties are not advisable in situations which require cooperation. Whenever there is still some chance of problem resolution, communication and negotiation should be used instead.
M5	Setting expectations Leading Appeal to technical prowess	Author's hindsight	'Could the problem with the automated system be overcome with the dedication of additional resources? Given that the system represented a significant departure from conventional technology, would reducing its size and complexity facilitate resolution of the problems that plagued it?'	Hypothesis: smaller size and complexity, additional resources	By offering a hypothetical reason for the project collapse early in the teaching case, the authors are likely to lead the reader towards these as a conclusion.
M6	Motivation Setting expectations	Denver 1980s	'An aging and saturated Stapleton Airport was increasingly seen as a liability that limited the attractiveness of the region to the many businesses that were flocking to it. Delays had become chronic.'	Perceptions and expectations of stakeholders. Strong motivation for the project.	External pressures could provide positive project motivation. It may however also lead to unduly strong stakeholder expectations, while haste could cause major project problems.
M7	Colourising Politics	Frederico Peña	'The airport was to become a grandiose project to revive the Colorado economy and a master showcase for the Public Works Department.'	Perceptions and expectations	Project overselling can elevate stakeholder expectations beyond common sense.

The revelations from the fifth cycle show that *collaborative hermeneutics* can yield substantial benefits. In this case, the two researchers developed independent derivative texts with completely individual approaches to their interpretations. The curious result of this textual analysis has been the revelation that a considerable amount of the original case study seems to be directed at colourising and novelisation of the reported events, at setting the reader's expectations and, from the very beginning, at leading the reader to reach very specific conclusions at the end of the case – mainly that the project should have been de-escalated before its ultimate failure. While many of these writers' strategies can be attributed to the intended use of the text in teaching IS students, the selectivity of the text and its clear omissions hint at yet another agenda. In particular, the majority of the case study text seems to rely on an interview with the then President and Project Manager for BAE, Gene Di Fonso. Much of the substance of Di Fonso's statements seem to be a defence of the BAE involvement in the project and an attempt to lay blame for various aspects of the failure on everyone else. If the authors' intentions were to direct the reader to sympathise with a wronged BAE then that goal has definitely been achieved.

In the process of 'peeling off' the layers of the case study authors' intentions and prejudices, and by reconciling the two distinct horizons of understanding as developed by both investigators, new observations started to emerge. In particular, we were struck by a large number of issues hinting at the inherent rigidity in the project administration and management.

Fusing the horizons led further to re-evaluating all the findings collected thus far. In particular, in cycles one and two, rigidity and/or flexibility seemed quite irrelevant and nearly all observations could have been explained by assuming the basic laws of project management had been violated. In cycle three, gender parity, work practice conformity, imposition of authority and autonomy reduction were rediscovered, and seen by the researchers as a serious decrease in flexibility.

While some of the inflexibilities could have been attributed to the nature of the project, such as its size, complexity, relative novelty and task granularity, other inflexibility factors, such as inflexible business processes, state and project policies, hiring policies, staff and contractor duties, schedules and expected deliverables, relationships and alliances, finances and contracts, designs, coordination and communication modality, could all only be explicated by the inexperienced and unwilling project management.

The fourth hermeneutic cycle further enhanced the understanding of the case and revealed that while there was initially considerable flexibility in the system as a whole, that flexibility was taken away in the later stages of the project when it was needed most. And that seemed to be inextricably linked to the death of Chief Engineer Slinger.

Sixth cycle

In the last project phase, the researchers sought to include additional documents that were substantively about the DIA project and to apply the hermeneutic principle of adding new knowledge into an existing system of understanding that has already been developed, and using Myers notion of continuing to make sense (1994a, p. 191), to either confirm understanding, or to extend the understanding to accommodate the new knowledge.

The new text document was by Montealegre, titled 'De-escalating Information Technology Projects: Lessons from the Denver International Airport' (Montealegre and Keil, 2000). The goal in the introduction of this new document was to determine if there was any new knowledge about the DIA project that had not been previously revealed, and whether this knowledge maintained consistency with the understanding built to date.

The focus of the document was to analyse the project failure from the standpoint of de-escalation. The first new piece of knowledge was the fact that several government agencies (Federal Grand Jury, SEC, Government Accounting Office and the Federal Aviation Administration) had started or requested investigations into the project (Montealegre and Keil, 2000, p. 424). There was, however, no inkling of government dissatisfaction in the original case study.

This new fact caused us to reassess our understanding about the amount of public concern that existed during the latter days of the project. In particular, it made us aware that there must have been considerable pressure brought to bear on the management of the project. The consequences of this pressure could have been to panic, or take some other course of action. The original document describes the Webb administration bringing in external consultants to look at the baggage handling system in an almost 'matter-of-fact' way. There was no indication of weight of pressure present at the time.

The second new piece of knowledge that emerged from the document was that Moody's, the credit rating agency, reduced the DIA bonds to level BAA, just one level short of 'no-investment status'. This added pressure of dried up funds sources again served to add the words 'crisis' and 'panic' to the prevailing atmosphere.

The third new addition was that Mayor Webb established a task force to look at alternatives that could be deployed with the express purpose of opening the airport as quickly as possible. There was no mention of this task force in the case study, even though it preceded the report tabled by the LogPlan company. This was truly the first piece of evidence of high level flexibility being brought to bear on the problem – if a problem becomes intractable, try to get around it.

The new horizons added by this further knowledge provided a relief to the tension that developed around what appeared at first sight to be an inflexible administration and management.

Reflections

It was not until the researchers actually engaged with the original case study document in such detail that the real benefits of the hermeneutic investigative process became apparent. The detailed creation of the derivative texts that focused on one perspective at a time forced us to review and in a way to confront our own prejudices. Each hermeneutic cycle, as evidenced by the different perspectives and subsequent derivative documents, enhanced the understanding. It was as if each text created its own horizon and in that process this fusion occurred very quietly.

The introduction of the second hermeneutic investigator who created another derivative text from a completely different perspective allowed an almost three dimensional view of the problem. This contribution had the potential to create a conflict not unlike a debate, where one seeks a winner. But when the principles of dialectic were enforced, rather than a debate ensuing, it seems that fusion occurred, leading to an even broader understanding.

Another interesting side effect of this *collaborative hermeneutics* was that each of the researchers again had another view of their own prejudices, as well as what turned out to be a quite stimulating debate, not on the respective validity of these perspectives, but on the sheer value and importance of dialectics.

The first researcher then wanted to locate and feed every possible available document on the Denver International Airport into the investigation just to make sure that nothing had been left unchecked and that there were no more hidden reasons for the events that occurred.

Conclusions

This article has presented a case for the use of critical hermeneutics to the study of IS development projects. In particular, we used the infamous case study of Denver International Airport (DIA) and its Baggage Handling System to illustrate the hermeneutic process, its numerous cycles of understanding and the insights gained and recorded as new text that could be further analysed and reconciled.

The method demonstrated that the hermeneutic approach is eminently well suited to the task of analysing IS processes, environment, actors and events – the truly factual aspects of recorded project information. The example also showed that pre-existing text can be screened for prejudices and biases, which may hide the richness of new insights and information.

In the case of DIA, the hermeneutic approach led to the discovery of new factors, such as those related to project inflexibility, which could explain the downfall of the DIA development project, but which seem to have eluded the original project investigators, either due to unintentional omission, educational objectives of the case, or possibly due to the political pressures imposed on the authors by various project stakeholders.

On reflection, in the course of our study, we came to the conclusion that critical hermeneutics can be effectively employed in IS research to determine IS project characteristics, to identify the associated project events and their actors. It is also a very useful approach to assist IS researchers in sifting through the secondary data of possibly biased and prejudiced project reports and in peeling off these biases to reveal and interpret the true nature of project events.

7. Information systems technology grounded on institutional facts

Robert M. Colomb, *School of Information Technology and Electrical Engineering, The University of Queensland*

Abstract

This paper presents a theory explaining the success of information systems development based on SQL-type database technology by showing that the assumptions underlying that technology correspond very closely to the way Searle's institutional facts are created. The theory presented is a theory of action and design, so its productivity is shown by retrodiction of the necessity for business process engineering to achieve integration of information systems within an organisation, and prediction that interorganisational integration of information systems using the internet can succeed only if the applications share institutional facts. The theory is used to predict that autonomous intelligent agent applications can succeed in the information spaces populated by these common institutional facts.

Introduction

Information systems are generally and very successfully implemented using a particular sort of technology typified by relational database systems, which I will call *logical databases* for reasons that will be explained below. There are alternative technologies. Why have logical database systems been successful?

Information systems have, for the most part, been successful in relatively restricted organisational subunits. A large organisation therefore may have hundreds of information systems. Over the past two decades organisations have been trying to develop information systems implemented by logical databases at the scale of the whole, typically by integrating the successful local systems. There are successes, but it has turned out that it requires an enormous effort, including changes in the way the organisation sees itself (e.g. through business process re-engineering), in order to achieve success. The question is: why is it so hard to extend successful local information systems to an organisation-scale system?

Organisations interoperate with other organisations in a global economy. A global communication infrastructure now exists which makes it easy for anyone to communicate with anyone else. There is a strong business case to interconnect the logical database-implemented systems of multiple organisations for a wide variety of purposes. But if it is hard to integrate systems within a single organisation, what hope is there for integration across organisations? After all, many of the things done to achieve single-organisation integration depend strongly on central management commitment. There is by definition no central management where the problem is to integrate systems across organisations. What can we hope to achieve?

We have a technology that works extremely well on a small scale, is difficult but possible to adapt to an organisational scale, and which we now want to further adapt to a global scale. The thesis of this paper is that in order to understand what is feasible on the global scale we need to understand why the technology is so successful on a local scale, and why it is difficult to adapt to an organisation-wide or larger scale.

Success at the local scale

Why are logical databases the technology of choice for implementing information systems?

Information systems are generally about the management of records. Records can be records of just about anything: a company's accounts, medical records, criminal records, a census, the archives of a newspaper, or the contents of a museum. Just about anything can be a record; the Babylonians used clay tablets to record their business dealings, some medical records are images, most of the contents of most museums are physical artefacts of various kinds. But contemporary information systems are generally concerned with documents that contain most of their information in the form of text. Physical objects like the contents of a museum are generally represented in information systems by documents called catalogue entries.

So, more specifically, information systems are about the management of records that are documents containing information mostly in textual form. The general technology for processing collections of text records is the text database.

The model of information-seeking behaviour supported by text databases has the following steps:

1. The user has an information need.
2. The user formulates the information need as a query consisting of a collection of terms.
3. The system returns the subset of its collection of documents containing all and only those documents that contain the query terms.
4. The user then reviews the documents returned, and makes a judgment as to whether each document satisfies the information need or not. The expectation is that many of the documents returned will be irrelevant (*limited precision*). The expectation is also that some of the documents in the collection that would have satisfied the information need were not returned, because the query did not contain appropriate terms (*limited recall*).

Precision and recall are measured on a percentage scale. A precision of 0% means that none of the documents retrieved met the information need. A precision of 100% means that all did. A recall of 0% means that none of the relevant documents were retrieved. A recall of 100% means that all were. Returning the entire collection guarantees 100% recall, but gives a very low precision. Text database systems are considered to perform very well if their average precision and average recall are as high as 40%.

Computer-based information systems generally make use of technologies such as relational databases. There is a wide variety of such systems, but they are generally characterised by data models based on classes and instances, with relationships among classes. Typically the data model is expressed in a language like UML, one of the varieties of entity-relationship modeling, or object-role modeling. The populations of particular systems are generally managed by systems based more or less on the first-order predicate calculus, such as relational database systems or object-oriented database systems, which we here call *logical databases*.

In text database terms, a query on a logical database is expected to have 100% precision and 100% recall. A class list is the definitive statement of which students are enrolled in a course. A person may attend lectures, submit assignments and sit an examination, but if they are not on the class list then they are not enrolled and cannot be assigned a grade. Another person may never attend classes, submit no assignments and not sit the examination but, being on the class list, is considered enrolled and will be given a grade, perhaps one signifying 'no assessment submitted'.

Because a query on a logical database returns all and only the documents satisfying the information need, it is possible to construct much more complex queries. Combining information from two different tables requires 100% precision and 100% recall. So does the reliable use of negation, and complex selection conditions.

The claim here is that logical databases are the preferred technology for managing collections of records using information systems. But all we have established so far is that an information system manages a collection of records. We need to look at these collections in more detail.

Consider a particular kind of collection of documents that are records of activity of an organisation, namely the correspondence incoming and outgoing. Imagine we have a UML model for this collection, and consider a particular document, namely a letter from a potential customer enquiring about the possible existence of a product that the company does not at present supply. Call this letter Q. We want to compare this with a letter from an established customer placing an order for an existing product. Call this letter P.

We want to look at what the organisation can do with letter Q compared to what it can do with letter P. Letter P can be cross-referenced with other documents associated with the established customer, and with other documents associated with the existing product. Some of the former will be invoices, statements, payments, and so on. Some of the latter will be picking lists, shipping orders, purchase orders and so on. The organisation will have standard queries associated with these documents, for example all orders that have been delivered but not paid for, or all orders for a customer that have not yet been shipped.

By contrast, it is not at all clear what to do with letter Q. It might routinely be answered with a polite negative reply. If the prospective customer will potentially place large orders, the letter might be sent to the product development group for a feasibility study. The product may or may not be technically feasible. If technically feasible, there may or may not be the capital available for development, or there may be higher return uses for the capital that could be used for the project. It would be hard to know with what other kinds of documents letter Q would be associated, and hard to see what routine queries might retrieve it.

Letter P fits well into the class/instance/relationship data model, while letter Q does not. The class/instance/relationship data model permits the construction of complex queries, the reliable definition of negation, and so on. Information systems generally exclude documents like letter Q from consideration, concentrating on documents like letter P.

So, the preliminary answer to the question as to why information systems are implemented using logical rather than text databases is that the subset of records considered by information systems are very largely those that are usefully modeled using the assumptions underlying logical databases, and so can profit from the much richer querying capability of logical databases.

However, this is hardly a satisfactory explanation since it is circular. Information systems use logical databases because they are about managing the sorts of records that can be well managed by logical databases. We need a deeper understanding of these sorts of records.

If logical databases are the solution, what is the problem?

What characterises logical databases in relation to text databases is that logical databases need the concept of logical equality and the subsumption of individual by class, so the data for which a logical database is to be used must support these concepts. Text databases do not make these assumptions. This is the reason text database systems suffer from problems of limited precision and limited recall.

For an object to be represented in a logical database, it must be completely characterised by the classes of which it is an instance. Letter P of the previous section is completely characterised by its membership in the class *order* and its membership in associations between the class *order* and the classes *product*, *customer* and so on. To the university student record system, a person is completely characterised by membership in the class *student* and membership in associations between *student* and the classes *enrolment*, *program* and so on. This is why we can expect 100% precision and 100% recall.

In a text database, we can't even reliably identify a document as a member of a class, much less characterise its content by class and association.

The ability to completely characterise an object by the class in which it is an instance is the basis for logical equality, which in turn is necessary for the computations performed in logical databases. The number of students enrolled in a course can be computed because the class list defines the enrolment, and all students' enrolments are equivalent. A grade point average can be computed because a student's performance in a course is completely characterised by the grade awarded, and the same grade awarded in different courses is logically the same.

So the first answer to the question as to what problems a logical database is a solution for is those applications where the assumptions hold that class and association membership completely characterise the objects. This might be somewhat less circular, but is still not satisfactory. What sort of world produces records that are completely characterised by class and association membership?

What sorts of applications satisfy the requirements for logical databases?

The world is a messy place. We tend to make order in it by classifying things. Most animals classify the world into at least the categories *food*, *predator* and *mate*. But these sorts of classifications are not enough for logical information systems since they do not completely characterise the objects in the world. A botanist may classify a forest by genus and species, but there is room for error. Observations of specimens in different ways can lead to a change in its classification. The object in the world is primary. We can use logical databases for applications like this, but we have to ignore the individual objects and treat them only as instances of classes.

We need to keep in mind that our information systems contain not the world, but statements about the world. That is, Popper's third world (McDonald, 2002). (Popper's first world is reality, his second is internal psychological states caused by an organism interacting with the first world. The third world is what the organism says about its experience.) Both letters P and Q are in the third, as well as the first, world.

What differentiates letter P from letter Q is that letter P is an instance of an institutional fact as described by Searle (1995). An institutional fact is a statement about the world, but the world it is a statement about is a social world. It has no meaning apart from the society in which it occurs. (There are enormous differences in approach between Popper and Searle, but at a first approximation, the claim that an institutional fact is one kind of statement about the world seems reasonable.)

Searle distinguishes institutional facts from brute facts. A brute fact is a statement about something in the world outside of human society. Examples of brute facts are: 'Thylacines are extinct', 'Canberra is cold in the winter', 'This is a 2.5 centimeter diameter gold-coloured metal disk', 'This is a piece of white paper with black marks on it'. All of these statements would continue to be true if our society disappeared. (Of course there would have to be some sentient being to make the statements, perhaps robots or extraterrestrials.)

All objects, including statements, are for Searle brute facts. A written statement can be black marks on white paper. A spoken statement is acoustic waves in the atmosphere at a particular place at a particular time. What makes a brute fact an institutional fact is how it is taken by the people concerned about it. In particular, an institutional fact is taken as a record of an instance of a standardised speech act performed by a social institution in a human society. A 2.5 centimeter diameter gold-coloured metal disk is taken to be a dollar coin in Australian society in 2004. A piece of white paper with black marks on it is taken as an order for particular goods by Acme Manufacturing Company at a particular time.

Searle's formulation starts with speech acts. A speech act is an action made by a designated person on behalf of a social institution that changes the social reality managed by that institution. The quintessential speech act is giving a new baby a name. The action is entering writing in blank spaces on a form, then lodging the form at the office of the Registrar of Births in the jurisdiction in which the baby was born. The designated person is one of the parents of the baby. The form is supplied by the Registrar of Births. The form is lodged by handing it to a designated officer of the Registrar in their designated office during the designated office hours. The social reality changed is that a new person now exists with the name indicated on the form. The institutional reality managed by the Registrar of Births is the population of citizens of the country of whose government it is an arm. That the person into whom that baby develops is named its name is an institutional fact. Records of this institutional fact are stored by the agency and on birth certificate and passport documents, but also exist in people's memories and are created whenever the name is used, especially in other official documents.

Searle's formulation is 'brute fact X counts as institutional fact Y in context C'. In our naming example, the brute fact is the filling in and lodging of the form. The institutional fact is that the baby has the designated name. The context is everything else: the person lodging the form is a parent, the office is the proper office, the form is given to the proper person at the proper time, and so on.

What most clearly differentiates letter P from letter Q is that letter P is an institutional fact. Sending and receipt of letter P by the appropriate people counts as the speech act of placing an order. When this occurs, the world changes, in that the receiver of letter P (the supplier) is entitled to ship the nominated quantity of the nominated product to the sender (the purchaser) and expect payment in return. The copy of letter P (brute fact) held by the supplier is a record of the institutional fact of the purchase order having been made. The context includes the supplier being in the business of selling the nominated product, the purchaser being a properly constituted customer, and so on.

The whole business is regulated by the laws of commerce in the relevant jurisdictions. In addition, it is regulated by a body of largely implicit customary practice. This body of customary practice is called *background* by Searle. Background is a significant aspect of any context.

Institutional facts are a subclass of what Searle calls *social facts*. Social facts are informal, while institutional facts are formal acts of formally constituted institutions. That my nickname is 'Bob' is a social fact, but that my official name is 'Robert Michael Colomb' is also an institutional fact. 'A is a friend of B' is a social fact, but 'A is the spouse of B' is an institutional fact as well. 'A is influential' is a social fact, but 'A is prime minister' is also an institutional fact. The institution or network of institutions that provides the context for institutional facts is a complex system of social behaviour. Different institutional environments have different informal patterns and norms of behaviour (*culture*) that are the background aspect of the context of the institutional facts it creates and maintains.

One key characteristic of institutional facts, at least in our present society, is that they are designed to be completely characterised by the classes to which they belong. Every name is completely characterised by the speech act of registration with a birth certificate as record of the institutional fact of having been named. Every purchase is completely characterised by the various classes by which the supplier and purchaser do business. Every student is completely characterised by the program and courses in which they have enrolled. This is the defining feature of modern bureaucracy. This is the reason people worry about 'being just a number'.

Nearly all information systems are used to store, retrieve, and now often create institutional facts. Society agrees that nothing is relevant except that 'brute fact X counts as institutional fact Y in context C'. There are a finite number of well-defined context types. All contexts of the same type are the same, so all institutional facts resulting from these contexts are the same. To make this work requires a highly disciplined form of behaviour, and a rigorous enforcement of the framing rules defining the contexts. This is the reason for the complex system of commercial law, standardisation of accounting rules, requirements for audit, and so on. But the standardisation also relies on the informal behaviour patterns and norms constituting the background.

That institutional facts are completely characterised by the classes constituting the operating rules for the institutions creating them corresponds exactly with the assumption underlying logical databases, that their contents are completely characterised by the classes of which they are instances. I submit that this is the reason for the overwhelming dominance of logical database technology in information systems.

In the following we are going to need some perhaps unfamiliar terminology. An *ontology* is a representation of the world with which a system is concerned. The rules of chess or cricket are an ontology. For an information system, the ontology consists of its data model, business rules, and a characterisation of the individuals with which the system deals. An ontology is *transcendent* if it contains the constituting rules for the relevant behavioural interactions, and the routine behavioural interactions cannot change their constituting rules. The rules for chess or cricket or the grammars of programming languages are transcendent. An ontology is *immanent* if the routine behavioural interactions can change the rules. Human natural language is an immanent ontology, since the grammar rules are patterns abstracted from practice and practice can change them, albeit slowly. The ontology of news topics in a newsfeed change as events happen in the world. The ontology given by the directory structure of a person's personal computer is immanent, because the user of the computer is free to change the directory structure.

The schemas defining types of institutional facts define a transcendent ontology for the information systems supporting the creation of institutional facts and keeping records of them. Data models for particular systems are representations of and implementations of aspects of the ontology. The technology implementing these data models works only because of the behavioural disciplines that implement the framing rules of the various speech acts. If each letter placing an order requires separate consideration and is treated in a unique way, the order entry system of the supplier can't work the way we expect it to. But of course the transcendent ontology is only the formal part of the system. The context of all speech acts includes the background, which is characteristic of particular institutions and differs between institutions.

How does this view help?

The theory described in this paper can be considered as a theory for design and action in the taxonomy of Gregor (2002). As such, it should be useful in guiding future designs.

One thing the theory does is explain why SQL and other logical databases are overwhelmingly the platform of choice in information systems implementations. This, however, does not seem to be a controversial situation. It is not a matter for concern, and there are no serious proposals for any other kind of platform. So to have value, the theory in this paper must do more.

The success of logical databases in information systems is most apparent in systems that serve highly focused organisational subunits. These are the subunits responsible for limited classes of speech acts, so needing records of limited classes of institutional facts. These are also the levels of institutional structure where the informal behaviour patterns and norms are the most stable, so where the background aspect of the context for the institutional facts is the most uniform.

As a result of success at this scale, there has been for many years a push to tie the information systems together. More recently, the availablity of cheap and powerful communication facilities has led to a push for tying together information systems of separate organisations into what may be thought of as world-scale computing. Although there have been successes at both of these enterprises, there have been many failures, with projects abandoned after vast expenditure. The idea that logical databases work well because they manage institutional facts can explain the successes and failures, and can be used to predict *a priori* whether a given project proposal has a chance of success.

The first of these enterprises, that of tying together the information systems in a single large organisation, was given a formulation as an extension of logical database technology in the federated database movement whose strategies are summarised by Sheth and Larsen (1990). The idea was that if we had many individual information systems, we could build a single big system by federating the data models and schemas of the local systems without requiring changes in the local systems. These efforts often failed, an example being the CS90 project of Westpac Bank in Australia in the late 1980s, which was abandoned after several years at a cost reported to be about A$500 million. Other major banking projects of the type were similarly abandoned at even higher costs.

In terms of the present theory, the reason these projects failed is that the speech acts performed by the organisation did not extend to the appropriate scale. The organisational subunits are in fact generally created to perform the limited class of speech act, and the framing rules for the speech act are often largely limited to things within the scope of that organisational unit. In a bank of the 1970s the savings accounts would be managed by a department, which would define what a customer was, the rules for interest payments, what addresses were kept, and so on. The home mortgage department would have analogous definitions, but there would have been no mechanisms to synchronise them. Also, different types of speech act have framing rules that take different things into account. A two-year-old might be a valid customer for a savings account, but not for a home mortgage, for example. Large organisations typically support hundreds of separate information systems serving low-level organisational units or specialised staff functions, and the speech acts performed by these subunits are typically uncoordinated. Furthermore, each organisational subunit has its own culture, so contributes a different background to the context of the speech acts for which it is responsible.

To integrate the information systems supporting these organisational subunits required far too much negotiation and resolution of different views of what were in principle common concerns, beyond what was needed to support the speech acts for which these units were actually responsible.

Tying together the information systems of a large organisation turned out not to be primarily a technical problem. It did require a large investment in technology, but was also predicated on extending the scope of the speech acts performed by the organisation to encompass all of the interactions needed to serve particular stakeholders. This involves not only the formal rules but requires creating a common culture so as to create a uniform background. This extension of scope is called business process reorganisation. If a bank wants to provide a web interface integrating all the services it provides to a given customer, the various departments need to come to a common definition of what a customer is, how they are named, what addresses they can have, under what conditions a customer is enabled to access a particular product, and so on. Making these decisions then reorganising the organisational subunits to work from the now larger scale ontology is a major cost to the organisation. Investment in technology is an enabling factor for business process reorganisation, but is not the major cost.

The prediction of the theory is that no proposal to integrate the separate information systems of organisational subunits is likely to succeed unless the organisation is rebuilt so that the speech acts it performs are at the scale of the whole of business interaction with classes of stakeholders. Once the speech acts are at the right scale, the consequently revised schemas and models will be able to be integrated in a relatively straightforward way. So the failure of the federated database approach to information systems integration can be retrodicted by the theory.

A similar problem has arisen more recently with the Internet. Since it has become technically feasible to interconnect systems operated by different organisations, people have been talking about interoperation. Of course people have been able to find resources using text database technology (search engines), and to compose individually selected services for particular purposes, but the dream is to be able to interoperate automatically using logical database technology. (This is often called use of intelligent agents.)

There are a number of manifestations of this dream, the most recent and concrete of which is the semantic web (Berners-Lee and Fischetti, 1999). There are a fair number of developments of what might be thought of as infrastructure for interoperation, for example XML, RDF, OWL, SOAP and WSDL [1]. There is a sometimes not clearly expressed dream that if you represent your web site or database in XML, or if you put descriptors on your site using RDF or OWL, then you can interoperate using logical database technology with anybody else who does so too.

---

[1] More details of any of these can be obtained from www.w3c.org

The theory of this paper, that logical databases work because they store institutional facts, leads to the conclusion that interoperability using logical database technology is only possible if the interoperating sites share speech acts and consequently share in the creation of institutional facts. In particular, they must have sufficient shared culture so that the background is sufficiently uniform. (For another view of this issue, see Colomb, 1997.) Some of the kinds of situations where this condition is satisfied include:

1. The sites do business together. This is what Electronic Data Interchange (EDI) is all about. For example, a group of businesses agree on common terms and common business messages with agreed semantics, and can then buy and sell from each other by the interoperation of their respective purchasing and order entry systems. E-commerce exchanges are built on this basis. The agreement on common terms and common business messages with agreed semantics constitutes the synchronisation of the framing rules for speech acts, so that the interoperation can make speech acts and there is an agreed semantics for the consequent institutional facts. The agreement is a transcendent ontology, supported by a common background. The ontology is transcendent because the only way to change the common world is to change the ontology, which is done by the management body outside of the routine interoperation of the sites.

2. All sites report to a central body using a common ontology. Tax returns in a given jurisdiction or financial reports to a given stock exchange are examples. The common ontology is the set of regulations and accounting standards established by the tax office or stock exchange and enforced by auditors and the commercial law institutions. This ontology is generally transcendent because it is imposed by the central body, and the participation in the relationship with the central body gives aspects of common culture so there is a stable background.

3. All sites operate as small players in a dense market. An example is residential property sales in a particular city. There are many agents, many sellers and many buyers, and each has the choice to deal with many of the others. In these markets, conventions develop so that to do business one must do it pretty well the way everyone else does. The speech acts and consequent institutional facts are similar by convention rather than by agreement. Any innovation either dies out quickly or is quickly adopted by everyone else due to competitive pressure. Here, the ontology is not transcendent, but immanent, derived from patterns in the background. It is possible to build, for example, services that will search for a house in many agents' sites. There are many ways to do this requiring more or less cooperation among the players. An immanent ontology is unstable in that a player may innovate at will, and that innovation may take off unpredictably. Background is the critical factor in this situation.

Unless there is some reason to assume the interoperating sites share institutional facts, there is no reason to think that interoperability using logical database technology is possible.

How can we build on this?

Our theory leads us to expect that we can build interorganisational information systems using logical database technology, enabling interoperation among organisations that share institutional facts. The sharing of institutional facts is represented by the participants' commitment to a common ontology. This ontology can be either transcendent or immanent. The question now is: given that we can interoperate where can we then go?

One possibility is to recognise that once an interoperating community is established, it can generate a large number of institutional facts. These institutional facts can be interpreted by any of the players who share the common ontology. These ontologies or institutional fact schemas constitute the atomic behavioural units, but do not necessarily determine behaviour. The rules of chess determine what constitutes a chess game, but there are lots of different games.

So we can use techniques like data mining that depend for their atomic data on the exact classification/logical equality nature of institutional facts, but which can find emergent patterns in the multiplicity of instances. These emergent patterns can be used as an immanent ontology for strategic or tactical decision making, for example advertising campaigns to encourage or discourage behaviour patterns, or as evidence of undesirable behaviour to be subjected to further investigation (e.g. fraud, money laundering).

Where the interoperating community consists of many small players, there may be an advantage to each player giving up its exclusive access to the institutional facts it creates in favour of a community-wide pool to which all players have common access. This is common, for example, in real estate where individual sales reports and auction success rates can be published for a whole city market area, enabling each player to see trends to which they can respond in their own fashion.

The information spaces opened up in this way give great scope for the development of interoperating autonomous intelligent agents. Each agent can develop its own immanent ontology, which it uses to govern the strategies and tactics it uses to interoperate with others to perform speech acts using the common transcendent ontology. The theory of this paper predicts that a research and development program along these lines would be likely to be productive.

8. Perhaps it's time for a fresh approach to IS/IT gender research?

Phyl Webb, *School of Information Systems, University of Tasmania*
Judy Young, *School of Information Systems, University of Tasmania*

Abstract

The aim of this paper is to demonstrate the value of the adoption of a feminist epistemology in information systems and information technology (IS/IT) gender research. Much of the research undertaken in IS/IT in relation to gender issues adopts a positivist philosophy. A feminist research approach is rarely used in IS/IT gender research. This is despite the fact that it is generally accepted that the IS/IT workplace is 'gendered' and embodies a tacit masculine norm. This paper adopts a feminist research approach in a case study that explores imbalance in Tasmanian (Australia) IS/IT workplaces. The aim of the research was to disclose common characteristics of women currently working within the industry and to consider the factors that could impact on women moving to or being placed in IS/IT positions. Clearly a research approach that enables the researcher to explore the perspective of the research participant and as a consequence offer some insights into the declining gender balance in the field offers significant benefits.

Introduction

Since the inception of the IS/IT industry women have been an under-represented human resource (Nielsen et al., 2000; Panteli et al., 1999; Ahuja, 2002; The Women in Science Engineering and Technology Advisory Group, 1995). In addition, many women who gain professional qualifications in the area and enter the industry do not remain (O'Neill and Walker, 2001). Largely, the problem has been attributed to a dominant male culture in the IS/IT field. The ongoing gendered environment in IS/IT has been defined as the perpetuation of the 'old corporate boys' club syndrome (O'Neill and Walker, 2001, p. 118). This implies that while women are not precluded from entering the industry, little action is taken to recruit them or foster their career advancement opportunities through involvement in managerial decision-making.

To date much of the research examining gender issues in IS/IT is framed within a positivist philosophy and uses quantitative methods. The value of this stream of research is the measurement and quantification of the extent of the gender imbalance in the industry. Generally the focus is on attempting to put in place policies and strategies to address the problem (Pringle et al., 2000). However this approach has been criticised because it largely seeks to 'add more women' and fails to acknowledge and address the need to change the gendered culture in IS/IT workplaces if, indeed, this is possible (Adam et al., 2002).

There are few examples of research that use a subjectivist approach and qualitative method focusing on the gender imbalance in the IS/IT industry. There are even fewer examples of research that have explicitly adopted a feminist research approach.

Adam (2001) argues that the adoption of feminist theory in the study of gender within IS has the potential to reap benefits in three ways. These are:

1. support for IS commitment to social and cultural aspects;
2. commitment to emancipatory action that results in the revelation of previously hidden viewpoints, thus contributing to knowledge; and
3. emphasis upon the minority or repressed being involved in the development of their own methods for liberation.

In response, the aim of this paper is to adopt a feminist epistemology to demonstrate that this approach has the capability to build a rich insight into the experiences of women currently working successfully in the IT industry in Tasmania. In the short term it is not feasible to expect a change in the dominance of a male culture in IS/IT. However, reporting the experiences of women who have achieved in the industry is a positive move to weaken the extent of this domination and potentially attract women in larger numbers to careers in the IS/IT field.

Background

The aim in this section of the paper is to briefly outline the nature of IS as an emerging discipline, the imbalance of women in the IS/IT industry, the scope of IS gender research and then to offer an insight into feminist research. From this background the research questions posed in this paper are then presented.

IS as an emerging discipline

As a relatively recent discipline, IS draws on a range of reference disciplines. The major sub-disciplines are in turn focused in a different set of sub-disciplines (Robinson and Richardson, 1999). The primary reference disciplines have been identified as computer science, management science, organisational science, cognitive science and economics. The secondary reference disciplines are sociology, information science, linguistics, anthropology, ergonomics and systems science (Khazanchi and Munkvold, 2000). This implies that research from an IS perspective draws on a wide range of domains of study, strategies and methods (Marble, 2000; Robinson and Richardson, 1999). Because of this, IS is often criticised for its diversity and fragmentation, which are seen as precluding an ability to become a mature discipline with a cumulative research tradition (Robinson and Richardson, 1999).

At the same time IS has been acknowledged as having 'subject matter that is so central to contemporary society' (Robinson and Richardson, 1999, p. 3) that is subjected to continuous change (O'Donovan and Roode, 2002). While there is pressure for IS to consolidate, this does not imply that IS research should be static, but rather it should be open to innovative ways of doing research. The application of a feminist epistemology, as demonstrated in this paper, is one example. The aim in adopting this approach is not to offer an alternative epistemology but to show that, in IS gender research, a feminist approach can be beneficially applied (Adam and Richardson, 2001).

The imbalance of women in the IS/IT industry

In most Western countries women remain a minority in the IT industry (Trauth et al., 2003). UK women were found to be a minority in all areas of the IT industry in the country (Panteli et al., 1999). In European countries only 25% of those working in the industry are women, while in the United States the figure has been reported as being as low as 20% (Ahuja, 2002). All indications are that the situation in Australia follows these patterns. In contrast to other areas within science and technology such as engineering, where numbers of women studying and working are increasing, the number of women studying and entering the IS/IT industry is actually declining (The Women in Science Engineering and Technology Advisory Group, 1995).

Little research has been done within the IS/IT industry that has explored the experience of women and how it can be used to address the continuing problem of gender imbalance. 'Most research on women in the information technology (IT) industry has been concerned with practical questions: measuring disadvantage, establishing causes, and attempting to put in place policies and strategies that will rectify the situation' (Pringle et al., 2000).

The scope of IS gender research

Much of the literature considering gender issues in IS/IT is framed within a positivist philosophy and uses quantitative methods to examine the research problem (Ahuja, 2002; Igbaria and Baroudi, 1995; Holmes, 1998; Khazanchi, 1995; Truman and Baroudi, 1994; Baroudi and Igbaria, 1994; Frenkel, 1991). While this research identifies the extent of the gender imbalance, it is largely based on dichotomising IT professionals on the basis of biological sex. This means that females are seen as a stereotypical group and individual differences are not considered (Adam et al., 2002). Accordingly, the effectiveness of this approach is limited as it precludes the opportunity to gain any insight into the personal experiences of women who have become IS professionals and subsequently continue to successfully work in the industry.

There is little evidence of IS gender-focused research based on a subjectivist approach using qualitative methods (Pringle et al., 2000; O'Neill and Walker, 2001; von Hellens et al., 2001; Trauth, 2002; Webb, 2002). Within these examples, while Trauth (2002) and Webb (2002) are explicitly presented as feminist research, the work reported by Pringle et al. (2000) implicitly adopted this stance. Subjectivist research enables the researcher to explore the research problem in greater detail from the perspective of the research subject. While subjectivist research cannot usually be easily generalised to the wider community it can, and does, have the capacity to highlight areas and issues that may benefit from further investigation and discussion.

Feminist research

A fundamental aspect of feminist research is that it is conducted for women rather than on women (Reinharz, 1992; Reynolds, 1993). It involves a broad and dynamic theory within which numerous positions exist (Millen, 1997). Central to feminist research are goals of social change and improved representation (Humphries, 1997). It must also be believed that women have been oppressed and not treated fairly, and that there is action that can be taken (Grimshaw, 1986). Further, the role of the researcher and the researcher's rapport and familiarity with the participant is also important in feminist research (Reinharz, 1992). Feminist research lends itself to the use of qualitative methods enabling the researcher to explore each woman's individual perspective. While quantitative research methods and a feminist epistemology are not mutually exclusive it would be uncommon to find quantitative methods, with its focus on hard, numerical data used for feminist research (Stanley, 1990; Neuman, 2000).

Feminist research often uses case studies to analyse change in a situation over a period of time, the significance of a situation for the future and the connections between components of a situation (Reinharz, 1992). The use of semi-structured interviewing in feminist research is significant. It enables the use of open questions and provides the capacity to encourage participants to give lengthy and full responses in their own words. 'Feminist researchers find interviewing appealing for reasons over and above the assets noted by social scientists who defend qualitative methods against positivist criticism' (Reinharz, 1992, p. 19). Semi-structured interviews are seen as offering access to people's ideas, thoughts, and memories and real life experiences in their own words rather than the words of the researcher (Reinharz, 1992; Dallimore, 2000). To achieve this outcome it is important that considerable rapport is developed between the researcher and the participant, as this is a fundamental prerequisite in feminist research.

From this background, the research presented in this paper draws on a feminist epistemology to demonstrate that it is an appropriate approach in IS gender research. In so doing it is acknowledged that there is gender imbalance in information systems workplaces and it is likely that there are factors at work that inhibit or reduce the likelihood that women will participate in equal numbers with men. It may be that oppression exists and this has contributed to the inequality. Further, it is recognised that, due to the exploratory nature of the research, no immediate change is likely to occur as a result of it. It may, however, lead to further research and subsequent actions to effect change and therefore meets yet another criterion in adding support for a feminist stance. When these conditions apply they represent the subtle distinction between a feminist epistemology and a subjectivist approach.

The aim of the research is to disclose common characteristics of women currently working within the industry and to consider the factors that impact on women moving to, or being placed in, IS/IT positions. To address this objective the following questions are posed:

1. What are the factors influencing the careers of women in IS/IT?
2. What are the characteristics of women working in IS/IT roles in Tasmania?

Method

To demonstrate the application of a feminist epistemology within IS gender research, the research presented in this paper uses a case study approach involving semi-structured interviews conducted with women who are successfully working in the IS/IT industry in Tasmania. The adoption of a case study strategy is supported by the view of Reinharz (1992) that feminists use case studies primarily to analyse the significance of a situation. While there is an absence of research that directly relates to gender imbalance within the IS/IT industry in Tasmania, this research is founded on an assumption that any discriminatory practices found in this state are likely to mirror the situation elsewhere.

Participant recruitment

To recruit participants for the case study the primary researcher attended a social event hosted by the Women in Information Technology Tasmania (WIITT) group. WIITT is a special interest group constituted under the auspices of the Australian Computer Society (ACS). At this event she was able to address the group and provide an outline of the research and invite the women in attendance to volunteer to participate. A brochure providing an overview of the research and the participants' expected contribution was made available at the event. Within a feminist research perspective this personal approach was an important initial step in the development of rapport with potential participants.

At this gathering between six and nine volunteers were sought to participate in interviews. This number of interviews was established by reference to the limitations of the time and the resources available for this research. Based on the qualitative literature, the appropriate number of interviews is dependent upon the projected depth of analysis and the proposed representativeness of the research (Connell et al., 2001). In any case, that evening six women volunteered to participate. It was interesting to observe that most of the women approached by, or who themselves approached, the researcher during the course of the evening expressed their interest in the research but also expressed their reservations regarding the relevance of their contribution. Comments like *'I don't think I'm the right person to speak to'* or *'I'm not sure if I really do the right kind of work – I'm not very technical'* were common although a few questions generally showed that the women were indeed employed in the IS/IT sector. Comments such as these are perhaps indicative of the fundamental difference in approach that women exhibit compared to men in similar roles in the industry.

The choice of research participants was based on the following criteria. The women needed to be currently working in IS/IT in either the public or private sectors in Hobart, readily accessible and willing to take part in the research and available for an interview during the required research time of the research.

Subsequent to the WIITT social event two more women volunteered to participate. This brought the total number of volunteers to eight. The potential participants were contacted shortly after the WIITT event to thank them for their offer of participation and to let them know that they would be contacted again to organise the interview. They all expressed their ongoing support for the research. In keeping with a feminist epistemology this second personal contact was yet another occasion to build rapport with the women who were prepared to contribute to the research.

Data collection and analysis

Data collection was based on the use of semi-structured interviews that aimed to encourage participants to provide their own views and perspectives of their experiences working in an IS/IT work environment. A combination of open and closed questions was used. The majority of the questions began with 'how' or 'what' as a reminder to keep the question broad and open, and were worded to encourage descriptive replies. For example: *'How did you get into information systems?'* and *'What do you envisage for yourself in your professional career?'*.

A prepared interview guide was also used to stimulate discussion. This was based on the personal experience and understanding of the primary researcher, gained from working for a number of years in the IS/IT industry. It provided a solid starting position, and offered the ability, when appropriate, to pursue interesting responses with probing questions.

Pilot Interview

Prior to the main interviews a pilot interview was conducted to ensure the questions were easily understood, to test the application of the interview guide and assess the pace necessary to complete the interview. The pilot took place with a female IS professional who had lengthy experience working in the IS/IT sector in Tasmania. It was completed within the projected 60-minute time frame and the interview schedule worked effectively in encouraging the woman to relate her personal experiences of working in the IS/IT industry.

Main interviews

The eight main interviews took place in June and July 2002 and were conducted at venues and times suitable to the participants. To maximise the level of comfort and increase the likelihood of full, comprehensive and frank responses, the women taking part were assured the interviews would be treated as confidential and no identifying information would be incorporated into transcripts or subsequent analysis.

With the permission of the participants the interviews were tape recorded to enable the researcher to capture the exchange with a high degree of accuracy. None of the participants declined to have the interviews recorded. The intention, where the participants indicated their willingness to do so, was that the transcripts would be provided to them for checking. This approach was used to fulfil a validity test involving collaboration.

Interview transcription

Each interview was transcribed within 48 hours of completion. This was done to complete the task while the memory of the researcher was still fresh, thereby reducing the risk of error in the transcription should any words be indistinct on the tape. This approach proved to be very successful with all but one of the tape recordings. The exceptional recording was indistinct in parts due to high levels of background noise in combination with a very softly spoken participant. Because the transcription was completed in a timely manner the majority of data from this interview was recovered.

Data coding and analysis

The interviews were transcribed into Microsoft Word and then entered into an Excel spreadsheet to facilitate the detailed breakdown of the data that qualitative analysis demands. The aim of coding in qualitative analysis is to shatter the data and then manipulate it into groupings that can be compared and regrouped (Maxwell, 1996). In coding the data, a three-stage bottom-up coding process was adopted: open, axial and finally selective.

Findings

The analysis and interpretation revealed three major themes in the data: *supermum factor*, *serendipity* and *culture*. The major themes incorporated ten sub-themes, which are summarised in Table 8.1.

Table 8.1. Research findings

Major themes	Sub-themes
Supermum factor	societal expectation; work-family balance; support
Serendipity	skills; adaptive behaviour; outlook
Culture	paucity; definition; gender traits; distinction

Even though relationships were revealed both within themes and between themes, for clarity and simplicity, each theme and the underlying sub-themes will now be presented individually.

Support for the identified themes will be presented through use of quotations drawn from the interview transcriptions. Due to the space limitations of this paper, the quotations provided are usually just one example from among many alternatives available from the findings. The use of quotations to support interpretation follows an established technique used to demonstrate the validity of the findings (Whittemore et al., 2001). It also provides the women participants a voice to examine, explain and explore the findings (Broido and Manning, 2002).

Supermum factor

The *Supermum factor* can be interpreted as the external influences on the work choice of the women. As shown in Table 8.2, it contains three sub-themes: social expectation, work-family balance and support. The supermum aspect of the findings recognises the impact and value of support from both the family and from employers in helping to achieve a sustainable balance between work and family. It acknowledges the struggle experienced by women striving for excellence in both the work and family areas of their life within a framework of societal expectation. The data subtly demonstrated the existence and impact of societal expectation and also illustrated the changing nature of societal expectation. The amount and form of support provided to the women was also impacted by societal expectation.

Table 8.2. Supermum sub-themes

Supermum sub-themes	Illustrations from the data
Social expectation	Participant #6: She actually had to leave work at the end of the year she got married.
Work and family balance	Participant #3: And I think that … as women are starting to or as society is starting to accept that … it is not automatic for women to have short-term careers and go off and have families during their twenties.
support	Participant #3: It has been damn hard to combine a family with study and with full-time work and I think that's a real challenge. I think that the community and the industry could reap so many benefits if they allowed a little flexibility.

Serendipity

This theme encapsulates the skills, qualities and attitudes of the participants as represented by the data. It has been so named because of the strong sense of the role of fate or luck expressed by the women.

Participant #6: 'well it's just… serendipity. I mean that's how life is isn't it?'

It can, however, be demonstrated from the data that luck probably contributed less to the women's progress and success in their careers than did the skills, outlook and the adaptive behaviours these women used to survive and thrive even though they were and remain a minority in a male dominated environment. The sub-themes, along with supporting quotations from the data, are shown in Table 8.3. While there were examples of a range of skills in the data (interpersonal communications, problem solving/analytical skills, and skills in mathematics and science) there did not appear to be a single core skill set among the participants. However, the outlook of the participants and any consequent adaptive behaviours evidently do not occur independently of the skill set of the individual women concerned.

The outlook sub-theme was arguably the most exciting finding in the research, revealing as it did a set of common qualities shared by the women participating in this research. It highlighted some strong aspects including displaying a positive attitude, excitement and enthusiasm for their work and life. The women welcomed change and opportunity to the extent that some participants spoke of the need for stimulation and a commitment to continuous learning. Paradoxically, there was also a sense of insecurity and lack of confidence among the participants. There was also some evidence of self-awareness and the recognition that insecurity and lack of confidence were not justified when skill and ability were considered.

Table 8.3. Serendipity sub-themes

Serendipity sub-themes	Illustrations from the data
Skills	Participant #1: And I get on equally well drinking at the pub with the riggers as I do talking to, when you're doing a customer presentation and talking to management.
	Participant #2: ... but I am a fairly, you know, organised kinda person so just organise yourself and you get by.
	Participant #7: I have a degree in maths and physics.
Outlook	Participant #4: I sort of suddenly began to realise that it was within my reach to do something that was ... in demand and current like to me it just seemed so ... oh, so exciting so ... my mind was set then.
	Participant #4: And yet ... it was so easy when I did it.
Adaptive behaviours	Participant #6: Because lovely though they are, if you were a real sensitive sort you would find some of their jokes really appalling.

Culture

As shown in Table 8.4, the final main theme of *Culture* is based on four sub-themes: paucity of women in IS/IT, definition of IS/IT, gender traits and the distinction in approach and support. These sub-themes combine to create the environment within which the women carry out their IS/IT work-related activities.

There was some sense that the low numbers of women in IS/IT may have impacted on the culture and environment within the IS/IT workplace. Potentially, it has served to perpetuate the dominant male culture. The nebulous nature of IS/IT was revealed by the data, with no common perception among the women participating in the research. From the data it was clear that there was a perception that men and women, in general do have subtle inherent differences and that this impacted on the way they operate and interact. There was also recognition that the description of gender traits relies heavily on generalisation and stereotyping.

The distinction sub-theme encompasses discriminatory behaviour that the participants had experienced. A common view from the data was that the women had not experienced barriers within their workplaces, although they acknowledged the existence of barriers in a more general sense.

Table 8.4. Culture sub-themes

Culture sub-themes	Illustrations from the data
Paucity of women in IS/IT	Participant #2: Yeah no, I suppose after 30 something years you get used to working in that environment.
Definition	Participant #8: ... this is where I struggle a bit with being classified as being in information technology (this participant included, among other responsibilities, management of a WAN as part of her duties).
Gender traits	Participant #2: So then most women I suppose it's part of being a woman, you kinda have a bit more ... you accept that you're going to be asked questions and you're prepared for it more whereas guys seem not to like that kind of thing.
Distinction	Participant #6: And he actually complimented me by telling me I was almost a bloke, almost a man, as far as my work went, you know.

Validity

Feminist research has been accused, in a similar way to interpretivism and critical social science, of being wanting in the area of validity (Dallimore, 2000). To address the issue in the present research, with reference to Dallimore (2000) and Neuman (2000), collaboration, natural history, and member validation were applied.

In purposefully building rapport with participants, as consistent with a feminist approach, the researcher addressed validity through collaboration. The relevant industry experience of the researcher helped to frame the questions and assisted in drawing out rich and detailed responses. This personal interest could be perceived as providing potential for bias. This was readily acknowledged and in so doing the likelihood that it would be successfully managed was increased. Validity can also be demonstrated in the manner that the findings truly represent the views of the participants. In this research participants were offered the transcript to review and provide feedback on its accuracy. Only one woman chose to review the transcript and that participant did not request any changes to its content.

In the present research, the researcher has provided a detailed description of the philosophy, processes, methods and approaches in order to comply with a natural history test of validity (Neuman, 2000). The researcher set out to faithfully record all aspects of the research to ensure validity in the eyes of other readers.

The final method of validation used within this research was that of member validation. When the findings of the research are provided to the participants and they are able to identify their situation as reflected in the findings, its validity is supported. Member validation can, however, be difficult to achieve. Despite the research presenting a truthful portrayal, participants may have personal motivations for disagreeing with the findings. This was evidently not the case in the present research:

> Thank you ... for sending me your findings. I can identify with a lot of what you say, especially 'It would appear from the data that being valued, encouraged and supported in their family and career was important ...'

and:

> I can definitely identify with the findings of your research and with the other women interviewed. Especially the serendipity theme – we all think we're just lucky but in reality we're pretty damn good aren't we?

Discussion

In addressing the objective of this research the application of a feminist research approach has proved to be beneficial. It could be argued that some of the factors influencing the careers of women in IS/IT and the characteristics of these women may have been identified using a positivist research approach, and others obtained from the use of a qualitative approach. However, it is proposed that the findings have extended to uncover subtle factors and characteristics of individual participants that could only come from the use of a feminist approach. Central to this is the fact that the research was conducted for women, not on women. In addition, in the context of feminist research the extent of rapport and element of trust between the participants and the researcher is critically important, and in the research reported here it was clearly very good. Unless this rapport and trust exists then participants do not feel comfortable giving comprehensive, open and truthful responses. The high level of rapport and trust is evidenced by the fact that the only woman who asked to read the transcription of the data subsequently did not request any changes to her interview dialogue. In addition the remaining participants obviously had confidence in the researcher to the point that they did not even want to review the transcription of their interviews. There was also a general consensus that the women readily identified themselves in the findings of the research. This implies that the women taking part were given a voice and not just treated as a stereotypical group based on their biological sex. This research has, therefore, provided a new perspective with the ability to extend understanding in IS gender research.

A number of factors were identified that influence the careers of women in IS/IT workplaces. One significant factor was that of societal expectation. While this was acknowledged as changing, it can still place considerable pressure on women who are attempting to balance work and family in pursuit of a career; the requirement to be a supermum. The findings have shown that support was crucial for the women in their career endeavours. However, it became evident from the transcripts that sometimes the extent of this support was less than ideal. The example quoted from participant #4 supports this view. While she acknowledged the support of her husband, there was still an expectation that she was responsible for going home to make dinner. Potentially this could imply that while the husband was prepared to be supportive, societal expectation was still influential in that there remained in his mind a clear division of labour on the basis of gender.

The women contributing to this research were a highly intelligent group holding tertiary qualifications, not necessarily in IS/IT, but in mathematics, physics or science. They were willing and interested to take part in this research even though initially they were unclear about their role within IS. As highlighted in the findings, the serendipitiy sub-theme 'outlook' was arguably the most exciting result in the research. While a particular core skill set was not found among the participants, when those they had were combined with a positive outlook, the women, as individuals, were able to use adaptive behaviours to succeed and thrive in what was often a discriminatory work environment. The women readily acknowledged that they were a minority in the IS/IT industry with many of the participants dismissing the male culture dominance as of no consequence.

Conclusions

A research approach that enables the researcher to explore, in some depth, the perspective of each female research participant and, as a consequence, offer some insights into the declining gender balance in the IS field, offers significant benefits.

Adopting a feminist research approach has enabled the researcher to:

1. develop and establish a rapport with the participants to a level and depth that would be difficult with alternative approaches; first in a convivial social situation and then on a personal one-on-one basis;
2. inform the research process based on her own experience and to extend and explore issues with participants based upon that experience, resulting in richer data and a greater insight into the research problem; and
3. gain a richer and more detailed insight into the research problem through the explicit adoption of a research approach that supports women in challenging and confronting a situation that requires social change.

This paper has provided an example of research conducted using a feminist approach and qualitative research methods to demonstrate that it is a viable alternative in IS gender research. The approach was beneficial in conducting this research as it enabled the researcher to explore the research problem more fully and in greater depth. The individual women participants were given a voice and as a group their combined wisdom was illuminating. However, as acknowledged at the beginning of this paper, due to the exploratory nature of the research and the nature of the issues investigated, little if any immediate change is likely to occur as a direct result of this study.

Nevertheless, perhaps now the time is right for researchers studying gender issues within IS to consider potentially useful alternative approaches to the more conventional ways. The worsening gender imbalance in the IS/IT discipline demands new and innov-

ative approaches and the need to ensure that the views of women are adequately represented in the workforce should provide a powerful catalyst to action.

9. Reflection in self-organised systems

Maureen Lynch, *School of Information Systems, University of South Australia*
Carmen Johan, *School of Information Systems, University of South Australia*

Abstract

Organisations operating in a dynamic environment need to be able to detect and respond to changes both internal and external. One effective decision making approach is self-organisation, which is appropriate where there is a state of constant awareness of the working environment and flexibility so that decision-making groups are formed spontaneously to solve problems and incorporate changes. Decision-making from this perspective is done on three levels: individual, group or cluster, and organisational. With each level, it is imperative that the situation is fully understood, alternative solutions are considered and compared with an ideal, and consequences are taken into account. The authors argue that this model of thinking and decision making is that recommended by Dewey – reflection. The evidence used in this argument comes from two bodies of knowledge, the reflection and self-organised systems literature. The paper describes the process of reflection on the three levels of organisational decision making and concludes that one of the most effective ways for organisations to optimise operations in a dynamic environment is to be open to self-organisation and reflective thinking.

Introduction

The complexity of information systems and technological changes confronting most organisations today means there is an increased urgency for them to be able to reflect and adapt. The aim of this paper is to explore the importance of reflection for successful problem solving in self-organised social human systems that face this urgency. Organisations are constantly exposed to new market opportunities and competitive dynamics, demanding that they learn quickly when there is new information provided by, and new opportunities caused by, changes in the external environment.

The increase in interconnectivity and the ubiquity of information systems across the globe is causing the competitive environment to become more complex and self-organising. In this paper, the authors highlight that, in order to operate effectively at the edge of these complexities, reflection at three levels of decision making (i.e. individual, cluster, and organisational) becomes not only necessary but fundamental. An iterative reflection process throughout problem solving, where the 'theory of action' of both individuals and the organisation are questioned and matched against an ideal outcome, allows more informed decisions to be made. This continuous cycle of reflection leads to spontaneous self-organising behaviours. Behaviours are self-organising when knowledge networks and communication channels are freely developed in organisations, even if this involves individuals (actors) crossing the organisational boundaries created by formal hierarchical structures.

Reflection

This paper refers to Dewey's (1997) method of thinking and problem solving – reflection that involves the spontaneous creation of a belief (Dewey, 1997), conjecture (Popper, 1969) or intuition (Georgiou, 2001) from one's consciousness and past experience, contemplating and pondering these thoughts, comparing them with an ideal, and finally challenging them in an attempt to substantiate or invalidate them.

Dewey (1997) expresses this reflection succinctly:

> Active, persistent and careful consideration of any belief or supposed form of knowledge in the light of the grounds that support it, and the further conclusions to which it tends, constitutes reflective thought. (p6)

The continuous cycle of experiencing, reflecting, forming possible solutions, and testing is illustrated in Kolb's model (see Figure 9.1) as depicted in Graeff (1997). Kolb (1984) argues that, rather than viewing experiential learning as a closed cycle, it should be seen as a spiral 'filling each episode of experience with the potential for movement, from blind impulse to a life of choice and purpose.'

Figure 9.1. Kolb's model of reflection.

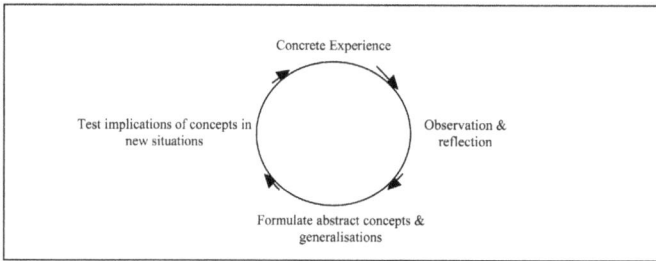

Reflective learning 'engages the person at the edge of their knowledge, their sense of self and the world as experienced by them' (Brockbank and McGill, 1998) where their ideas, beliefs or knowledge are challenged.

Reflection types

Simple reflection

Simple or single-loop reflection refers to increasing efficiency of an objective; 'Are we doing things right?' (Flood and Romm, 1996) – it is task oriented and is about the design of the process to retain reliability. It is simple reflection that may challenge assumptions and strategies to alter the plan of action but always 'in ways that leave the values of a theory of action unchanged' (Brockbank and McGill, 1998). Courtney et al. (1998) describe this as low-level as it involves keeping to a set of rules and is simply error correction. This reflection and learning are viewed as valuable for day-to-day activities and are necessary for progress to be made within the established frameworks (Brockbank and McGill, 1998). To illustrate this sort of reflection, Dooley (1999) uses the example of a buggy whip manufacturer in the early 21st century improving the manufacturing process in order to make finer buggy whips. The manufacturer does not look beyond his immediate task to take in the strategic perspective of, for example, the long term viability of buggy whip manufacturing. Similarly, an organisation may upgrade a transaction processing system to handle processes more efficiently without the effectiveness or even necessity of the processes being examined.

Double-loop reflection

Double-loop reflection is described by Argyris and Schon (1996), who use the term 'double loop learning', and Courtney et al. (1998) as a higher level of reflection than single-loop reflection – it incorporates the first loop (that centres on finding the best means of achieving an end) together with a second loop. This second loop centres on the examination and reflection of the theory or perspective in use. It is recognised that the action and consequences striven for in the first loop may not be valid – that there may be different perspectives regarding what the outcome should be and therefore assumptions, premises and context are questioned. Consequently, double-loop learning asks, 'Are we doing things right AND are we doing the right things' (Flood and Romm, 1996). While it is advised that the 'gate' into the second loop should be used frequently, it cannot be sustained constantly (Brockbank and McGill, 1998) as the required paradigmatic shift that the second loop requires is often disruptive to everyday activities. Dooley (1999) gives as an example of double-loop learning when, in the 1980s, Royal Dutch Shell delayed its plans for acquisition of oil fields when it foresaw the drop in oil prices and the demise of the Soviet Union. It examined what it was doing, as well as how it was doing it. See Figure 9.2 for an illustration of the combination of the two loops to form double-loop learning as depicted in Encyclopedia/Forum (2004).

Figure 9.2. Schon's double-loop reflection.

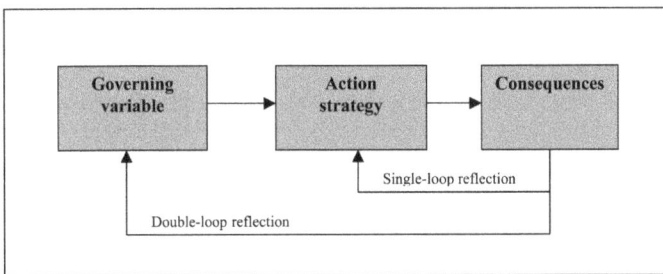

Reflecting against ideal

Morris and Moore (2000) maintain that research has shown that 'the way individuals make sense of experienced outcomes is greatly determined by thoughts of what could have been, by comparisons of actual outcomes to counterfactual alternatives'. When preparing for an action, 'upward counterfactual comparisons' as anticipatory reflection lead to enhanced outcomes. Therefore, reflection against an ideal, or counterfactual alternatives, when anticipating or reviewing action has been shown to improve the outcome of the process.

There is a double movement in all reflection: a movement from the given partial and confused data to a suggested comprehensive (or inclusive) entire situation; and back from this suggested whole – which, as suggested, is a meaning, and idea – to the particular facts, so as to connect these with one another and with additional facts to which the suggestion has directed attention (Dewey, 1997, p. 80).

Dewey (1997, p. 12) warns that it is impossible to reflect against an ideal if one has not had experience in a similar situation: 'But unless there has been experience in some degree analogous, which may now be represented in imagination, confusion remains mere confusion. There is nothing upon which to draw in order to clarify it'.

Learning from negative feedback

'It is a theory of experience that assigns to our observations the equally modest and almost equally important role of tests which may help us in the discovery of our mistakes. Though it stresses our fallibility it does not resign itself to scepticism, for it also stresses the fact that knowledge can grow and that science can progress – just because we can learn from our mistakes.' Popper (1969, p. vii)

Negative feedback in this paper is approached from the self-organisation perspective. The concept of reflection involves criticising one's conjectures, ideas, theories or past actions with a view to invalidating them or, in the case of action, to improve performance by learning from mistakes in previous action. Jung (1950), as cited in Fortune and Peters (1997), asserts that 'little or nothing is learnt from successes … while failures are, on the other hand, priceless experiences in that they not only open up the way to a deeper truth, but force (one) to change views and methods'. Popper (1969) concurs, maintaining that mistakes indicate a gap in knowledge and that learning occurs when those mistakes are rectified.

Fortune and Peters (1997) stress that the main deterrent to learning from failure is 'post-event rationalisation' where frequently the desire to discover the reasons for failure cause investigations to be carried out hastily; this leads to a false picture of the failure, its cause and the context in which it occurred. They cite the cases of the Bhopal chemical disaster and the British European Trident Papa India air crash as examples of hastily formed first impressions that led to completely erroneous findings. The writers advocate using the Systems Failure Method whose goal is 'a systemic interpretation of a failure and its context' (Fortune and Peters, 1997, p. 64) to learn from any failure or mistake. This applies systems thinking concepts to reflection – the focus of reflection is viewed as a 'system' and, when reflection is taking place, the boundary, environment, purpose and different perspectives are taken into account to describe the system in which the failure occurred. An idealised model of the system is designed, and then this and the failed system are compared. This comparison is used to identify or explain the causes of failure. The knowledge created from this reflection is used to recommend actions to improve the situation.

Reflective culture

This section will argue that the reflective culture of the individual and organisation is critical for effective reflective learning to take place (Schon, 1995; Mathiassen and Sandeep, 2002; Seibert, 1999; Raelin, 2001; Ayas and Zeniuk, 2001; Brockbank and McGill, 1998). Individual reflective culture is defined as 'the act of developing the intellectual and moral faculties' to reflect (Merriam-Webster). It can be difficult for an individual to acquire the skills of reflective learning (Alvesson and Skolberg, 2000) as these skills do not occur naturally. Accordingly, opportunities and education need to be provided to stimulate the practice and develop the individual's culture (Raelin, 2001). Ayas and Zeniuk (2001) agree that a reflective culture based on the search to improve knowledge by questioning one's assumptions and understandings, and the consequences of one's actions, starts at an individual level and can be practiced in the workplace in such situations as project development.

The reflective culture of an organisation is defined as: 'The set of shared attitudes, values, goals and practices that characterises a company or corporation' (Merriam-Webster). If reflective learning is to take place at an organisational level, the culture of the organisation needs to be sympathetic to reflection. Raelin (2001, p. 13) maintains that an individual's background has a significant effect on the propensity to reflect with others; some marginalised groups have difficulty in developing trust and a sense of security so reflective learning can be threatening unless the environment 'intellectually and emotionally supports individuals in their learning and development' by allowing them to challenge ideas and practices without the threat of reprisal. It is a common trend in the busy workplace for reflection-in-action and reflection-on-action to be discouraged and resisted due to time pressure (Brockbank and McGill, 1998; Ayas and Zeniuk, 2001), and any type of learning to be deferred to the future. Project work, in particular, allows opportunities for learning, but evidently these opportunities are rarely explored. Sharing of lessons learnt from experiences, successes and problems does not happen in many organisations (Mathiassen and Purao, 2002).

Mathiassen and Purao (2002) suggest that what organisations strive for is a culture that instigates the evolution of a 'community-of-practice'. This is where colleagues collaborate and share work experiences with the intention of combining individual learning in a localised context to allow the creation of knowledge that can be generalised to other organisational contexts and perhaps lead to changes in practices, modifications to design, etc. Communities-of-practice cannot be designed – they emerge as colleagues collaborate to solve problems together. Mathiassen (2002) explains 'membership [of communities-of-practice] is informal and based on participation in diagnosing situations and telling stories about them. The resulting communities are fluid rather than bounded, evolve rather than being designed and typically cross the formal boundaries of an organisation.'

Successful reflection, therefore, is dependant on culture at both an individual and organisational level. On an individual level, one needs to be in a philosophical position to feel comfortable about questioning long standing assumptions, values and understandings, and with using the reflection process to reach new knowledge. Individual reflective culture can determine organisational reflective culture but organisational culture can also dictate individual behaviour (Ayas and Zeniuk, 2001). If organisational learning is to take place, there needs to be an environment in which individuals feel psychologically safe to challenge organisational norms and practices so double-loop and triple-loop learning can take place.

Self-organisation

Technological systems become organised by commands from outside, as when human intentions lead to the building of structures or machines. But many natural systems become structured by their own internal processes: these are the self-organising systems, and the emergence of order within them is a complex phenomenon that intrigues scientists from many disciplines (Yates et al., 1987, cited in Camazine et al., 2001).

Self-organisation is a process that is set in motion when, confronted with change, components of a system (e.g. individuals, organisms, elements) spontaneously form patterns and structures in order to target their goals: *problem-solving*. One way of understanding self-organisation is to contemplate a common purpose or problem, initiating a strong relocation of energy and actions within a system, which leads to the formation of complex webs from elements that are sparsely coupled in order to achieve a common purpose. Following are four definitions that summarise the view of self-organisation as it is being used in this paper:

> Self-organisation refers to a broad range of pattern-formation processes in both physical and biological systems, such as sand grains assembling into rippled dunes, chemical reactants forming swirling spirals, cells making up highly organised tissues, and fish joining together in schools (Camazine et al., 2001).

Self-organisation literally denotes the process whereby a group of people organise themselves in pursuit of a common cause (Humphrey, 2000).

[Self-organisation is] the flexibility of a system to deal successfully with variety in transactions with the environment (Molleman, 1998).

Self-organisation is an emergence of order to deal with social complex systems (Yates et al., 1987).

The term, *pattern,* as used in this paper, denotes a particular organised assembly of elements taking place in a specific space and time. Based on local information, a system's components interact to create a pattern. As such, a pattern's formation is built with no external direct influence; that is, with no global information or directions from a leader. Patterns, from Kauffman's (1995) point of view, are the creation and physical representation of order; while order is then accounted to the theory of emergence as one of its creations. He argues that order arises naturally as an expression of the self-organisation that abounds in very complex networks. Similarly, in social systems and organisations, the formation of clusters by people themselves pursuing a common cause is a clear example of self-organising patterns.

Constructs of self-organisation

Rycroft and Kash (2004) state that the world is full of self-organising systems that form structures and processes in response to their own internal logic. A review of the literature (see, for example, Kauffman, 1993; Comfort, 1994; Hudson, 2000; Camazine et al., 2001) suggests that these types of systems have three basic components. Holland and Melhuish (1999) more specifically point out there are three distinctive signatures that complement the four basic characteristics of self-organisation. The three signatures are:

1. the creation of spatio-temporal structures;
2. the possible attainability of different stable states (*multiple stable interactions* within a system or parallel-processing systems, where various components perform various functions concurrently in order to achieve a desired outcome); and
3. the capacity for adaptation to the prevailing environment.

Spatio-temporal structures

Self-organisation is a problem solving process whereby components or elements at one particular level interact in order to create structures at a higher level, which may combine again to create even higher level structures. The structures emerging from these repeated interactions develop patterns that are then recognised as self-organisation. Jointly with the environment's space and time, they define the first signature of self-organisation: *spatio-temporal structures.* An example commonly cited is the spatio-temporal patterns of army ant raids. The coordinated, functional structure of their movement, which spontaneously forms a higher order structure, occurs with minimum external interference.

Multiple interactions

Self-organisation takes place in systems with multiple active interactions among many actors. Because there are many, often identical, actors there is no requirement for a single actor (e.g. a leader) to carry out a series of connected sequences of movements. For example, referring to an army of ants foraging without recruitment, *the rules of thumb* [1] are just simple cues that alone will ensure that a complete sequence of actions is executed,

---

[1] The rules of thumb are surprisingly simple interactions among systems components requiring limited access to global information (Kauffman, 1993; Camazine et al., 2001).

even though an action or movement may be performed by a different ant from the one initially involved in it. The execution of these rules, in this case, is conducted by the flow (cue) of an ant's pheromone. *Multiple stable interactions* arise when other ants interact with this cue and create new stimuli for further interactions to occur.

Ants leave their nest in order to find food. Once found, they load up and return to the nest leaving a trail of pheromone. For simplicity, assume that ants 'would raise an alarm for other ants to follow'; while this is a multiple interactive process, it could also be a *parallel-process* as other ants from the nest may find other food sources and also raise an alarm. However, as Holland and Melhuish (1999, p. 4) assert, '... if there are many locations with such cues, the subtask [2] will be performed faster at the location that has greatest numbers of agents present' due to the higher interaction rate and stability of the process.

Adaptation

Prigogine (1996, p. 711) argues that '... self-organising systems allow adaptation to the prevailing environment'. Comfort (1994, p. 3) explains that:

> ... self-organisation recognises that individual choices, communicated across organisational frameworks, affect the operation of the wider system [and] in this respect, voluntary selection allows individuals operating within organisational systems to cluster around points of energy that they find more attractive, creating a 'peak' of energy distribution over repeated interactions and aligning other members to that point in a 'basin' of attraction.

This explains why ants perform faster at the location that has greatest numbers of ants present: they cluster around the point of more attractive energy, adapting to environmental conditions (Kauffman, 1993; 1995). This actually becomes a powerful mechanism when coupled with one of the formal characteristics of self-organisation: positive feedback.

In summary, self-organisation is the result of utilising the system's capacity for patterns and structure formation; processing communication and multiple interactions by choices or cues; and the mutual adjustment in behaviour based on a shared goal among actors of a given system and environmental conditions. Based on these signatures, we can now start to identify the main four characteristics of that system.

Positive and negative feedback

While most self-organising systems use positive feedback, for such systems both negative and positive feedback are indispensable. Camazine, et al. (2001) point out that negative feedback often takes the form of regulation, competition, reduction or saturation. Continuing with the social insect analogy: in the ants' nest negative feedback dominates when there is competition among food sources, the food source is fully consumed, too many ants are feeding from a food source, there are not enough food sources in a particular area, lack of space or any other similar event that overtakes the positive feedback processes of the ants' nest. Consequently, the ants are forced to hunt for other food sources and commence the feeding cycle again. A different example used in the biology literature is the case of pillar formation in termite nests (e.g. Franks and Deneubourg, 1997; Camazine et al., 2001). In this event, negative feedback takes over when there is no more material in the area close to the formation of these types of pillars. It has also been observed that there seems to be a certain type of competition among termites

---

[2] This is the sequence of movements making up a task; in this case: search, food and nest.

building other pillars in the same area. This pattern of competition is recognised as negative feedback.

Positive feedback coupled with negative feedback provides a powerful mechanism for creating and balancing structures and patterns in many physical and biological systems. Kauffman (1995) points out that feedback and its consequences also apply to organisations – driven by simple behavioural rules, actions and activities. Examples include attraction, aggregation, self-enhancement, clustering and amplification, and they lead to the processes of self-organisation within an organisational system.

Information, communication and cooperation

Another characteristic of self-organisation is the reliance of organisational processes on multiple interaction and passing of information among individuals. In fact, as Fuchs (2003) points out, '... all self-organising systems are information-generating systems' and thus, '... information is a relationship that exists as a relationship between specific organisational units of matter'. Systems use communication to process meaning and perform internal and external operations, but it appears that it is the search for information that triggers the emergence of internal order.

Kauffman (1993; 1995) asserts that the patterns of communication of information in biological systems are characterised by cues and signals. It is the same for human systems. As Mingers (1997) describes it, the communication of information does not necessarily have to be characterised by language; symbolic interaction via cues or signs alone can generate the information transfer between individuals in a system.

Vanderstraeten (2000) asserts that the identity of information is established in the communication process. But what is the purpose of information? Based on systems theory (e.g. Checkland, 1981) information can be considered as the objective relationship between the elements inside the system's structure and the environment of the system. This basically means that the purpose of information is to establish the relationship of reflection between a system and its environment. This interaction causes structural changes, which result in order, to emerge in the system. It is important to highlight that a system's environment also refers to the surrounding self-organised systems – or neighbours – from which information can be gathered.

Camazine, et al. (2001) assert that, in a good number of the cases, the most important information comes directly from an individual's closest neighbours. So, it could be argued that information is a result of a cooperative process with an individual's neighbours, from which coordination emerges. Fuchs (2003) points out that a detailed study of nature shows that cooperation within animal species and biological organisms is a main aspect of self-organisation. Human beings differ from animals in various ways but cooperation is, of course, also necessary for the existence of social systems. Even competitive situations that create negative feedback (e.g. competition among termites when building pillars) can still be considered cooperative processes that generate information (i.e. termites' interaction) and cause a new order to emerge (i.e. new pillar constructions).

Fuchs (2003) asserts that, in a communication process, a portion of subjective, systemic information (cognition) is conveyed; hence cognition becomes the third aspect of information-generation in self-organising systems. He reiterates that '... information in self-organising systems has cognitive (subjective), communicative (new subjective information [= structures] emerges in systems due to interaction) and cooperative aspects (interaction results in synergies that cause the emergence of new, objectified information in the shared environment of the involved systems)'. These general aspects can be found in biological, physical and social self-organising systems. However, there are qualities unique to each of these systems and their correspondent environments.

Stigmergy

The term 'stigmergy' was originally proposed in 1959 by the French scientist, Grasse, in his study of social insects, and more specifically, while observing termite building behaviour. Grasse's stigmergy definition, as translated by Holland and Melhuish (1999, p. 2), indicates that:

> '... the coordination of tasks and the regulation of constructions does not depend directly on the workers, but on the constructions themselves. The worker does not direct his work, but is guided by it. It is to this special form of stimulation that we give the name Stigmergy (stigma, wound from a pointed object; ergon, work, product of labour = stimulating product of labor)'

This means that *stigmergy* describes the influence that information, derived from the local environmental effects of the activities of previous individuals, has on the current individuals' behaviour.

Camazine, et al.(2001) refer to stigmergy as the process of information gathering from work in progress. In other words, working stimulus comes from the information gathered when individuals interact with environmental effects rather than from fellow workers. This is a further step in communication and cooperation among individuals of a system. As Camazine, et al.(2001, p. 24) describe it, in continuing with the social insect analogy:

> '... instead of coordination through direct communication among nestmates, each individual can adjust its building *behaviour* to fit with that of its nestmates through the medium of the *work in progress*'.

Stigmergy appears to be an important mechanism that assists a system to structure itself through the collective behaviour of individuals within the system's environment. An individual could move through the environment, gathering or emitting information, but it can also interact with the environment. Both actions could be considered stigmergy.

Self-organisation is made possible by the coordination of activities that over time and space creates a pattern of construction. Stigmergy is effective in coordinating these construction activities and also in mediating interactions among workers through the environment. For that reason, it is an important component of self-organisation. However, it appears that stigmergy is not a complete explanation of such construction activities since there is no explanation of how construction ends, nor how errors made during construction are amended.

Stigmergy can explain the simpler aspects of transfer of information among individuals, where each individual needs to determine what to do and where a direct line of information from one individual to another individual does not exist; transfer instead occurs through the stimulus of previous individuals' information and construction activities embedded in the environment. Figure 9.3 summarises this process. Here the work previously accomplished by one or more individuals is imprinted in the environment as a cue and stimulus for other individuals. Thus individuals can interact socially by indirect transfer of information encountered in the environment through constructs made by others of their kind.

Figure 9.3. Stigmergy – information flow.

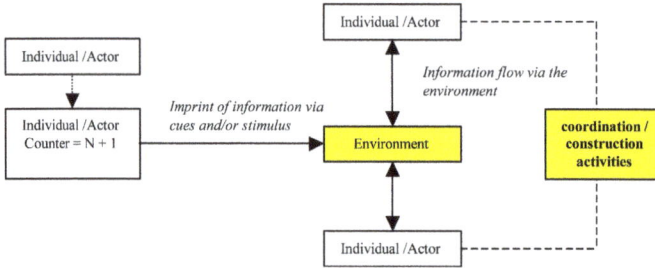

Decentralised control

Camazine, et al. (2001) refer to decentralised control as another important concept under-pinning self-organising systems. As with stigmergy, this concept addresses the flow of information within a system. In decentralised control mechanisms, the information gathered and shared by individuals does not follow a hierarchy of control. In fact, quite the opposite occurs; each individual gathers and acts on information independently. As a result, a natural coordination process of information shared and tasking among indi-viduals takes place without relying on instructions from a leader. Each individual selects essential information for decision-making. This information often originates from the interaction among individual members of the system. This decentralisation of information flow provides the basis for multiple interactions among the components of a self-organised system, making these systems *dynamic*.

The dynamics of the system (i.e. the interactions, cues and stimuli among individuals, and the environment) are a clear indication of the relationship between stigmergy, de-centralised control and self-organisation. As Camazine, et al. (2001, p. 61) point out:

> In a decentralised system, each individual gathers information on its own and decides for itself what to do. Stigmergy is one means of information flow within a decentralised system that involves gathering information from the shared environment ... These decentralised paths of information flow provide essential means of interaction among the components in a self-organising sys-tem.

Moreover, the multiple interactions are in themselves dynamic processes of pattern formation that constitute self-organising systems.

Reflection in self-organisation

The previous section has endeavoured to establish that spontaneous information flow within and between an organisation and its environment, that is essential for problem solving, is one of the main attributes that leads to a self-organised system. The effective-ness of the circulation of information and its outcome is dependent on the quality of the information. The authors recommend a method of thinking and problem solving that constitutes reflection, taking into account previous experience and actions of others (and includes stigmergy). In this section, it is argued that this approach of problem solving is ideal, and in fact necessary, in a self-organised system.

It is a common concept that, when a problem arises in an organisation, one or more groups of people are formed to improve organisational performance and establish a suitable problem solving approach. Where the self-organisational approach is adopted, one of the main advantages is the flexibility to adjust to any changes within the organisation and to the environment – *the real world* (Checkland, 1981) – and its capacity to explore, through reflection, ongoing changes according to the system's requirement and up-to-date needs. Figure 9.4 illustrates this important process. Self-organisation can be viewed as a basis for information systems development – it is flexible; a particular approach that adjusts to specific situations but is not necessarily information systems modelling nor planning. It is a spontaneous process organised by reflection, communication and analysis of socio-technical systems.

Self-organisation can also contribute to creating a conceptual framework for non-structural, self-evolving knowledge networks. To help organisations make decisions and solve problems in a collaborative way, these knowledge networks must be present and therefore be able to reflect and share required information. This also supports information systems by allowing the adequate development of communication channels, full participation across the organisation and interaction of individuals (i.e. actors) within and between systems and the environment.

Figure 9.4. The integration of reflection into self-organised processes.

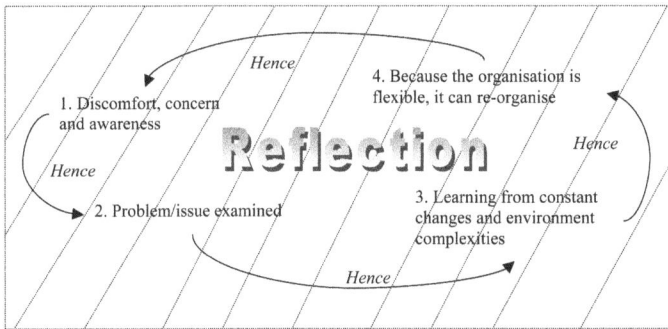

The interaction of reflection and self-organisation will be discussed by viewing the decision-making process in an organisation as being on three levels, as illustrated in Figure 9.5.

Figure 9.5. Levels of decision making in self-organised systems.

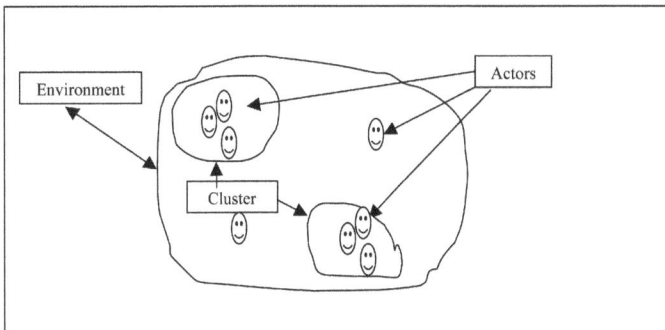

The first level consists of individuals (referred to as 'actors' in the previous section) who may be faced with an unusual or complex situation, or have an idea or conjecture about improvements to the area in which they work. The second level is composed of a grouping or cluster of individuals who have a common purpose or problem. The third level represents the complete system or organisation, which needs to maintain the effectiveness of its performance.

Description of process

For an organisational system to be suitable for both self-organisation and reflection, it needs to have a flat and decentralised structure, individuals need to be able to interact easily with others, and all parts of the system are necessary and sufficient for the operation of the whole but are not necessarily required to produce or replicate each other. The environment also needs to be conducive to reflective learning and cooperation between the parties. Seibert (1999) suggests the conditions that cultivate this environment are:

1. *autonomy* – ample freedom and discretion to structure one's work as one sees fit;
2. *feedback* – information on the results of one's actions – information is the raw material of reflection;
3. *interactions* with other people, entailing access to others – encounters with skilled and knowledgeable people; connection to others – at least one caring interpersonal relationship; and stimulation by others – encounters with people who provide new ideas and perspectives;
4. *momentary solitude* – periodic, brief occasions at or away from work to process new information alone.

Within an organisation that has these attributes, there will be individuals who, at any particular time, will become aware of a problem, a complex or unusual situation or perhaps an opportunity for improvement in their line of work. At this point, the individual conducts an analysis by examining the current situation, challenging their espoused theory of action, contemplating the ideal outcome and using their own experience and knowledge as well as knowledge from other sources (if it is reflection-on-action) to propose viable alternatives. The individual then tests each alternative to arrive at the optimal solution. The interaction of the individual with the information creates a spatiotemporal structure that has minimal interference from external sources. The iterative testing of alternatives within this structure creates a pattern from which cues are emitted and then perceived by other individuals in the organisation who are pursuing a similar purpose. The existence of patterns and emission of cues cause unintentional attraction between the individuals. These cues trigger an emergence of order – the creation of a cluster based on the common purpose. Within the cluster, links between individuals are strengthened as they work towards attaining a common meaning assigned to the problem or a modified purpose of this newly generated system.

This emergence of order initiates the second level. Clusters, based on various meanings are formed – each has its own purpose. Knowledge and information needs of each cluster may become part of the internal environment (stigmergy) or may form actual communication patterns (channels within the organisation) that are used to trigger the coordination and construction of activities targeting problem solving. Actors within the cluster work together, reflecting on each other's suggestions and comparing them with the ideal, often coming to a satisfactory conclusion. However, there may not be sufficient information available within the cluster, necessitating further exploration – possibly from another cluster. One important factor to consider, and that is often missed in the self-organising literature, is that cooperation is a necessary condition for the existence of a social system and therefore for the presence of clusters. Cooperation facilitates the interaction among clusters and ensures *information flow* so that each cluster's issues and concerns are known across the organisation. Under these conditions, clusters are better informed in a problem situation as their *multiple interactions* support further generation of information and knowledge, which is then embedded in the organisational environment.

Faced with a problem, the purpose of one particular cluster in the system will have an impact on other clusters, and vice versa (i.e. organisational networks are affected by each cluster's reflection on information and ideal). These trigger self-organisation of clusters at a different level with a much more informed image of the problem-solving ideal. Because of the cooperation among clusters, reflection from different perspectives arises, allowing the emergence of new alternatives.

At this point it is worth noting that clusters constantly accommodate in order to target best alternatives. They can therefore structure themselves, generating new patterns, stimuli, actions, and eventually new clusters. The clusters come together because of problems at an organisational level. This initiates the third level. The cooperative system carried on from the second level strengthens the availability of information from past experience, facilitating the forecasting and reflection on business trends.

At this level, an organisation is in a position to reflect upon complex environmental changes and put itself in a position where blueprints and information systems templates are no longer required. Consistent reflective processes allow the system to monitor and be aware of changes in the environment and are therefore an important asset for the organisation as they assist further development of capabilities and help ensure market position.

As pointed out earlier, decentralisation is one of the key characteristics of self-organised systems, and one that enhances reflection. A decentralised organisation does not follow a hierarchical system. In fact, they focus on a more linear structure. Here, actors are empowered to act based on their own knowledge and perceptions, and no longer have to go through extended decision channels. They start to offer solutions as soon as they are faced with a problem and they are no longer inhibited or held back waiting for instructions from superiors. There is now an internal culture for constant information-knowledge development. Being able to self-reflect indicates that the organisation has placed itself in an advantaged position by establishing a circle of learning, auto-analysis and multiple ideals for problem solving.

With each level of problem solving, there are three opportunities for reflection (Raelin, 2001):

1. *Anticipatory* reflection occurs prior to the relevant experience (often at the planning stage).
2. *Contemporaneous* reflection occurs at the moment of the relevant experience (as with Schon's reflection-in-action).
3. *Retrospective* reflection looks back at the relevant experience (as with reflection-on-action).

Mathiassen (2002) explains that, in systems development, the timing of reflection depends on whether the task is constructive, evolutionary or an intervention. When the task is constructive, requirements need to be taken into account to design the system required, and therefore reflection needs to be done before construction or action takes place. When dealing with evolutionary systems, the situation is already ongoing, and probably not stable, so the developer needs to reflect as the development takes place – it requires reflection-in-action. With intervention, the current situation and the problems associated with it need to be explored, alternatives suggested and implemented. This requires both reflection-in-action and reflection-on-action.

Dewey urges that reflection take place ad infinitum. He believes one can never be certain of the 'truth' and therefore should continually search in an attempt to invalidate an idea. Each time the reflection supports the belief, it is strengthened, but reflection should never stop.

Self-organisation should also be perceived as a continual process. The systems thinking literature (e.g. Checkland, 1981) highlights the importance of flexibility within a system. Reflection supports self-organising systems' flexibility by not imposing time in the actual process of analysis and pattern formation. In a self-organising system, the flexibility of actors to adjust to the environment and anticipate problems and their solutions can only be possible by reflecting:

1. *before* the construction of actions takes place (i.e. prior problem recognition and awareness);
2. *while* the actions are taking place (i.e. during emergence of order); and
3. *after* actions have impacted the environment and system (i.e. learning from actions).

Actors should be able to benefit from reflecting at different times. A continuous reflecting process would guarantee the argumentation and negotiation required among actors for self-organisation to emerge. It supports the creativity needed for problem solving and helps the understanding of the underlying assumptions in complex environments. Reflection leaves actors in the position of reading the environment at any time and able to record and retrieve information and knowledge to address the ongoing requirements of the system. This type of flexibility, as described by Checkland (1981), results in the effectiveness, efficiency and efficacy of the system. Furthermore, it can support the reorganisation of systems while new patterns evolve. Success for a range of soft systems applications, issues such as complexity, variables and long-term system monitoring, are therefore addressed by the reflection rooted in self-organising systems.

Conclusion

To reiterate our argument in this paper: we suggest that a continuous reflection process is critical for successful problem solving and knowledge creation on individual, group or cluster and organisational levels in self-organised systems. An iterative reflection process allows patterns created by some individuals to attract other individuals, resulting in emergent forms that are based on a common interest. Self-organisation in human systems requires pre-existing freedom in ideas, thoughts, beliefs and actions that allows equilibrium: the system incorporates the negative and positive feedback relations that balance any fluctuations. This equilibrium results in multifunctionality, versatility and flexibility that allow the system to adapt.

A self-organising system is self-contained – it emerges as an integrated flow where actors and their collective behaviours and ideals are formed into organisational patterns and structures without any influence imposed from external sources. For this to happen, reflection within the system needs to continue but the system also needs to reflect on the state of the environment in order to be able to adapt to necessary changes. The capacity for adaptation is enhanced by the reflection process – in a self-organised system all the necessary information is available, the actor reflects on this information and is in a position to select that required for problem solution.

Within this process, communication channels support the flow of information. The ease of information flow is one of a self-organising system's characteristics and consequently it is necessary that the needed channels are available so that the most appropriate medium (verbal, email, phone, correspondence, voice mail, body language) can be utilised at any particular time.

To summarise, reflection is integral to the success of self-organising systems (they are *intertwined*). Reflection enhances:

1. the freedom of internal actors' decision-making processes (generating creativity, innovation and motivation);
2. clarification of purpose;
3. the capability of the system to adapt to the environment; and
4. expands communication channels into the environment.

Future research

Although we believe that reflection is fundamental to self-organisation, there is still much work to be done in validating this principle both in theory and in practice. Furthermore, in the information systems field, self-organisation is not clearly accepted as a problem-solving approach. We believe this approach to be feasible in the real work setting if an appropriate organisational culture is in place. It can readily be seen that reflection already occurs successfully in some organisations when addressing problems. Hence, self-organisation could easily be the next step. There will be, of course, far-ranging implications for organisations seeking to adopt this approach in terms of internal structures, information systems already in place and indeed the motivation to do so.

Acknowledgement: The authors would like to acknowledge Dr Mike Metcalfe's contribution of ideas on this topic.

10. Strategic knowledge sharing: a small-worlds perspective

Mike Metcalfe, *School of Management, University of South Australia*

Abstract

This paper is about designing knowledge sharing in wicked systems. The perspective the paper takes is that of the self-organising 'small-worlds' phenomenon. Specifically, this paper argues that strategic knowledge sharing can be viewed as designing small-worlds networks so as to allow a wicked socio-technical system to self organise a coordinated strategic response to unpredictable environmental changes. The evidence used comes from the softer systems literature, biology (insect) literature and social-network literature.

Introduction

Centralised governance of effective knowledge sharing is very difficult in times of rapid change, especially for purposeful, information rich, socio-technical wicked systems. The lines of communication quickly become clogged, leaders suffer information overload and are unable to fully appreciate problems at the local level. Decentralisation of knowledge sharing runs the risk of causing local overload, with key information not being prioritised or depending on actors who only have experience at processing local problems. Alternatives such as 'middle-out' (Keen, 1999) have been suggested, where strategically informed middle level actors play a coordination role between the top and bottom level actors. This paper explores an alternative, using the small-worlds phenomenon, which is itself seen as a self-organisational response that enables actors in a wicked and dynamic socio-technical system to share knowledge and thereby generate an effective strategic response to environmental surprises.

For those who are concerned about the deep-rooted assumption that all socio-technical systems need a hierarchy to become organised, this paper can be seen as a small contribution to the anti 'hands on' top-down view of leadership, where a 'John Wayne' figure leads the herds of awestruck battlers through some life-threatening disaster. Rather, leadership is seen as a socio-technical system that is capable of allowing knowledgeable actors to interact strategically, as they see the situation, using their different experiences. To those who have some appreciation of the very limited impact even caring 'hierarchical leaders' can really have on the activities of any complex system such as regional government, this paper may provide some improved sense of the complexity of leadership in these dynamic situations. That said, this paper is not primarily about how to organise a response, but rather how to envisage a self-organising socio-technical wicked system. Examples of wicked problems in which this self-organisation design is believed to be required include broad area wildfires, rapidly evolving environmental disasters such as the one outlined below, blitzkrieg warfare, industry reorganisations and national IT policy in recent times.

Wicked problems and wicked systems

A wicked problem is defined by Rittel and Webber (1973) as one characterised by the following:

1. There is no definitive formulation.
2. Any solution is not true-or-false, but rather good-or-bad.
3. There is no immediate and ultimate test of any solution.
4. It is a 'one-shot operation' since there is no opportunity to learn by trial and error.
5. There is no enumerable (or an exhaustively describable) set of potential solutions, nor is there a well-described set of permissible operations that may be incorporated into the plan.
6. It is essentially unique.
7. It can be considered to be a symptom of another problem.
8. It results from a discrepancy that can be explained in numerous ways, and the choice of explanation determines the nature of the problem's resolution.
9. It does not allow the planner the right to be wrong.

Item 8, where the explanation of the problem is crucial to perceptions of how it can be resolved, is central to the design thinking in this paper. A wicked socio-technical system is, therefore, one that is made up of people, supported by technology, who appreciate that they are dealing mainly with these wicked problems. This includes most human organisations. Although not explicitly mentioned in the list above, these problems are also dynamic; they change over time due to a mixture of events, including new technology, new knowledge and possible shifts in participants' perspectives. The design task is, therefore, to allow actors in a wicked strategic problem situation to self-organise in order to produce what they see as an acceptable resolution.

This paper will discuss self-organisation and small-worlds phenomenon, providing two examples of wicked problems.

Self-organisation

The concept of 'self-organising systems' is in danger of losing its effectiveness and becoming as vague a term as 'general systems theory' and 'autopoesis', with their abstract talk of generic open and closed systems. For example, Georges and Romme (1995) define a self-organising system as one that is both open and closed; evoking the old debate about what constitutes a closed system. Mingers (1997) definition of *autopoesis* (self-re-producing) would appear to subsume self-organising systems. However, doing so may hide some of the advantages of using the perspective of self-organising systems for automatic knowledge sharing when wicked systems pose problems that need to be solved. In order to be able to reproduce, a system needs to be organised, and it may be hierarchical. A self-organised system, however, is one that does not need a hierarchy to respond to environmental surprises. It is the assumption of the need for a hierarchy to direct knowledge sharing that is being challenged here. Self-organisation is not being used here in the sense of the development of identity in a hostile environment, (such as the establishment of the early Christian Church, the labour movement or the feminist movement). Rather, this paper is concerned with how a wicked socio-technical system might be designed to share knowledge so as to provide an effective response to environmental surprises when there is no explicit internal hierarchy. Ideas about how these systems might be designed come from analogies with the world of insects. Some swarm, as in ant nests, and some bee nests have no boss, no corporate plan, and no strategic planner, but a higher level organisation has *emerged* that serves to enable the unsuspecting insects to make a strategic response to unpredictable large scale problems that suddenly impinge upon their world.

There is an extensive literature (e.g. Mingers, 1997) on self-reproducing, self-replicating, and similar systems. This paper will bypass revisiting these and merely synthesise from two other related areas. The first is the empirical scientific biological literature about what insect colonies do to share knowledge to provide an effective strategic response to problems. The second is the small-worlds literature, which has recently moved from the sociometric to the sciences, as more and more biological systems are seen to use the small-worlds structure to share knowledge. These will be discussed in terms of a story from the crisis management literature, which tells what actually happens in response to a rapidly changing, community-based problem, in particular when the strategic response has voided any pretence of controlled top-down knowledge sharing.

The insect literature

There has been a lot written about self-organisation in the biological and related sciences. Much of this literature is presented as a mathematical analysis of patterns that emerge, e.g. waves, sand dunes, tree structures and the markings on animals. Camazine et al. (2001), however, provide an empirically based explanation using insect systems. This paper's interpretation of what is meant by self-organisation draws heavily on this, and thus draws on analogies from the world of the insect nest. Camazine et al. (2001) observe that some complex actions emerge through simple interactions internal to the system, without intervention by external directing influences. More formally they define self-organisation as:

> ... a process in which pattern at the global level of a system emerges solely from numerous interactions among the lower level components of the system. Moreover, the rules specifying interactions among the systems components are executed using only local information. [p8]

Camazine et al. (2001) do not accept that the queen insect in an ant's nest or beehive is somehow 'giving instructions' to the millions of insects who have never been near her. The term 'queen' is misleading; the term 'womb' would be more acceptable from a knowledge sharing perspective. Each individual ant or bee bases its behaviour on its perception of the position and behaviour of its nearest neighbour, rather than on knowledge of the global behaviour of the whole group. Local dynamic knowledge sharing is all that is present, yet the insects are able to make strategic responses to a global threat to the whole nest. A strategic response somehow 'emerges' from lower level actions, evidenced by the very existence of a nest that has specialised integrated operations. The individual ants, for example, are not even thinking about this higher order purpose; rather they are only concerned with their own small function in the nest. If this emerging strategy appears different to the actions of lower level activities, then the system may be described as complex. Individual ants forage for food, build the nest, care for the eggs and milk the queen, yet somehow these activities have become coordinated to produce a species that has survived, and very successfully, for millions of years.

Camazine et. al. (2001) summarise the now significant amount of empirical research that has been conducted on insect nests to better understand how a strategic response can emerge. For example, a few ants placed in a Petri dish were found to move sand around in a random fashion, achieving nothing. But when enough ants were added, the probability of the production of a randomly constructed shape that the ants recognised and would respond to, increased. The presence of these particular shapes then acted to suddenly start the ants working in a coherent manner, constructing recognisable elaborate structures. In another example, an ant's nest was deliberately damaged and metal plates used to divide the damaged area in such a way that knowledge sharing between the two damaged areas was impossible. The strategic response, the reconstruction, matched perfectly. When the dividing plate was removed, the rebuilt sections looked like one singular rebuilding exercise, perfectly orchestrated. In summarising this empirical literature, Camazine et al. (2001) identify a series of conditions necessary to enable the emergence of a knowledge sharing system from the insect activity that results in a coherent strategic response. These include the presence of:

1. group influence;
2. stigmergy;
3. decentralised control, dense heterarchies; and
4. dynamic knowledge sharing.

Group influence

Camazine et al. (2001) do not clearly label this attribute of a self-organising group; rather they sum it up as 'I do what you do'. The idea starts with noticing that members of a group copy or mimic those around them; they are influenced by the actions of others. Children do what their parents do, artisans learn from their masters, business schools teach the 'echo of lies' of how management is done, and when at work we learn a corporate culture, we become team players. We learn the preferred way of doing things if we want to 'get along'. Examples of our compliance to our local group norms include our dress, religion, food and ethics. However, we can from time to time insert some small minor variation based on experiences we have had elsewhere. This is analogous to our genetic make-up; we are only minor variants of our parents, but we are variants. An invention, a new recipe or a clothes fashion change are examples of an individual changing a group's behaviour, but if we are honest, one person usually makes very little difference to the generic behaviours of a community. This 'get along, go along' behaviour seems related to our very strong 'inclusion' needs; we need to belong to a group. Horses are trained by threats to exclude them from the herd, which is far more sustaining as a threat than physical pain. Arguably, the worst punishment we inflict on other humans is solitary confinement. The need to belong is seen as an explanation of why herd species and insect colonies are influenced as they evidently are by the behaviour of the whole group; expressed as 'I do what you do'.

Being influenced by the behaviours of others, especially those immediately around us, is central to self-organisation. An insect seems to be born perceiving that the world will be intimately integrated with what the insects colony around are doing. An ant will merely do what the ants immediately around her do, using whatever genetically received devices she has at her disposal. More empirical evidence of this from insect research includes the behaviour of fire flies. When swarmed, fire flies, with their flashing tails, will all end up synchronising their flashes. The fire flies will alter their flash time and speed under the influence of the group. Infectious yawns, synchronised reproductive cycles, synchronous breathing and 'mobbing' are all examples of human group behaviour that influence individual behaviour. Wilson (1983), giving the example of a librarian thinking about the demand for books, uses the term 'cognitive authority' to identify who of those around us we choose to mimic. In an insect colony it is assumed the individual insects can only choose to mimic, to listen to, those immediately around them. Modern people, who have access to the media, books and different corporate cultures, and are able to travel to numerous different communities, have a much wider choice of cognitive influences to mimic.

In this social setting, knowledge sharing between those in immediate contact is expected to have already largely occurred. When a crisis occurs, more than one insect knows the same things.

Stigmergy

Camazine et al. (2001) are very cautious about the idea that colonies of insects carry in their heads a detailed recipe or fully laid out blueprint of what, for example, a nest should look like; a detailed vision of what the finished construction should do and be. This is justified with the empirical evidence for how nests respond to different physical situations. The insects build allowing for the physical conditions encountered, so every nest is slightly different. Yet overall common design features are observable. This is not attributed to the insects' knowledge sharing, but to their merely responding with a set of alternatives.

Stigmergy is a term attributed by Camazine et al. (2001) to Grasse. It refers to the mechanism whereby a swarm insect (such as an ant or bee) is stimulated to work constructively towards a common purpose by the presence of work in progress. The half completed work of other similar insects is recognised as an 'event' that induces automatic *responses* from those that see and recognise it. For example, an ant may see a pair of pillars and respond by building an arch between them, without having communicated directly with the earlier builders. This is an indirect form of knowledge sharing; an event is driving asynchronous knowledge sharing. The human equivalent may be the response of rescuers when a building is seen to collapse or a child is seen to be treated badly. In place of stigmergy, Michener uses the expression, 'indirect social interactions'. In systems management this may be called asynchronous knowledge, or sharing through design. For insects, it may be the result of the quantity of pheromones on the half finished building works, or it may be the physical shape that acts as the asynchronous stimulus.

It is possible to appreciate the importance of asynchronous knowledge sharing to the running of a complex system (one that has emergent properties), such as an ant nest, by drawing on the analogy of a modern corporation. The existence of multinational corporations has been attributed to asynchronous knowledge sharing of faxes, (e)mail and web pages. The size of organisation that can be controlled by means of oral knowledge sharing, is restricted. In large organisations, while oral synchronous knowledge sharing remains very important, time zones, legal records and very detailed specification require 'written', asynchronous knowledge sharing. Nations that have developed joint synchronous and asynchronous knowledge sharing have been dominant in economic and scientific terms. At a more modest level (in insects) Camazine et al. (2001) are suggesting a more subtle form of asynchronous social interaction, and thus motivation in the presence of half completed tunnels, pheromone paths and other work in progress.

Given the centrality of purposeful activity to systems thinking and design (Ulrich, 2002; Checkland, 2000), it seems necessary to mention that purposeful activity is presented by Checkland and Ulrich as an emergent property from the large, self-conscious human brain. This is thought to enable us to appreciate the purpose (drivers) of our actions and stand outside ourselves. But should insects be thought to be engaged in purposeful activity, rather than operating like parts of an alarm clock? Are insects living out genetic drivers to bring up young and continue the gene pool? Surely any human self-organising system would need to anticipate that the participants would be able to ask themselves why they should act. Moreover, in human systems, language could be used to provide a driver to act. Therefore, in human self-organising systems it may be necessary to emphasise why people should act if it is not otherwise obvious to them that they should. However, Camazine et al. (2001) understate the influence of purposeful activity, even those of genetic survival, for insects compared to group interaction influences of humans. They place much more emphasis on the insects' response than to their driving forces for achievement. The genetic drivers of gene survival are not emphasised, possibly because most of the insects never see or come in contact with the young.

Decentralised control and dense heterarchies

The decentralised control attribute identified by Camazine et al. (2001) is defined as a particular 'architecture of information flow'. Each insect responds to other insects immediately around it to learn what is to be done, rather than from messages from well-informed individuals (leaders) in the upper echelons of a control hierarchy. The organisation chart is one of small clusters of interacting insects responding to one stimulus, such as a half built arch in one part of the nest, or a food retrieval clique at another location in the nest. There is no tree of hierarchical knowledge flowing up and down; rather the structure is more a series of independent clusters of workers who, ninety percent of the time, only communicate directly with the other members of their cluster (described as cliques, or *small-worlds*). Only when they are unable to solve a problem with local knowledge sharing will they venture out to ask another cluster. The dense heterarchies attribute reinforces the image of a series of separate yet connected small clusters, each focusing on different but loosely interconnected tasks. Heterarchies are inter-independent groups; they are neither hierarchical and nor totally independent clusters. This raises concerns about how a strategic response from these roughly independent responding clusters is possible. The small-world literature may help here.

Small-worlds

The previous section briefly introduced some of the findings from empirical biological research as presented by Camazine et al. (2001). The next thread of the synthesis presented in this paper is that derived from the sociometric literature. In order to develop some appreciation of the knowledge sharing system considered so central to insect nest life, it is perhaps necessary to discuss this literature, or at least one part of it: the small-worlds literature.

The small-worlds phenomenon emerged as a result of Stanley Milgram's experiments (Milgram, 1967), and was later captured in the play and film 'Six Degrees Of Separation' (Watts, 1999). The idea proposed is that it appears that any two people picked at random are connectable via a chain of, on average, six intermediate acquaintances. This seems counter-intuitive given that, for most of us, frequent direct two-way conversation only occurs with fewer than 20 people; our small- world cluster. In sociometric network terms, this suggests an overall population network that can neither be described as 'everyone knows everyone else', nor, at the other extreme, one where local clusters of socially interactive persons have no means of contacting other clusters. The reality is a mix of the two, with imperfect knowledge shared between clusters. In rather simplistic terms, a small world network can be illustrated as in Figure 10.1. If one cluster were pressed to send a message to another, it would be possible to find a 'weak link' between the clusters; someone who can carry a message between them. In Figure 10.1, if A wants to send a message to F, whom he does not know, then first he would ask friends in cluster 1. B says she knows someone, C, in cluster 2, who may be able to pass the message on. When C gets the message, she asks her friends, and D suggests E, who does know F.

Solid lines represent knowledge sharing between people who talk to each other very frequently and dotted lines are between people who talk very infrequently.

Figure 10.1. Small-worlds.

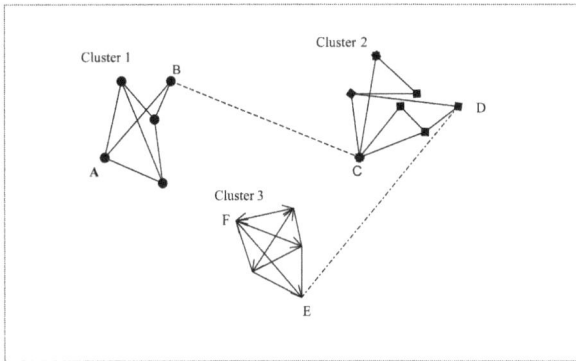

The small-worlds phenomenon provides a way of seeing knowledge sharing between small groups of ants working one particular project cluster, and occasional sharing with other groups of ants working within a different project cluster. It is perhaps predictable from the knowledge-sharing theory literature (Hare, 1976), which highlights that we can only have direct two-way knowledge sharing with a limited number of people. This is due to the exponential growth of knowledge sharing channels as the number of people involved increases. When three people wish to communicate with each other freely, there are only three knowledge sharing channels that need to be kept open (A to/from B, A to/from C, and B to/from C). For four people there are six, and for five there are 10 channels that need to be serviced. For people, that may mean exchanging pleasantries, as well as being able physically to get to and from the others at the same time and in the same place. Having to service a lot of channels becomes time consuming.

So with an ants' nest it is possible to imagine a situation where an ant responds to the ants immediately around it, obeying self-organisation driver number one (I do what you do), and joins in doing whatever they are doing; for example building a new passageway. When a problem arises with the harmony of this activity, no individual in the ant's immediate cluster knows what to do. One of them communicates to an ant nearby that was not involved in the passage building, an ant from another cluster it only knows weakly. The weakly known stranger may communicate that it is very busy collecting food. This then stimulates the passage builders to start collecting food. When a crisis occurs in this task, the ants look around for previously weak messages about other tasks.

The small-worlds research (Killworth and Bernard, 1979; Watts, 1999; Matsuo et al., 2001; Richardson and Lissack, 2001; Buchanan, 2002) extends the social network research (e.g. Mizruchi, 1994; Scott, 1996; Durrington, 2000; Cross et al., 2002) by suggesting what network shapes have self-organised in human groups, in the natural environment, in written communication and in biological systems. Management literature increasingly regards knowledge management as a social networking problem. Hansen (1999), Roubelat (2000) and Reagans and McEvily(2003) have studied management issues related to knowledge sharing using weak links.

To summarise, the discussion above suggests that small-worlds networks allow for effective knowledge sharing both in times of routine and when a strategic response is required. This further suggests that anyone responsible for designing the knowledge-sharing network in their organisation might use this lens to evaluate their communications systems.

Examples

Two very simple examples are now discussed. The first is an account of the response to a community level problem, with special emphasis on knowledge-sharing issues. Hopefully, the analogy to ants' nests and small-worlds phenomena is apparent.

Comfort (1994) argues that the citizens' response to a oil spill near Pittsburgh in 1988 was a self-organised one, as the situation developed too rapidly and was too complicated for a simple top-down leadership response. She reports that the crisis began with a four million gallon diesel fuel tank collapsing. This resulted in a seventeen-mile-long emulsified oil and water mixture flowing down and over the locks and dams of the Monongahela River, extending bank to bank. The river provided drinking water for the Pittsburgh metropolitan region but the risk of damage to water filtration systems made the water authorities shut down the water intakes, resulting in a lack of water for either drinking or fire suppression. For two weeks alternative arrangements had to be organised, requiring the coordination of 25 different types of organisations – public, private, and community non-profit. The zoo, the fire service, medical services, the coastguard, hazard waste services, car washes, and bottled water companies all had to be coordinated.

One can easily imagine groups of concerned persons establishing informal clusters around their particular concern, or expertise. The bottled water people may be one cluster, the fire services another and so on. Most of their knowledge sharing would be within their cluster, perhaps on a one-to-one basis. Every now and then one of these clusters would need information from another concerned cluster; for example, the bottled water people might need an estimate of how long the crisis would last, or need to know how to get access to extra transport, or bottle manufacturing facilities. They would then use their 'weak link' to make contact with another cluster, as they would need to keep an overall appreciation of what was going on. The whole system would only work if there were both the locally knowledgeable clusters and the presence of weak but effective inter-cluster links.

One knowledge-sharing centre handled an estimated 37 000 thousand incoming and outgoing messages during the crisis; averaging 154 per hour, 24 hours a day, seven days a week. This would have been a fraction of the knowledge sharing involved. Comfort (1994) emphasises the need for a dynamic decentralised information system, one that provided up-to-date local and overall information as the situation changed, able to record messages asynchronously and then supply relevant messages to inquirers at a later time. The danger was that critical information would not be stored and located effectively and so not be correctly identified due to the sheer mass of messages generated. Achieving this was not possible through one hierarchical knowledge sharing hub. A self-organisation or small-world knowledge-sharing system was required; one that needed to use human memory and awareness.

Another simple but familiar wicked problem example may help. A university is made up of numerous groups undertaking research in their own discipline area. This typically involves small groups ranging in size from perhaps only two to laboratories containing 10 to 20 or more members. These groups know much the same 'stuff', the discipline-specific research methods, the literature and the worldwide experts in their field. View these research groups as small-worlds knowledge clusters. The strategic imperative, or common purpose some of these wicked system clusters may appreciate is the need for multi-discipline research to provide a comprehensive research effort to deal with wicked problems such as poverty, terrorism or natural disaster response. This common purpose may spread through the weak inter-cluster links. The Research Dean may also further encourage this concern by allocating increased resources to multi-discipline research solutions. Each cluster has specialist knowledge and any excessive attempt to insist all its members spend a significant proportion of their time getting to know other cluster's research in detail may distract them from developing their own knowledge. However, these clusters do need to be 'weak linked' both with each other and with clusters knowledgeable about research resources. These weak links will need to be synchronous and asynchronous (stigmergy), using web pages, internal research newspapers, publication listings, signage, question-asking software like 'askme.com', web publishing of seminar PowerPoint slides, financial rewards and Listserv public acknowledgement of achievements. All of these are examples of the asynchronous (stigmergy) weak linking. Telephone lists by knowledge area, cross discipline coffee groups and conferences are examples of synchronous weak linking. The role of the Research Dean is merely to provide effective responses to those that do multi-discipline research compared to those that do not, and to encourage weak linking (not strong linking) between groups that would not normally even appreciate each others existence. Given the common purpose and the presence of weak links, the self-organisation perspective anticipates that members of the clusters will knowledge-share and self-organise an appropriate response for the improvement of the knowledge holding of the entire university.

Implications and conclusion

There is not much new about many of these activities, perhaps because weak linking across clusters is naturally efficient, an unappreciated theory in use (Argyris and Schon, 1978). However, this paper has attempted to make this theory explicit, and provide a clearer picture that makes sense of the phenomena of interest. This, it is hoped, will make the governance of strategic knowledge sharing more explicit. Given the complexity of wicked problems and the creativity needed to respond to them, hierarchical control of either participant's actions or of their knowledge sharing is considered naïve. The exact opposite of a 'need to know' knowledge sharing policy is required. Participants are to be encouraged to decide for themselves what they need to know and to be aware where they can get that information easily, as in the oil spill example.

This paper has argued that strategic knowledge sharing can be viewed as a task in designing small-worlds networks so as to allow a self-organised strategic response to wicked problems. Knowledgeable clusters and synchronous or asynchronous weak links can both identify wicked problems and respond strategically. A designer of this sort of network needs to encourage knowledgeable clusters that are only weak linked together, whether synchronously, asynchronously or both. Perhaps, for a commercial organisation, the designer may allocate resources to encourage a particular common purpose. Two examples of wicked problems being handled by wicked systems were outlined. In one, the wicked problem was a rather obvious oil spill threatening many dimensions of a community. In the other, the wicked problem required innovation and creativity. It is argued here that neither should be managed in a hierarchical sense.

Future research may continue the work to make explicit the design of existing social networks in public and research communities, so as to better appreciate if they follow a small-world structure. The limits of synchronous and asynchronous 'weak links' may also warrant further investigation, as might the role of information and communication technology from this point of view. Other suggestions may include: how people communicate, and with whom, when involved in a crisis; and what information they need or could not obtain. How the self-organisation process works also needs to be made more explicit.

11. A unified open systems model for explaining organisational change

Doy Sundarasaradula, *School of Economics and Information Systems, University of Wollongong*
Helen Hasan, *School of Economics and Information Systems, University of Wollongong*

Abstract

This paper presents an approach to developing a unified conceptual model to describe and explain change in organisations, viewed as complex systems. The authors propose a model that brings together the traditional open systems model (based on principles of homeostasis, steady state, and cybernetics) and the dissipative systems model (based on thermodynamic non-equilibrium principles) to explain distinctively different phases of change. Gradual and incremental change can be explained by using the traditional open systems model, whereas dramatic and discontinuous change can be explained by the adoption of the dissipative systems model. These two phases of change occur naturally, depending on the nature and pattern of external and internal disturbances. Since the implementation of any information system involves some degree of organisational change, it would be valuable to the IS community to more clearly understand organisational change processes, thereby increasing the possibility of success.

Introduction

We currently dwell in a turbulent environment, one in which change constantly occurs and elements in the environment are increasingly interrelated (Emery and Trist, 1971; Terreberry; 1971; Robbins, 1990). The nature of change has recently tended to be revolutionary rather than evolutionary. One possible explanation is that the progress in information and telecommunication technologies, together with the inception of the Internet as a global computer network, has made the world substantially more interconnected than ever before. This acts as a catalyst in fostering further change so that change is now the norm rather than an occasional occurrence. This poses an immense challenge to academics and practitioners alike in successfully understanding and managing organisations as complex entities.

One of the prime sources of change in organisations is the introduction of new technology (especially information technology) into the organisation (Davenport, 1993; Gasco, 2003; Bertschek and Kaiser, 2004). Recently, the concept of re-engineering was introduced as a means of achieving a dramatic improvement in organisations' productivity and effectiveness by radically redesigning business processes through extensive application of information technology (Hammer, 1990; Hammer and Champy, 1993; Davenport, 1993). However, the chance that a re-engineering project can be successfully implemented in an organisation is surprisingly low, as organisational inertia and resistance to change must be overcome, and the ability to do this varies from one organisation to another (Robbins, 1990). Moreover, successful implementation of information systems projects in organisations depends on factors apart from technological ones (Johnson, 1996). Therefore, an alternative and distinctive organisational change model is proposed here.

Like living systems, organisations experience gradual, incremental types of change as reflected in their growth, maturity, and decline (Miller, 1978). In addition, they experience an oscillatory type of change due to the operation of feedback mechanisms that work to achieve a steady state or homeostasis (Bertalanffy, 1973; Kramer and De Smith, 1977; Skyttner, 2001). However, if the environmental changes are so great that they are beyond the limits within which the homeostatic mechanisms can cope, the organisation as a system has to transform itself into another form that is more suitable to the new environment. Thus a pattern-breaking type of change can be expected (Leifer, 1989). This kind of change does not occur regularly, although evidence reveals that it now occurs more frequently since the progress in telecommunication and transportation technology acts as a catalyst in fostering the rapid evolution of economic, social and political environments (Rosenberg, 1986; Zuboff, 1988; Ohmae, 1991). These developments are making the world smaller in terms of space and time, and the effects of change in one part of the world can be felt rapidly in the others.

Changes in an organisation consist of two distinctive kinds, namely 'convergence' which is typified by an incremental, gradual and adaptive type of change, and 'reorientation' which is characterised by a disruptive, discontinuous and transformational type of change (Tushman and Romaneli, 1985, 1994; Tushman and O'Reilly III, 2002). We propose that neither of these models of types of change is, alone, either adequate to explain changes in complex organisations, or can completely explain the phenomena that occur in the change process. Our belief is that the traditional open systems model, which focuses on incremental change, and the dissipative systems model, which focuses on disruptive change, should be applied together as a unified model in order to account for all types of organisational change.

Closed systems and organisational theories

Before an extensive analysis of theories of open systems is conducted, it is useful to briefly consider some attributes of closed systems. In physics, a closed system is one where there is no exchange of matter between the system and its environment (Cengel and Boles, 2002). However, Kramer and De Smith (1977) define a closed system as a system that has no interaction at all with its environment. But they explain further that a system can be deliberately considered as a closed one by researchers if the relations that exist between the system and its environment are disregarded for the sake of simplicity in their analysis. For example, a production or assembly line, which is built on the theory of scientific management and operations research, can be treated as a closed system if it is insulated from fluctuations in demand and supply (environmental contingencies) through the stockpiling of raw materials and finished-goods to keep it in a relatively static environment.

Even though it is impossible to treat a work organisation as a completely closed system, in the past several organisational theories have assumed this view (Robbins, 1990; Scott, 1998). Between 1900 and 1930, the most dominant theories, which were based on closed-rational system models, were Taylor's scientific management approach, Weber's model of bureaucracy, and Fayol's administrative theory. From the 1930s through the 1950s, the most influential theories were based on a new perspective of closed-natural system models, such as Barnard's theory of cooperative systems and Mayo's human relations model. It is reasonable to say that the ideas of scientific management and bureaucracy are rooted in engineering where the system designer believes that, through proper design and without referring to external factors, a purposive system will perform in an efficient and effective manner. This belief has become the foundation of the machine metaphor or the mechanistic organisation (Morgan, 1997).

A prevalent example of a management system built on a closed system model is a machine bureaucracy, which is still, to various degrees the prevailing paradigm in most organisations (Brown, 1992; Beetham, 1996; Du Gay, 2000). The main objective of a bureaucracy is to promote efficiency and control in systems through the following: a fixed division of labour; a hierarchy of offices; a set of general rules that govern performance; a separation of personal from official property and rights; selection of personnel on the basis of technical qualifications; and employment viewed as a career by participants (Scott, 1998). From an engineering viewpoint, it is a superbly designed system based on technical rationality, aimed at maximising operational efficiency and control. However, the emphasis on internal operational efficiency without referring to external factors can result in system-environment misalignment. In addition, the sole concentration on control without flexibility may well cause poor adaptation, which leads to unsatisfactory performance in the long run.

Closed systems and change

One possible explanation for the existence of organisations that continuously remain in a steady state condition is that they reside in a relatively static environment (e.g. some not-for-profit organisations). When the environment is relatively static, stable, and predictable, interactions and relationships between the organisation and its environment are trivial and, thus, can be ignored or otherwise managed (Robbins, 1990). The closed system model was universally adopted in management theory development during the early 20th century. However, the environment has changed dramatically over the past century and the direction of change is toward an increase in both complexity and dynamism (Neumann, 1997; Robbins, 1990). A model that was valid in the past might not be effective in describing, explaining, and predicting organisational phenomena in a changing context. For example, the Just-in-Time (JIT) inventory system increases the alignment between the production system and its environment, giving a substantial increase in operational efficiency and a reduction in inventory cost (Chase and Aquilano, 1989; Greene, 1997; Gaither and Frazier, 1999).

If the human or work organisation is assumed to be a closed system, the direction of change should go toward an equilibrium state in which entropy will maximised, according to the second law of thermodynamics. In this case, the organisation as a system should deteriorate rather than prosper over time. The increase in entropy suggests that the organisation and order of the system will be degraded and the system will run down.

Open systems and organisation theories

It was realised, by the 1960s, that the assumption that organisations are closed systems was no longer tenable. The fact that organisations exchange resources with their environment is incompatible with the assumption in the closed systems model of lack of interaction and interdependence between the system and its environment. This realisation could possibly be explained by the increase in the complexity and dynamism of the environment (e.g. technological, social, economic, and political) and the impact of these changes on organisations required organisational theorists to rethink the validity of the previous model and its assumptions. This led to the inception of a new generation of theories, which were based on the open systems model, that were dominant during the 1960s and through the 1970s.

Characteristics and mechanics of open systems

The concept of equilibrium and steady state conditions need to be clarified before we go further into how open systems operate. In a closed system, equilibrium is achieved when opposing variables in the system are in balance (Miller, 1978). In addition, the equilibrium can be static or dynamic. The former is commonly found in closed systems while the latter is a property of an open system. Since living systems are open systems, with a recurrent alteration of fluxes of matter, energy, and information, their equilibrium is dynamic. Miller (1978) termed the dynamic equilibrium a 'flux equilibria' or 'steady state'. The term dynamic equilibrium has, however, also been utilised interchangeably in both closed and open systems (Bertalanffy, 1973). We argue that both closed and open systems can exhibit equilibrium; however, in the latter case, the equilibrium is 'quasi' rather than being a true one as in closed systems.

In the previous paragraph, a steady state was characterised as a dynamic equilibrium that exists in open systems. According to Kramer and De Smith (1977), a steady state refers to an open system maintaining an unchanging state even when input and output are still in operation. This makes the system appear static to the observer despite the fact that the flow of resources through the system is dynamic and continuous. A popular example of this is the maintenance of the human body temperature at 37° Celsius. In this case, the amount of heat generated by the body's metabolism is kept equal to the heat lost to the environment. As a result, a constant body temperature can be maintained.

The most important quality of an open system is that it can perform work, which is unachievable in a closed system in an equilibrium state because a closed system in equilibrium does not need energy for the preservation of its state, nor can energy be obtained from it. In order for it to perform work, it is necessary that an open system is not in an equilibrium state. Nevertheless, the system has a tendency to attain such a state. As a result, the equilibrium found in an organism (or any open system) is not a true equilibrium, incapable of performing work. Rather, it is a dynamic pseudo-equilibrium (or quasi-equilibrium) kept constant at a certain distance from the true equilibrium. In order to achieve this, the continuous importation of energy from the environment is required (Bertalanffy, 1950, 1973).

The homology between an open system and human or work organisations can be drawn from the chain of logic mentioned in the previous paragraph. A fictitious organisation, which is largely closed to the external environment, will eventually lose its alignment with the environment because only limited or no resources (i.e. materials, energy, and information) from the environment are allowed to cross the boundary into the organisation. This leads to a misalignment between organisational strategy-structure and the environment, which results in substandard performance as the acquisition and usage of resources become inconsistent with the demand from the environment. The organisation that persistently performs poorly will deteriorate over time and, we argue, is on the way to equilibrium according to the second law. On the other hand, a viable organisation needs a continuous inflow of new members for new ideas, skills and innovations, raw materials and energy to produce new products and/or services, and new information for reasonable planning, strategy formulation and coordination. Only the importation of these resources from the environment can keep it away from equilibrium and can allow it to perform its activities in a viable manner.

It should be noted at this point that the meaning of equilibrium as it is used here, is 'entropic equilibrium' in which equilibrium is maintained at the expense of structure (Grey, 1974; Van Gigch, 1978). In other words, the system's structure and organisation will deteriorate over time, according to the second law, if there is no importation of energy and materials from the environment and processing of information. Another type of equilibrium will be introduced in the next section.

Homeostasis and the behaviour of open systems

It is necessary for many systems to maintain their equilibrium in changing environments or disturbances, otherwise they cannot function properly or their goals cannot be attained. In living systems, the process of self-maintenance or 'homeostasis' is essential to ensure their survival and viability. The term homeostasis is referred to by Flood and Carson (1993) as a process by which a system preserves its existence through the maintenance of its dynamic equilibrium. This equilibrium is termed 'homeostatic equilibrium' (Van Gigch, 1978). Thus, a mature organism as an open system appears to be unchanged over a period of time because there is a continuous exchange and replacement of matter, energy, and information between the system and the environment. Homeostasis can be explained mathematically as follows (Flood and Carson, 1993): If we define $x(t)$ as the state vector at time t and $x(t+s)$ as the state vector at time $t+s$, the preservation of the system's condition over a relatively short period of time can be represented by a statement: $x(t) = x(t+s)$, which means that at $t+s$, the identity of the organism may appear to be unchanged; however, the actual materials that constitute the organism at time t will be partially or entirely replaced by time $t+s$. This can be shown graphically as in Figure 11.1.

Figure 11.1. Homeostasis in an open system at *t* and *t*+*s*. Adapted from Flood and Carson (1993).

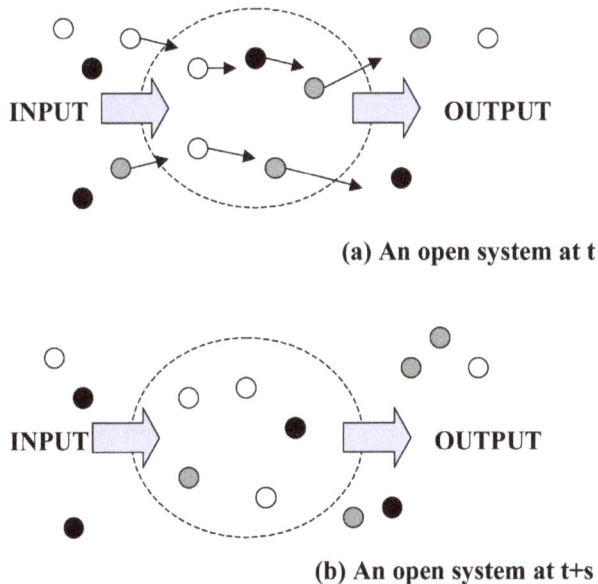

(a) An open system at t

(b) An open system at t+s

Homeostasis is not only one of the most important properties of any living organism, but is also readily applicable to human or work organisations treated as open systems. The organisation needs to recruit new employees to replace those who retire; it also needs raw materials, energy, and information for use in its processes and operations to maintain a steady state. In fact, an organisation that appears externally static and unchanged to outside observers is internally in a state of flux, in a state of dynamic equilibrium.

Another significant aspect of an open system in a state of dynamic equilibrium is that it relies on feedback mechanisms to remain in that state. Based on Boulding's system hierarchy, which classifies the system according to its complexity, it is not surprising to find that properties exhibited by systems lower in the hierarchy are also found in those higher in the hierarchy because the latter are built on the former (Boulding, 1956). Therefore, a system that is classified as an open system would possess all the qualities that belong to the system at a cybernetic (or self-regulated systems) level. The behaviour of open systems is, to a great extent, determined by the feedback mechanisms present in them. There are two types of feedback that operate in most systems, namely negative and positive. Negative feedback reduces or eliminates the system's deviation from a given norm, so a negative feedback mechanism tends to neutralise the effect of disturbance from the environment so the system can maintain its normal course of operation. On the other hand, positive feedback amplifies or accentuates change, which leads to a continuous divergence from the starting state. Positive feedback works together with negative feedback in living systems (e.g. in organisms, and organisations too, both types of feedback are present during growth even though the net result is positive). However, the operation of positive feedback alone will eventually result in the system's disintegration or collapse. Negative feedback plays the key role in the system's ability to achieve a steady state, or homeostasis.

Organisational life cycle: growth, maturity, decline and death

Organisations exhibit a similar, though not identical, life-cycle pattern of changes to living organisms. They grow, mature, decline, and eventually pass away. However, there are some differences that require attention. Firstly, the duration of each stage is less precise than that of typical organisms. In human beings, physiological growth reaches its climax at about the age of 25 whereas the growth phase of an organisation can vary to a great extent. Secondly, the mechanics upon which changes are based are different. Living organisms are typical biological machines with their own physics and chemistry, while organisations are not. According to Boulding (1956), organisations are at a higher level of complexity than living organisms.

Genetic factors and available resources both influence growth in organisms. Organisms develop from fertilisation to maturity through a programmed or predetermined genetic code, a process termed 'ontogenic development' (Ayres, 1994). Apart from this, it is also necessary that the organism acquire sufficient necessary resources from the environment to sustain its life and remain viable. Although the concept of ontogenic development may not be directly applicable to the growth of real organisations due to the difference in basic constituents and mechanisms (i.e. biological vs. socio-technical), there is a similar idea upon which the description of growth in organisations can be based. Greiner (1972) proposed a growth model that explained the growth in business organisations as a predetermined series of evolution and revolution (Figure 11.2). In order to grow, the organisation is supposed to pass through a series of identifiable phases or stages of development and crisis, which is similar, to some degree, to the concept of ontogenic development. Thus, it is interesting to see that systems at different levels of complexity (Boulding, 1956) can exhibit a similar pattern of change. This is also consistent with General System Theory, which attempts to unify the bodies of knowledge in various disciplines (Bertalanffy, 1973).

Figure 11.2. The five phases of organisational growth (adapted from Greiner, 1972).

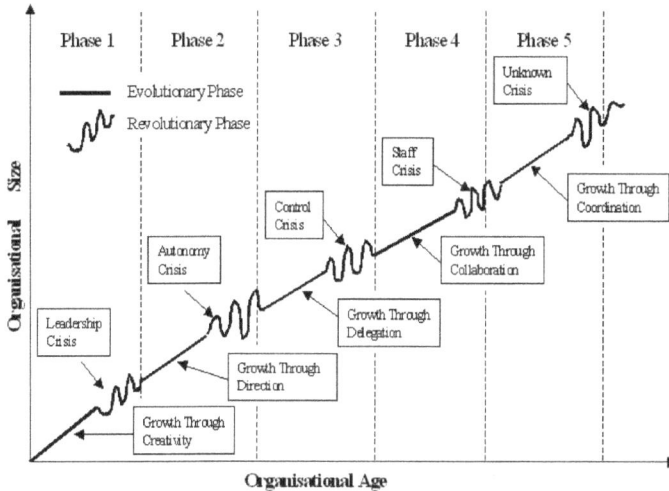

Greiner's model suggests how organisations grow, but the basic reasons behind the growth process and its mechanics remain unclear. As mentioned previously, growth in a living organism is a result of the interplay between the ontogenic factor and the environment. Here, positive feedback plays a vital role in explaining changes in a living system. Although both positive and negative feedback work in concert in any living system, in order to grow (or to effect other changes in a system), the net type of feedback must be positive (Skyttner, 2001). In organisms, starting at birth, the importation of materials and energy from the environment not only sustains life but also contributes to growth. As they keep growing, so does their ability to acquire resources. This means that the more they grow, the more capacity in resources acquisition they have and the more resources they can access. This growth and the increase in resource acquisition capabilities provides a positive feedback loop, which continues until the organism matures. The positive feedback loop will be active again when the organism starts to decline, which will be mentioned later.

An analogy can be made between the process of growth in a business organisation and that in an organism (provided that the business organisation pursues a growth strategy). If the resources in a niche or a domain are abundant, a business organisation in that niche is likely to run at a profit (provided that the relevant costs are under control). An increase in profit results in an improvement in return on investment (ROI), which tends to attract more funds from the investors. The firm can use these funds to reinvest for expansion, to gain more market control, and make even more profit. This positive feedback will continue until limiting factors (e.g. an increase in competition or the depletion of resources within a particular niche) take effect.

A living system cannot perpetually maintain growth, nor can it ensure its survival and viability forever. After its growth, the system matures, declines, and eventually ends. This can be explained by using the concept of 'homeokinesis' (Cardon, et al., 1972; Van Gigch, 1978, 1991; Skyttner, 2001). It has already been argued that one of the most important characteristics of any living system is that it has to be in a homeostatic, or dynamic, equilibrium condition to remain viable. Nonetheless, the fact that a living system deteriorates over time and eventually expires indicates that there is a limit to this. Rather than maintaining its dynamic equilibrium, it is argued that a living system is really in a state of disequilibrium, a state of evolution termed 'homeokinesis'. Rather than being a living system's normal state, homeostasis is the ideal or climax state that the system is trying to achieve, but that is never actually achievable. Homeostasis can be described in homeokinetic terms as a 'homeokinetic plateau' (Figure 11.3) – the region within which negative feedback dominates in the living system. In human physiology, after age 25 (the physiological climax state), the body starts to deteriorate but can still function. After achieving maturity, it seems that a living system has more factors and contingencies to deal with, and that require more energy and effort to keep under control. Beyond the 'upper threshold' (see Figure 11.3), it is apparent that the system is again operating in a positive feedback region, and is deteriorating. Even though the living system is trying its best to maintain its viability, this effort, nonetheless, cannot counterbalance or defeat the entropically increasing trend. The system gradually and continuously loses its integration and proper functioning, which eventually results in the system's expiry.

Although we argue that the concept of homeokinesis and net positive feedback can also be applied to the explanation of deterioration and demise in organisations, as noted earlier it is very difficult to make a direct homology between changes in organisms and changes in organisations. Rather than being biological machines, which can be described and explained, to a large extent if not (arguably) completely, in terms of physics and chemistry, organisations are much more complex socio-technical systems comprising ensembles of people, artefacts, and technology working together in an organised manner.

Figure 11.3. Control requires that the system be maintained within the bounds of the homokinetic plateau. Adapted from Van Gigch (1991).

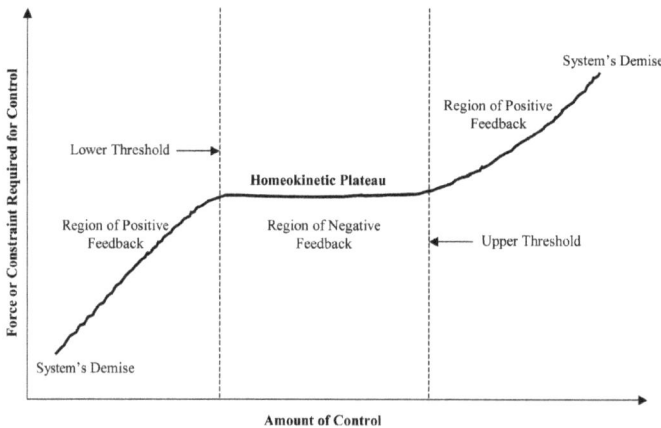

As mentioned earlier, after its maturity, the organism gradually and continuously loses its ability to keep its integration and organisation under control (to counterbalance the entropically increasing trend) and this finally leads to its demise. While this phenomenon is normal in biological systems, even though organisations in general may experience decline and death (as many empires and civilisations did in history), it appears that the entropic process in organisations is less definite and more complicated than that in organisms. Kiel (1991) suggests that this dissimilarity can be explained in terms of systems' differences in their abilities to extract and utilise energy, and the capacity to reorganise as a result of unexpected and chaotic contextual factors. This suggests that biological systems are less resilient and capable than social systems with respect to natural decline.

This may be reflected in the difference in timing and duration of each of their developmental phases. For example, while the duration of each phase in the life cycle, and the life expectancy, are relatively definite for a particular type of organism, such duration is very difficult, if not impossible, to specify for organisations. A small business may, on average, last from several months to a number of years whereas, in contrast, the Roman Catholic Church has lasted for centuries (Scott, 1998). It may be that the size and form of the organisation are influential factors in this respect, a proposition that still requires further empirical investigation.

To be in the region of the homeokinetic plateau, the proper amount of control for a well-functioning and sustainable living systems must be present, and similarly for organisations. Too little control will lead to poor integration and a chaotic situation whereas too much control results in poor adaptation and inflexibility.

The dissipative systems model

The theory of dissipative structure upon which the current discussion is based can be treated as the open systems model extended with a capability to continuously impose a revolutionary change or transformation.

The theory of dissipative structure

Pioneered by the Brussels school of thought in the 1970s (Prigogine, 1976; Nicolis and Prigogine, 1977, 1989; Prigogine and Stengers, 1984), this theory is firmly rooted in physics and chemistry. Nevertheless, it was later applied to urban spatial evolution (Allen and Sanglier, 1978, 1979a, 1979b, 1981), organisational change and transformation (Gemmill and Smith, 1985; Leifer, 1989; Macintosh and Maclean, 1999), changes in small groups and group dynamics (Smith and Gemmill, 1991), and political revolutions and change in political systems (Artigiani, 1987a, 1987b; Byeon, 1999).

Dissipative structure in physical systems

The most prominent example of dissipative structure in a physical system is convection in a liquid (Nicolis and Prigogine, 1977; Jantsch, 1980; Prigogine and Stengers, 1984). If cooking oil is heated in a shallow pan, the following macroscopic changes occur. Firstly, while the temperature of liquid is relatively uniform, heat is transmitted through the body of liquid by means of conduction in which the molecules' heat energy (molecular vibration) is transmitted to neighbouring molecules via collision without major change of position. We can say that the system is still in a thermodynamic equilibrium. Next, as the pan is heated further, the temperature gradient between the upper and lower portion of the oil in the pan becomes more pronounced and thermal non-equilibrium increases. At a certain temperature gradient, convection starts and heat is then transferred by the bulk movement of molecules. Evidently, however, the surrounding environment at first suppresses the smaller convection streams, but beyond a certain temperature gradient, the fluctuations are reinforced rather than suppressed. The system moves into a dynamic regime, switching from conduction to convection, and a new macroscopic order called 'Benard cells' (i.e. a pattern of regular hexagonal cells that appear on the surface of liquid) emerges, caused by a macroscopic fluctuation and stabilised by an exchange of energy with the environment. Such a structure is called a hydrodynamic dissipative structure, and is a version of spatial structure (Haken, 1980).

Order in a non-equilibrium state

As mentioned earlier, open systems make an effort to avoid a transition into thermodynamic equilibrium by a continuous exchange of materials and energy with the environment. By doing this, a negative entropy condition can be maintained. It has been understood for a long time that entropy is a quantification of randomness, uncertainty, and disorganisation, and negative entropy therefore corresponds to (relative) order, certainty, and organisation (Bertalanffy, 1973; Kramer and De Smith, 1977; Nicolis and Prigogine, 1977; Prigogine and Stengers, 1984; Miller, 1978; Van Gigch, 1978, 1991; Flood and Carson, 1993). However, the mechanics underlying this idea had not been clear until it was explained in the work of Nicolis and Prigogine (1977), Prigogine and Stengers (1984), and Jantsch (1980) in the theory of dissipative structure and order that exists in the non-equilibrium condition.

According to the theory of dissipative structure, an open system has a capability to continuously import free energy from the environment and, at the same time, export entropy. As a consequence, the entropy of an open system can either be maintained at the same level or decreased (negative entropy), unlike the entropy of an isolated system (i.e. one that is completely sealed off from its environment), which tends to increase toward a maximum at thermodynamic equilibrium. This phenomenon can be represented in quantitative terms as follows (Nicolis and Prigogine, 1977; Jantsch, 1980; Prigogine and Stengers, 1984). According to the second law of thermodynamics, in any open system, change in entropy dS in a certain time interval consists of entropy production due to an irreversible process in the system (an internal component) d_iS and entropy flow due to exchange with the environment (an external component) d_eS. Thus, a change in entropy in a certain time interval can be represented as $dS = d_eS + d_iS$ (where $d_iS > 0$). However, unlike d_iS, the external component (d_eS) can be either positive or negative. Therefore, if d_eS is negative and as numerically large as, or larger than, d_iS, the total entropy may either be stationary ($dS = 0$) or decrease ($dS < 0$). In the former case, we can say that the internal production of entropy and entropy exported to the environment are in balance. An open system in a dissipative structure sense can be viewed as shown in Figure 11.4.

Figure 11.4. An open system's entropy production and dissipation.

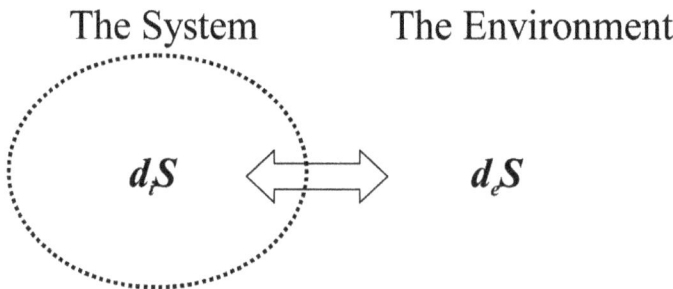

It can be concluded that order in an open system can be maintained only in a non-equilibrium condition. In other words, an open system needs to maintain an exchange of energy and resources with the environment in order to be able to continuously renew itself.

Entropy and sustainability of dissipative systems

The internal structure and development of dissipative systems, as well as the process by which they come into existence, evolve, and expire, are governed by the transfer of energy from the environment. Unlike isolated systems (or closed systems in a broader sense), which are always on the path to thermal equilibrium, dissipative systems have a potential to offset the increasing entropic trend by consuming energy and using it to export entropy to their environment, thus creating negative entropy or negentropy, which prevents the system from moving toward an equilibrium state. A negentropic process is, therefore, the foundation for growth and evolution in thermodynamic systems.

For dissipative systems to sustain their growth, they must not only increase their negentropic potential, but they must also eliminate the positive entropy that naturally accumulates over time as systems are trying to sustain themselves. The build up of the system's internal complexity as it grows is always accompanied by the production of positive entropy ($d_iS > 0$), which must be dissipated out of the system as waste or low-grade energy. Otherwise, the accumulation of positive entropy in the system will eventually bring it to thermodynamic equilibrium, a state in which the system cannot maintain its order and organisation (Harvey and Reed, 1997).

Implications for organisations

Although the argument so far is fundamentally based on chemical or biological systems, we argue it also applicable to the organisation as an open system. It is suggested by Leifer (1989) that the net resource used by an organisation can be viewed as being divided into two parts. First is that concerned with the maintenance of the internal environment, and second, that which is transacted with the external environment. The former is treated as the change of entropy due to necessary maintenance and support processes (d_iS), which is always positive due to the nature of indirect costs, and the latter as the change of entropy in the input-transformation-output process (d_eS), which may be positive or negative (e.g. a firm may experience profit or loss). It is suggested, further, that d_iS refers to all the activities that are necessary to keep the organisation maintained and supported (e.g. management, administration, research and development, etc.) and d_eS refers to all the activities where there is interaction with the environment (e.g. purchasing, selling, recruiting, etc.) and production of products and services. We further maintain that, in order for the organisation to remain viable, the flow component of entropy must be negative and greater in magnitude than that of the maintenance and support component since the support and maintenance activities always result in a net drain or loss to the organisation due to the exploitation of resources, but the input-transformation-output process (i.e. production and sales activities) may result in a net gain for the organisation if its earning is greater than its cost (Leifer, 1989). In summary, we conclude, albeit perhaps at a metaphorical level, that in order for an organisation to maintain its order it must be in a non-equilibrium state.

Order through fluctuations and system transformation

This section will address how fluctuations can lead to significant change in systems, which results in higher degrees of order and complexity, and how this relates to the concept of the systems' transformation and self-organisation. Fluctuation in this case can be defined in general as a spontaneous deviation from average behaviour (Nicolis, 1979). In chemistry, it can be defined as follows (Jantsch, 1980, pp. 42-3):

> The fluctuations referred to here are not fluctuations in concentration or other macroscopic parameters, but fluctuations in the mechanisms, which result in modifications of kinetic behaviour (e.g. reaction or diffusion rates). Such fluctuations may hit the system more or less randomly from without, as through the addition of a new reaction participant or changes in the quantitative ratios of the old reaction system. But they may also build up within the system through positive feedback, which, in this case, is called evolutionary feedback.

However, the theory of dissipative structure has the potential to be applied to systems beyond those of concern to natural science (Nicolis and Prigogine, 1977; Jantsch, 1980; Prigogine and Stengers, 1984). In this theory, fluctuations play a vital role in causing significant system change because, when a system is driven to a critical instability point (bifurcation point or point of singularity), the non-equilibrium system can be regarded as testing various configurations by fluctuations, which results in a new space and time structure (Haken, 1984, 1987). In other words fluctuations, which lead to instabilities, may be introduced to the system in order to yield new types of function and structure. In this sense, no system is structurally stable. Rather, the evolution of dissipative structure is a self-determining sequence of its function and boundary testing, spatio-temporal structure, and fluctuations (Nicolis and Prigogine, 1977; Allen, 1981) as illustrated in Figure 11.5.

Figure 11.5. The role of fluctuations in creating order.

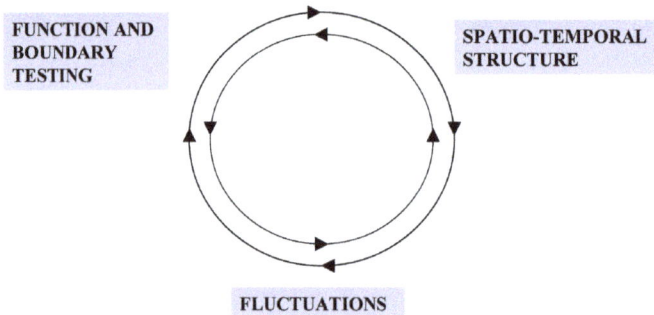

FUNCTION AND BOUNDARY TESTING

SPATIO-TEMPORAL STRUCTURE

FLUCTUATIONS

In addition, the source of fluctuations can be internal or external (Allen, 1981). In organisations, sources of internal fluctuations may come from the action of leaders or managers or the dynamic of power and political struggle and activities. External sources may arise from both the macro-environment (i.e. economic, technological, political, and socio-cultural) and the micro-environment (i.e. customers, suppliers, competitors, etc.).

Figure 11.6 shows how macroscopic order can be created through fluctuations and how it is related to the system's ability to cope with complexity and environmental contingencies. At α_1 an organisation, as a complex system, has a capacity to cope with complexity at level L_1, within a range of environmental contingencies R_1. As the environmental contingencies increase, the system can still maintain a steady state, a state within which negative feedback operates. This is represented by the straight-line portion of the graph within range R_1. However, as the environmental contingencies keep on increasing, the system starts to destabilise and fluctuations start to occur. If fluctuations are accentuated, this is because positive feedback is now dominating in the system. This process will continue until it reaches a bifurcation point (or point of singularity), where the system either self-organises and transforms (evolves) into a new form (i.e. new spatio-temporal structure), which is more complex and more capable of coping with the new level of complexity (a state of α_2 at level L_2) and the next range of increased environmental contingencies R_2, or it deteriorates and runs down because it fails to self-organise. This process will continue as long as the system succeeds in self-organising itself to handle the increase in environmental contingencies (i.e. it can achieve a state of α_2 , α_3 , ...).

Figure 11.6. System transformation and production of macroscopic order.

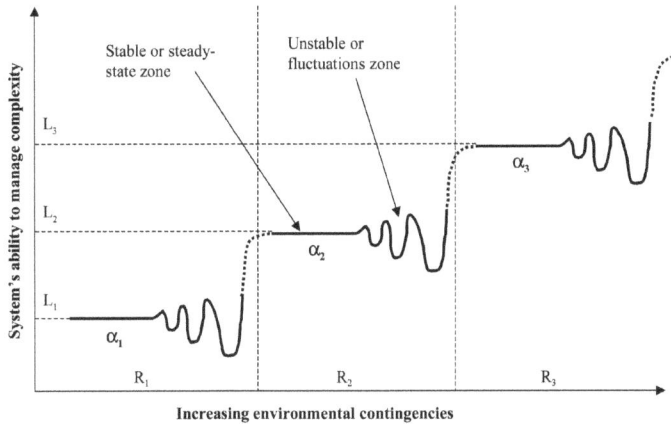

Based on the theory of dissipative structure, the system needs energy from the external environment to achieve a higher-level state or to be transformed into a new form with higher complexity and more capability to deal with increased environmental contingencies. In organisational theory, energy can be considered analogous to resources, efforts, change strategy, leadership, knowledge and information, and power required to effect fluctuations, which result in a transition from one state to another.

Model synthesis and discussion

The justification for adopting a unified or integrated approach in modelling change and evolution in organisations comes from the pattern of change characterised by the Theory of Punctuated Equilibrium, which was originally proposed in the field of palaeontology and biological evolution in the mid-20th century to explain a discontinuous change of patterns usually found in fossils (Mayr, 1942, 1982; Gould and Eldredge, 1977; Hoffman, 1989).

Theory of punctuated equilibrium and rationale for model synthesis

It is proposed in the Theory of Punctuated Equilibrium that biological species can remain unchanged, or only have a marginal change in their form, over a lengthy time period. This period is called 'stasis'. However, in order to survive and avoid extinction when the environment becomes unfavourable, the pace of evolutionary change needs to be accelerated. This results in a relatively discontinuous change in the species form. In other words, a new species comes into existence. Thus, according to this theory, a pattern of relatively long and stable periods punctuated by rapid and discontinuous change is typical of natural biological systems.

A similar pattern of change occurs in organisational dynamics (e.g. Miller and Friesen, 1984; Tushman and Romaneli, 1985, 1994; Gersick, 1988, 1991). As mentioned earlier, change in organisations is often characterised by a lengthy period of incremental, gradual and adaptive change (convergence) alternated or punctuated by a short period of a widespread, discontinuous and transformational change (reorientation). Modelling both phases of change thus poses a challenge because the traditional open systems model, which is based on the concepts of homeostasis and steady state, can only describe and explain the 'stasis' or 'convergence' phase. It does not encompass the type of change that occurs in 'transformational' or 'reorientation' phases. Consequently, we incorporate the theory of dissipative structure into the model.

Homeostasis, adaptation, and transformation

The degree of systemic change depends on the magnitude of environmental contingencies or external fluctuations although we have also argued that internal fluctuations play a vital role in inducing change in complex systems. Based on the argument made previously in the open systems and dissipative structure model, the organisation as a complex system can neither always maintain itself in a steady state (or homeostasis) nor keep on transforming without reference to the magnitude of fluctuations or disturbances that impinge upon it (see Tushman and Romaneli, 1985 for more details).

It is much more difficult for major transformational change to occur, or be implemented, because it typically involves a profound reformulation of the organisation's mission, structure and management, and fundamental changes in the basic social, political, and cultural aspects of the organisation (Levy, 1986; Levy and Merry, 1986). Hence, the concept of transformation covers both operational processes and psychological dimensions of the organisations. According to the theory of dissipative structure, transformational change requires energy (both human and non-human) to push the organisation across the instability threshold by means of necessary fluctuations, from within and without, to inflict a morphological change. In contrast, the concept of adaptation deals only with the modification of the system's structure or structural properties in such a way that the functional properties of the system are left largely or entirely unaltered when facing environmental disturbances (Van Gigch, 1978). Therefore, organisations as systems can only maintain their steady state or remain in a homeostatic equilibrium.

Adaptability is related to organisational structure in that it is about bringing the organisation into harmony with the changing environment, and the adaptive function works in two directions. First, it modifies internal structures to correspond with external changes, and second, it attempts to control the environment (Van Gigch, 1991). Moreover, the concept of adaptation is not limited to structural change but also relates to other factors as well (e.g. procedures and technology).

Figure 11.7. Punctuated equilibrium model showing adaptive (convergence) phase A and transformational (reorientation) phase B.

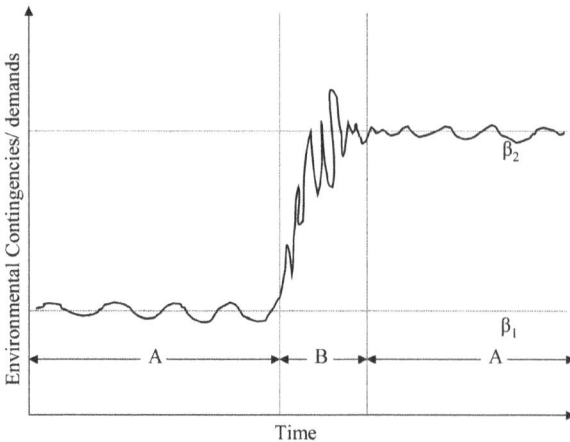

Figure 11.7 portrays how homeostasis, adaptation and transformation constitute the punctuated equilibrium model, and how they are interrelated. The graph represents the systemic behaviour, caused by the interaction among the organisation's subsystems and between them and the external environment. The pattern of such interaction is fundamentally determined by the system's structure (Cavaleri and Obloj, 1993) and can be measured by the system's output (Kramer and De Smith, 1977). The interaction between organisations and their environment results in variation in the system's behaviour. Phase A represents a system in a convergence period (β_1), which is mainly typified by its maintenance of a homeostatic condition (or steady state) − a condition in which the system is attempting to realign or adapt itself to the minor changes in the environment. Phase B represents a reorientation, which is characterised by a discontinuous and disruptive change that results in a reformulation of the organisation's basic constituents (i.e. structure, strategy, process/technology and psychological component) and is transient in nature. If the transformational change is successful the organisation will attain another equilibrium state (or convergence period) β_2 and remain in this state until conditions prompt another transformation. At β_2 a new organisational form, which is more complex and more capable of dealing with the environmental contingencies would be expected to have emerged. Therefore, the unified model, which constitutes the traditional open systems model and the dissipative structure model, can portray the whole change phenomenon.

Tools for system manipulation

Organisations as complex systems can be manipulated by using the 'Management Systems Model' or MSM (Cavaleri and Obloj, 1993). The MSM has five systemic tools or factors, which are available for managers to manage or manipulate organisations in a desired way, namely:

1. Strategy
2. Structure
3. Procedures (technology/process)
4. Culture
5. Leadership

This model implies that each systemic tool should be applied in a harmonised and thoughtful manner to yield the best possible result as each particular tool or factor, when applied, would yield a different systemic result. While leadership and strategy are generally tools for inflicting changes or destabilisation on organisations, culture, procedures or technology and structure are systemic tools that are typically used to impose stability and regulation in the organisation. Moreover, the dynamic behaviour of the organisation is a result of the interplay between these endogenous factors and the environment and the interaction among these endogenous factors themselves (e.g. the interaction among strategy, leadership, structure, procedures and culture).

Rather than being considered as one of the manipulating tools, each factor can also be treated as an organisational property that can be changed to suit both external and internal contingencies. However, the effort required to change each property varies from one to another. For example, in adaptation, or shallow change, it is common for an organisation to realign itself with the changing environment by adjusting one or more of its properties (e.g. procedures/ technology, strategy, structure), which requires energy and effort, although relatively little compared to transformational change. Transformation (or deep change), however, requires a tremendous amount of energy, in terms of resources and effort, to change organisational culture and the political network as well (Svyantek and DeShon, 1993), as illustrated in Figure 11.8.

Figure 11.8. System interface and hierarchy of efforts required for change in an organisation.

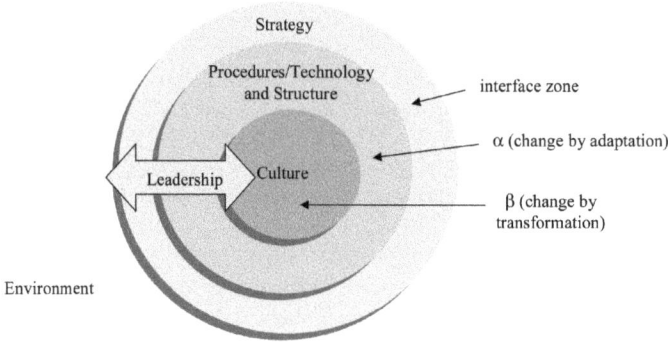

In order for an organisation to operate successfully in a specific environment, it needs an interface between its subsystems and the environment. Organisational strategy is such an interface (Cavaleri and Obloj, 1993). The next layer (α layer) is the zone in which the interplay between technology, process and structure to carry out the organisation's operations exists and is active. Variables and factors in this zone are more sensitive to the disturbance from both internal and external sources and less difficult to manage and change than those from the inner core (or β zone). This ensemble of variables can be changed, with a certain effort, to achieve a proper alignment with the environment – a process called adaptation. Figure 11.8 also shows that all elements in both the α and β zones are exposed to the environment although the degree of exposure may vary (e.g. the production line is shielded from fluctuations in demand and supply to a certain extent). Lastly, the core of this diagram (or β zone) represents organisational culture, an element that is very influential for the survival and performance of the organisation (Peters and Waterman, 1982; Handy, 1995, 1999; Hofstede, 1997). The impact of culture on organisations is pervasive because it controls people's beliefs and shared values, and it is also transferable from one generation to the next. It is thus unlikely that culture can easily be changed or adjusted to conform to the changing environment. It requires a great deal of energy, effort and time to change the existing culture, and this is beyond the adaptive mechanism (Svyantek and DeShon, 1993). That is why we call a change at a cultural level a 'deep change.' As a consequence, it is proposed in this model that only transformation as a means of systemic change can have a profound effect on the organisation's culture.

As far as change is concerned, leadership is an essential factor in influencing change in other variables or factors. In Figure 11.8, leadership provides a linkage between the external environment, strategy and internal factors in both the α and β zones, and is also a source of power and authority required to effect change at various levels. Tushman and Romaneli (1985) assert that strong leadership is essential, especially for the reorientation or transformational phase of change, because not only must a clear vision be declared and communicated to organisational members, but also adequate power and authority is required to alter dysfunctional political networks and overcome resistance to change. Without strong leadership, it is unlikely that change can be implemented successfully in the organisation.

Organisational politics, power and control are related to self-awareness in systems. In this regard, organisations are treated as open-natural systems whose collective behaviour is characterised by political relationships and their interaction (Scott, 1998). This can make the system behave in an apparently irrational manner as groups or political networks work to protect and maintain control over their domains rather than pursue the organisation's mission and goal (Pfeffer, 1981). If the domain of interest to the organisation is under control, it is unlikely that the status quo will be changed and this contributes to a resistance to change. Organisational culture that incorporates this feature is thus potentially dysfunctional, and requires a transformational approach to change. However, the psychological aspect of self-awareness in systems is beyond the scope of the proposed model.

Bifurcations and self-organisation

As illustrated in Figure 11.6, if organisations can be successfully transformed, they become more sophisticated and their ability to survive and prosper in a more demanding environment is enhanced. A successful transformation means that organisations can self-organise into another form that is more complex and sophisticated. We propose that the increase in capability can be interpreted in a more concrete way as follows:

1. an increase in the ability to utilise resources and energy more effectively and efficiently;
2. an increase in the ability to seek, process, and make sense of information;
3. an increase in the organisation's knowledge as a result of learning and relearning from history.

Figure 11.6 can be displayed in another form as Figure 11.9 – a bifurcation diagram.

Figure 11.9. Bifurcation diagrams showing (a) the possibility of successful or unsuccessful change, and (b) change, entropy and self-organisation.

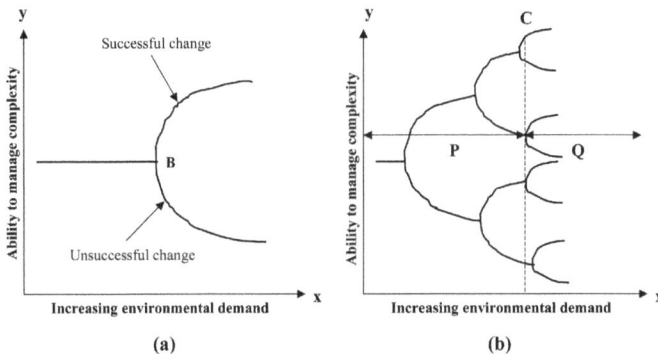

As the level of environmental contingency and turbulence increases, adaptation becomes less effective in coping with the change. If this situation continues until a critical point, which is called a bifurcation point (point B in Figure 11.9 (a)), is reached and the system is either radically changed to a more complex and sophisticated form with higher capability and capacity for survival (see also Figure 11.6, which displays only successful changes) or it fails to make a successful change and experiences a decline. The change displayed in diagram Figure 11.9 (a) represents only a simple version of organisational change using a bifurcation diagram. A more elaborate version, which explains change in organisation in detail, can be found in Guastello (1995, 2002).

Figure 11.9 (b) displays the relationship between the change in entropy level and the organisation change process. The distance between the y-axis and the vertical line C, which is represented by P, is the entropy build-up zone. An increase in entropy is necessary to bring the system to a far-from-equilibrium state. The area behind line C (represented by Q) is a chaotic zone in which self-organisation takes place and the system experiences a transformation to another state. This phenomenon corresponds to the development of the Benard cells mentioned earlier, in which a continuous supply of energy is required for the development of a new spatio-temporal structure.

Conclusion

Closed systems do not realistically represent real organisations because organisations are open rather than closed. Thus, any theories or models that treat organisations as closed systems are inadequate. Furthermore, although closed system models work best in a relatively static environment, such environments are rare and likely to become even less so.

Depending on environmental demand or contingency, organisations respond to perturbations in the environment either via an adaptation process, which can be viewed using an open systems model or homeostatic equilibrium model, or transformation, which is best viewed using a dissipative systems thermodynamic non-equilibrium model. Adaptation operates in response to limited environmental disturbances, but beyond these limits organisations need to transform themselves into more sophisticated forms that are more complex and capable of managing higher levels of environmental contingencies. However, a complex system must be in a far-from-equilibrium condition, which is characterised by instability, so that transformation can occur.

In adaptation, changes in the environment require that organisations modify some of their properties (strategy, structure, procedures or technology, and size) to be aligned with that environment. But adaptation cannot accommodate cultural change, which involves changing of people's beliefs held at a deep level. When organisations have to cope with an extremely high environmental contingency, transformation, which is a more substantial and pervasive form of change that includes the change of organisational culture and its political web, must be introduced to ensure their survival.

Since the environment of organisations is ever more complex and dynamic, we argue that a unified model, which encompasses both adaptation and transformation, should be developed and empirically tested with the aim of better representing and understanding change in organisations.

Acknowledgement

The authors are greatly indebted to Prof. Joan K. Pierson, Dr Ulrich Nehmzow, Joseph A. Meloche, and anonymous reviewers for valuable feedback and editing work, which, to a great extent, contributed to the improvement, readability and completeness of this paper.

Part III. Linking information systems theory and practice

12. Research as an information systems domain

Craig McDonald, *School of Information Sciences and Engineering, University of Canberra*

Abstract

There is growing interest in the use of ICT in the domains of science and research. Little of that interest is currently focused on the systems aspects of those domains, but instead looks piecemeal at the way they may make use of particular ICT tools. Two important opportunities exist here for the information systems discipline; firstly, to analyse it as a human activity system to see how ICT can be systematically employed in its activities, and secondly, to view the deployment and adoption in society of knowledge created by research as a matter of information systems inter-operation. This paper looks at how the foundation ideas of IS might be mobilised to improve the vital domain of research.

Introduction

Information systems is a discipline that interests itself in the interaction of information technologies with human activity systems. The purpose of this paper is to examine some aspects of *research* as a human activity system and the role information systems might play in it.

e-Science and e-Research

Both the Chair of the ARC and Australia's Chief Scientist have spoken recently about e-Science and e-Research. Cram's (2003) 'A Roadmap for e-Research' and Batterham's (2003) 'E-Science: A Frontier Technology for Achieving the National Research Priorities' set the scene for the section on e-Science in the 'Smart Use of Information Technology Systems' (SUITS) bid. Both of these sources, from peak government advisors, emphasise the use of information and communication technologies (ICT) in the way research and innovation will be conducted in the future.

The terms e-Science and e-Research are not well differentiated. *E-Science* is usually understood to be related to the use of ICT in scientific research, particularly that needing high computing power and vast data sources in a highly distributed grid environment (e.g. the National E-Science Center). Typical domains include astronomy, physics, geology, and so on. The Australian Partnership for Advanced Computing (APAC), Australasian Workshop on Grid Computing and e-Research (AusGrid) and, presumably, National ICT Australia (NICTA), are the kinds of organisations involved in e-Science. The technologies they are developing and promoting include broadband, middleware, repositories of scientific data, sensors and instrumentation, distributed computational power, and so on.

The UK e-Science Grid conceives of:

> an e-Scientist's workbench ... [that] aims to support: the scientific process of experimental investigation, evidence accumulation and result assimilation;

the scientist's use of the community's information; and scientific collaboration, allowing dynamic groupings to tackle emergent research problems.

E-Research is a broader term that, Cram (2003) says, 'concerns the ways that Researchers, Research Students, Scholars and Entrepreneurs use and will use Information and Communications Technologies (ICT)' in the context of innovation and knowledge application'. He argues 'Research is to Innovation as Sunlight is to Photosynthesis'. The first theme of this paper, then, is: *recognising research as a systematic, human activity that can make use of the 'big ICT' envisaged in e-Science*

In a major Australian Department of Education, Science and Training (DEST) study, 'Changing Research Practices in the Digital Information and Communication Environment', released in late 2003, Prof. John W. Horton has reviewed the current and future directions for research. The changing nature of research, who does it, how it is funded, what research practices are in use and the role of ICT are discussed at length, and key findings about the systems needed to underlie research in the future are presented.

To an information systems person, however, Horton is trapped in a traditional view of knowledge. While his study covers knowledge production and its dissemination in documents, it does not cover its *use*. His view is that ICT can contribute to collaboration between researchers' access to knowledge as part of the production process and the publishing of knowledge. But what of its deployment and use to achieve human ends? Consequently, the second theme of this paper is: *recognising the use of research, not just its production.*

For the reasons underlying the two themes of this paper, research is a suitable domain for IS attention. This paper will use the term *e-Research* to mean IS work in the research domain.

Information systems

Information Systems (IS) is an active, interventionist discipline that mobilises information and knowledge so people can effectively take knowledgeable, informed actions in their organisational and social setting. It is concerned with understanding and formalising areas of human activity and developing IT-based systems that responsibly intervene in those areas for the benefit of all stakeholders. The shape of IS practice is a bit like the middle loop in Figure 12.1: analysis, modelling, systems construction and intervention in a human activity system.

Figure 12.1. A general model of information systems activity.

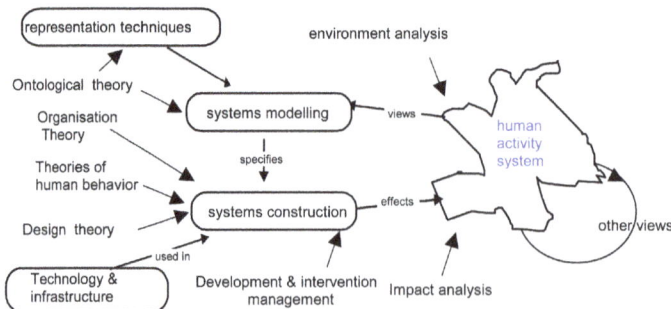

The outer components in the diagram show some of the generic theories, tools and techniques used in the process of IS work. The theories and understandings from onto-

logy, organisational behaviour, ethics, and so on inform IS practice. Information technology and infrastructure are a driving force in the IS process, having a particular effect
on representational techniques and the systems specification possibilities.

Looked at from an IS practice perspective, research is a human activity and the research
world a human activity system. As such, it is susceptible to IS intervention. Just as we
have e-business, e-learning or health informatics, so we can have e-research.

Using this model, we can examine research as a human activity system, and look at the
current technologies in use.

Research, human activity systems, and ICT

A human activity system can be analysed at different levels of granularity, from the
most fine-grained, personal level to the societal level.

Research at the *personal* level involves issues of motivation, personality, knowledge and
skill that the individual researcher brings to their work. The kinds of activities researchers
undertake include literature work, research design, data collection and analysis and research reporting. The technologies they use are:

1. document management technologies, which are used for document access and re-
    trieval (the Web, library databases), document tracking (Endnote and Procite), and
    document generation and publication;
2. data collection and management tools, including data loggers of various kinds, Web
    surveys and focus groups, data mining and the recording of laboratory records in
    image, text, recordings and video;
3. analytic tools, for dealing with quantitative data (SPSS) and qualitative content
    analysis (NVivo and Leximancer), and visualisation and simulation software, which
    are examples of special purpose technologies used in particular kinds of projects.

The *social* level of human activity consists of the personal networks, the public behaviours, norms and culture that are exhibited by research groups and collaborations.
These are supported by communication technologies, email, videoconferencing and
collaborative tools such as Sharepoint, Yahoo and CommunityZero.

The *organisational* level of human activity systems concerns the processes, accountability
and power structures in organisations such as universities, the Commonwealth Scientific
and Industrial Research Organisation (CSIRO), Defense and parts of industry. Typically,
ICT infrastructure is owned at this level. Systems like ResearchMaster are well established
in universities to help manage the flow of research projects, publications, and so on,
but such systems are probably not part of the research human activity system as they
are not concerned with research content.

The *societal* level addresses questions about who pays for, and who benefits from, research.

These levels are not hierarchical. For example, a social network exists independently of
organisations and societies. Nor is it necessary that human activity systems are purposeful.
In fact, from an IS perspective, we are often more interested in the 'metabolism' of these
systems than their justification. The ways people act are what IS contributes to, and
social, political and cultural factors are always active in all human activity systems
(Checkland and Scholes, 1990) .

As demonstrated above, the research human activity system, like all data, information
and knowledge systems, can make effective piecemeal use of information technologies.

ICT is most active at the personal level, with the adoption of tools for individual tasks. Research infrastructure is a feature of the organisational level where there is finance and ongoing structures to manage the assets. Technology is an *instrumental* component of the IS approach to human activity systems; one that offers opportunities and limitations. At the foundation of the IS approach, however, are the very significant human, social and use aspects of technologies, and IS as a discipline has the role of systematising a range of ICT breakthroughs that, combined, can address a problem more effectively than can individual technologies. In the research human activity system there is plenty of technology push, but little systems-pull.

Information systems in research

The possibilities of systems-pull (or, inversely, the problem of 'systems failures') in the research domain are rampant. The fact that data sets are typically not warehoused and re-used is an example of failure at the *data level*.

At the *information level*, McDonald (2003) argued that current methods of organising and mobilising this research are flawed. Considered as a whole, the applied science literature is:

1. *Dispersed:* It is scattered across different kinds of literature such as books, periodicals, research papers, technical reports, proceedings, which are located all over the globe. It is possible that research is unwittingly being duplicated because the original was not found in the literature review.
2. *Dated:* Some knowledge, created long ago, has been superseded by more recent work but still remains in the literature with a corresponding potential to mislead.
3. *Underutilised:* Studies indicate that no more than 20 per cent of the knowledge available in research institutes is really being put to use. Therefore, the full weight of current human knowledge is not being brought to bear on problem solving.
4. *Expanding rapidly:* The quantity of knowledge is increasing at an exponential rate.
5. *Variable in quality:* The reliability of public knowledge is complex. 'Textbook Science' is more reliable than primary (e.g. research papers) and secondary literature (e.g. review articles). Furthermore, knowledge that is reliable in one context may not be so reliable in another.
6. *Inconsistent:* Considerable contradictions have been found within published knowledge, and between the published knowledge and expert opinion.
7. *Incomplete:* There are considerable gaps in published knowledge.
8. *Slow to be published and applied:* The path from applied science research to decision making in the field can be long and inefficient. Publication in scientific journals can take 12 to 18 months after acceptance, which itself may have taken a year to achieve.

Clearly, there is a large knowledge management problem to be addressed here, even if the information management systems (document collection, indexing, bibliographic and full-text databases that store and deliver papers) were effective. We are stuck in a very outmoded system that serves neither researchers nor practitioners adequately.

There are attempts to address these problems. The Cochrane Collaboration has successfully adopted 'systematic reviews' or meta-analyses as a method for getting the best scientific results to practitioners and other researchers. Meyers, in the *Communications of the AIS* has papers that are regularly revised, and WIKI systems allow multiple people to continuously contribute to and revise a paper.

An IS approach to these problems would use a variety of technologies and methods, but IS theories, tools and techniques will need to be deployed, reviewed and, probably, new IS approaches developed. Some parts of an IS approach to e-Research might be:

1. research data warehouses;
2. ontological systems for content organisation;
3. meta-analysis to bring together work with a similar ontological basis;
4. more advanced techniques of domain analysis;
5. knowledge management mechanisms for evidence-based research;
6. serious e-libraries (see DSpace);
7. development of domain-specific patterns.

It is at the *knowledge* level, that e-research may well have its greatest impact. Knowledge management systems (KMS) technologies may be at the heart of a new kind of system. This system would be charged with representing the knowledge reported in a domain of research and, through a set of interface systems, employ the knowledge base in different ways to meet some of the needs in a range of human activity systems. For example, a decision support system would use the KMS as a model of a domain to allow scenario processing; an expert system would give advice using the KMS as a knowledge base and justify the advice on the basis of the publications from which the KMS has been built; a Computer Aided Instruction (CAI) interface would allow the KMS to form the basis of courses in the domain; researchers and research bodies could use the KMS as a source for literature reviews and hypothesis testing. Each of these interface systems would have specific systems components suitable to their purposes but would rely on the core KMS as the source for their domain knowledge. The KMS would be self-maintaining as each new research report that became available would be represented as a new document-related knowledge base and so participate immediately in the various uses to which the system is being put. Such a system would be domain specific, rather like the 'specialist libraries' of the past. The various needs of the different stakeholders could be met from a single core of knowledge.

Proposals like this are not new. A century ago, Paul Otlet was presenting a similar notion (see various papers by W. Boyd Rayward). We may now, however, be in a position to bring new technologies to bear on e-Research, but only if IS takes a major role in the intervention that such technology might make to the research human activity system. Without IS, another technology failure would most likely be imminent.

Research and practice interoperability

The KMS described above introduces the second e-Research issue that IS needs to address – the interaction of the research and practice domains.

The idea that research results need to be socially useful is not new either. The nature of knowledge, its production and use, has long been a topic of debate and academic research. In Australia, research has been largely a publicly funded activity, and government is now casting an increasingly critical eye over the way it is currently performed. DEST's research network initiative (the context in which this paper is written) is the latest in a series of moves to promote interdisciplinary research that aims to create and apply knowledge to address problems of national significance. Ronayne (1997) put it this way:

> In Mode 1 problems are set and solved in a context governed by the interests of a largely academic community. By contrast, Mode 2 knowledge production is carried out within the context of application. It is intended to be useful to

someone other than specifically the practitioner, be this industry, government or society generally; and this requirement is present from the beginning.

Batterham (2003) describes Mode 1 as 'discipline based; distinguishes between theoretical core and its conversion to application' while Mode 2 is 'multidisciplinary, team based; Constant flow between basic & applied; Discovery occurs where knowledge is developed and put to use'. The search for integration between research and practice is a priority.

But these are two very different worlds – human activity systems that share knowledge, but not purpose, method or people. The relationship has normally been one of knowledge provision on one side and adoption on the other. There are many examples of effective interoperation projects (for example, in most of Australia's Cooperative Research Centres).

In this way of thinking, the relationship between research and practice is like that between two organisations engaged in e-Commerce. The currency is knowledge, with practice providing relevance and raw data to theory, and research providing economically useful, causally based knowledge and interventions to practice. Figure 12.2 shows two information systems planes, one for research, the other for practice, with the suggestion of a third interoperation system in between.

Figure 12.2. Traditional interoperation of research and practice systems.

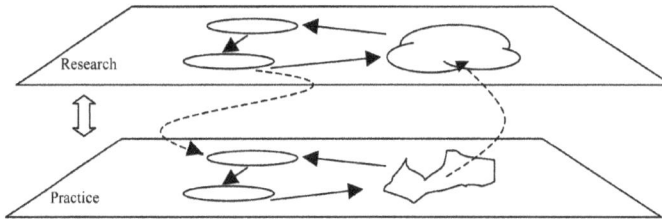

E-Commerce, like interoperation between systems, has become a significant part of IS. Recent work in terms of ontologies and the Web (Moody, 2000) and in object orientation, agents, XML, and so on, is accelerating the field. So patterns to support this kind of relationship between research and practice already exist.

But the KMS described earlier implies a different view. It concentrates not on the trading between systems but on sharing what they have in common. It suggests a deeper association of human activity systems, not just ICT mediated communication.

Conclusion

From an IS *research* perspective the research domain presents an opportunity to develop and test new ideas in IS. Our challenge is to make a serious effort to create systems architectures, define and mobilise technologies and specify processes that address e-Research.

ICT does not work effectively in human activity systems without IS. It can work at the individual and social levels, but not at the organisational or societal levels. So there is a demand and supply relationship between ICT and IS. From the IS perspective, new ICT offers opportunities for building new types of systems, and it can be argued that IS has been slow to adopt some of these technologies. However, IS has certainly been slow in demanding that ICT produce tools for solving new types of problem. Looking at research as an IS domain challenges us to think of, and to start driving, the next steps in informatics development.

This paper has looked at IS and its application to the research domain. Some IS foundations this review has exposed are: ICT as tools verses ICT as instruments in systems; aspects of human activity systems as they present in research; the need for integration of systems that address data, information and knowledge; and an approach to integrating research and practice.

The way forward would be to select a small research area, see it as a human activity system and knowledge domain, look to understanding and formalising it in IS terms, and developing IT-based systems that responsibly intervene in it for the benefit of all stakeholders.

13. A procedural model for ontological analyses

Michael Rosemann, *Centre for Information Technology Innovation, Queensland University of Technology*
Peter Green, *UQ Business School, The University of Queensland*
Marta Indulska, *UQ Business School, The University of Queensland*

Abstract

In recent years, there has been a significant increase in the popularity of ontological analysis of conceptual modelling techniques. To date, related research explores the ontological deficiencies of classical techniques such as ER or UML modelling, as well as business process modelling techniques such as ARIS or even Web Services standards such as BPEL4WS, BPML, ebXML, BPSS and WSCI. While the ontologies that form the basis of these analyses are reasonably mature, it is the actual process of an ontological analysis that still lacks rigour. The current procedure is prone to individual interpretations and is one reason for criticism of the entire ontological analysis. This paper presents a procedural model for ontological analysis based on the use of meta models, multiple coders and metrics. The model is supported by examples from various ontological analyses.

Introduction

As techniques for conceptual modelling, enterprise modelling, and business process modelling have proliferated over the years (e.g. Olle et al., 1991), researchers and practitioners alike have attempted to determine objective bases on which to compare, evaluate, and determine when to use these different techniques (e.g. Karam and Casselman, 1993; Gorla et al., 1995) . However, throughout the 1980s, 1990s, and into the new millennium, it has become increasingly apparent to many researchers that without a theoretical foundation on which to base the specification for these various modelling techniques, incomplete evaluative frameworks of factors, features, and facets will continue to proliferate. Furthermore, without a theoretical foundation, one framework of factors, features, or facets is just as justifiable for use as another (e.g. Bansler and Bodker, 1993).

Wand and Weber (1989; 1990; 1993; 1995) have investigated the branch of philosophy known as ontology as a foundation for understanding the process of developing an information system. Ontology is a well-established theoretical domain within philosophy dealing with identifying and understanding elements of the real world. However, interest in, and the applicability of, ontologies today extends to areas far beyond philosophy. As Gruninger and Lee (2002, p. 13) point out, '…a Web search engine will return over 64 000 pages given 'ontology' as a keyword … the first few pages are phrases such as "enabling virtual business", "gene ontology consortium", and "enterprise ontology".'

The usefulness of ontology as a theoretical foundation for knowledge representation and natural language processing is a fervently debated topic at the present time in the artificial intelligence research community (Guarino and Welty, 2002). The use of ontologies as a basis for the analysis of techniques that purport to assist analysts to develop models that emulate portions of the real world has been growing steadily more popular. The Bunge-Wand-Weber (BWW) ontological models (Weber, 1997), for example, have been applied extensively in the context of the analysis of various modelling techniques. Wand and Weber (1989; 1990; 1993; 1995) and Weber (1997) have applied the BWW representation model to the 'classical' descriptions of entity-relationship (ER) modelling and logical data flow diagramming (LDFD). Weber and Zhang (1996) also examined the Nijssen Information Analysis Method (NIAM) using the ontology. Green (1997) extended the work of Weber and Zhang (1996) and Wand and Weber (1993; 1995) by analysing various modelling techniques as they have been extended and implemented in upper CASE tools. Furthermore, Parsons and Wand (1997) proposed a formal model of objects and they use the ontological models to identify representation-oriented characteristics of objects. Along similar lines, Opdahl and Henderson-Sellers (2001) have used the BWW representation model to examine the individual modelling constructs within the OPEN Modelling Language (OML) version 1.1, which is based on 'conventional' object-oriented constructs. Green and Rosemann (2000) have extended the analytical work into the area of integrated process modelling based on the techniques presented in Scheer (2000). Most recently, Green et al. (2003) have extended the use of this evaluative base into the area of enterprise systems interoperability using business process modelling languages like ebXML, BPML, BPEL4WS, and WSCI. Clearly, ontology is a fruitful theoretical basis on which to perform such analyses. However, while ontological analyses are frequently utilised, particularly in the area of conceptual modelling technique analysis, the actual process of performing the analysis remains problematic. The current process of ontological analysis is open to the individual interpretations of the researchers who undertake the analysis. Consequently, such analyses are criticised as being subjective, *ad hoc*, and lacking in relevance. There is a need, therefore, for the systematic identification of shortcomings of the current ontological analysis process. The identification of such weaknesses, and their subsequent mitigation, will lead to a more rigorous, objective, and replicable analytical process.

Accordingly, this paper has several objectives. First, we aim to identify comprehensively the shortcomings in the current practice of ontological analysis. The identification of such shortcomings will provide a basis upon which the practice of ontological analysis can be improved. Second, we want to develop several propositions and methodology extensions that enhance the ontological analysis process by making it more objective and structured.

There are several contributions this paper aims to make. They are based on previous experiences with ontological analyses as well as observations derived from published analyses. First, the work presents a detailed analysis of the actual process of performing an ontological evaluation. We identify eight shortcomings of the current ontological analysis process, *viz*. lack of understandability, lack of comparability, lack of completeness, lack of guidance, lack of objectivity, lack of adequate result representation, lack of result classification, and lack of relevance. Each of the identified shortcomings is then classified as belonging to one of three phases of analysis, *viz*., input, process, and output. Second, the paper presents recommendations on how each of the shortcomings in the three phases can be overcome. The recommendations, *inter alia*, include an extended methodology for improving the objectivity of the analysis as well as a weighting model that aims to improve the classification of the results of any ontological analysis.

The remainder of the paper is structured as follows. The next section identifies eight current shortcomings of ontological analyses that are classified with respect to the three phases of analysis. The third section provides recommendations concerning how to overcome the identified shortcomings in each of the three phases. The final section provides a brief summary of the work and outlines possible future research in this area.

Shortcomings of current ontological analyses

An ontological analysis is, in principle, the evaluation of a selected modelling grammar from the viewpoint of a pre-defined and well-established ontology. The current focus of ontological analyses is on the bi-directional comparison of ontological constructs with the elements of the modelling grammar that is under analysis. Weber (1997) clarifies two major situations that may occur when a grammar is analysed according to an ontology. After a particular grammar has been analysed, an assessment of the modelling strengths and weaknesses of the grammar can be made according to whether some or any of the following situations arise out of the analysis.

1. *Ontological incompleteness (or construct deficit)* exists unless there is at least one grammatical construct for each ontological construct.
2. *Ontological clarity* is determined by the extent to which the grammar does not exhibit one or more of the following deficiencies:

a. *Construct overload* exists in a grammar if one grammatical construct represents more than one ontological construct.
b. *Construct redundancy* exists if more than one grammatical construct represents the same ontological construct.
c. *Construct excess* exists in a grammar when a grammatical construct is present that does not map to any ontological construct.

Though this type of ontological analysis is widely established, it still has a range of shortcomings. These shortcomings can be categorised into the three main phases of an ontological analysis: preparation of the input data, the process of conducting the analysis, and the evaluation and interpretation of the results. The first two identified shortcomings refer to the quality of the input data.

Lack of understandability

Most of the ontologies that are currently used for analysing modelling grammars have been specified in formal languages. While such formalisation is beneficial for a complete and precise specification of the ontology, it is not a very natural or intuitive specification. An ontology that is not clear and intuitive can lead to misinterpretations as the involved stakeholders have problems with the specifications. Furthermore, it forms a hurdle for the application of the ontology as it requires a deep understanding of the formal language in which it is specified.

Lack of comparability

The specification of an ontology typically requires a formal syntax, which allows the precise specification of the elements and relationships of the ontology. Such specifications are required, but are not necessarily intuitive. Consequently, textual descriptions of the ontology in 'plain English' often extend the formal specification. However, even if an ontology is specified in an intuitive and understandable language, the actual comparison with the selected modelling grammar remains a problem. Unless the ontology and the grammar are specified in the *same* language, it will be up to the coder to 'mentally convert' the two specifications into each other for comparison purposes, which adds a subjective element to the analysis. Different languages can also lead to different levels of detail and further complicate the analysis. In any case, they make a more automated comparison practically impossible. This is the typical situation in nearly all previous analyses.

The three further shortcomings identified below are related to the process of the ontological analysis and refer to what should be analysed, how it should be analysed as well as who should conduct the analysis.

Lack of completeness

The first decision that has to be made in the process of an ontological analysis is on the scope and depth of the analysis. Even though most ontologies have been discussed for many decades, they still undergo modifications and extensions. It is up to the researcher to clearly specify the selected version of the ontology and the scope and level of detail of the analysis. In our work in the area of Web Services, for example, it was often not clear what constructs form the core of the standard and, in fact, two researchers who conducted independent analyses of the same Web Services standard selected a different number of constructs.

Moreover, many ontological analyses focus solely on the constructs of the ontology and the constructs of the grammar but do not sufficiently consider the relationships between these constructs. The difficulty of clearly specifying the boundaries of the analysis, as well as the limited consideration of relationships between the ontological constructs, can lead to a lack of completeness.

Lack of guidance

After the scope and the level of detail of the analysis have been specified, it is typically up to the coder to decide on the procedure of the analysis, i.e. in what sequence will the ontological constructs and relationships be analysed? Currently, there are hardly any recommendations on where to start the analysis. This lack of procedural clarity underlies most analyses and has two consequences. First, a novice analyst lacks guidance in the process of conducting the ontological evaluation. Second, the procedure of the analysis can potentially have an impact on the results of the analysis. Thus, it is possible that two analyses of the same modelling grammar using the same ontological base, but that follow different processes, may lead to different outcomes.

Lack of objectivity

An ontological analysis of a grammar requires not only detailed knowledge of the selected ontology and grammar, but also a good understanding of the languages in which the ontology and the grammar are specified. This requirement explains why most analyses are carried out by single researchers as opposed to research teams. Consequently, these analyses are based on the individual interpretations of the involved researcher, which adds significant subjectivity to the results. This problem is further compounded by the fact that, unlike other qualitative research projects, ontological analyses typically do not include attempts to further validate the results.

The five shortcomings identified above have a common flavour in that they heavily depend on the researcher conducting the ontological evaluation. Three further shortcomings have been identified, namely lack of result representation, lack of result classification and lack of relevance. These shortcomings are detailed below and refer to the outcomes of the analysis

Lack of adequate result representation

The results of a complete ontological analysis, i.e. representation mapping and interpretation mapping, are typically summarised in two tables. These tables list all the ontological constructs (first table) and all the grammatical constructs (second table) and the corresponding constructs of the other meta model. Such tables can become quite lengthy and are typically not sorted in any particular order. They don't provide any insights into the importance of identified deficiencies and they also don't cluster the findings.

Lack of result classification

As indicated above, it is common practice to derive ontological deficiencies based on a comparison of the constructs in the ontology and the grammar. Ontological weaknesses are identified when corresponding constructs are missing in the mapping obtained between the ontology and the grammar or one-to-many (or many-to-one or even many-many) relationships exist in the mapping between the two. Such identified deficiencies are the typical starting point for the derivation of propositions and then hypotheses. In general, the ontological analysis does not make any statements regarding the relative importance of these findings in comparison with each other. Though this seems to be the established practice, it lacks more detailed insights into the significance of the results. It is to be expected, however, that missing support for a core construct of an ontology should be rated of higher importance than missing a construct corresponding to a minor ontological construct or a relationship. This lack of a more detailed statement regarding the significance of a potential shortcoming makes it difficult to judge quickly the outcomes of the results of two different sets of analyses (e.g. an ontological analysis of ARIS compared to an ontological analysis of UML).

Lack of relevance

Finally, the results of an ontological analysis should be perceived as relevant by the related stakeholders. However, if an ontological analysis leads, for example, to the outcome that Entity Relationship Models do not support the description of behaviour then it would hardly be surprising if the IS community developed a rather critical opinion of the worth of the analysis since this is both obvious and well known. It seems that an ontological analysis has to consider the purpose of the grammar as well as the background of the modeller who is applying this grammar. The application of a high-level and generic ontology does not consider this individual context and there is a danger that the outcomes can be perceived as trivial.

Reference methodology for conducting ontological analyses

The shortcomings identified above have motivated the development of an enhanced methodology for ontological analysis. The main purpose of this methodology is to increase the rigour, the overall objectivity and the level of detail of the analysis. The proposed methodology for ontological analyses is structured in three phases: input, process and output.

Input

The formal specification of ontologies, together with the differences in the languages used to specify the ontologies and the grammars under analysis, have been classified as issues pertaining to the lack of understandability and comparability.

In order to overcome these shortcomings, it is proposed to convert the ontology as well as the selected modelling grammar to meta models using the same language (e.g. ER Models or UML Class Diagrams). This facilitates a pattern-matching approach towards the ontological analyses of completeness and clarity of a grammar. As a first step we converted, for example, the Bunge-Wand-Weber ontology into an ER-based meta model. This meta model includes 50 entity types and 92 relationship types. It has clusters such as system, property or class/kind. Such a meta model explains, in a language familiar to the information systems (IS) community, the core constructs of the ontology. It also highlights the underlying focus of the ontology. In the case of the BWW model, for example, it is obvious from a visual inspection of the meta model that the ontology is centred around the existence of a *thing*, which is the central entity type in the meta model.

The obtained meta model can now be used for a variety of ontological analyses. Moreover, it allows a critical review of the BWW model by a wider community. The approach, however, is not without its limitations. Commonly used modelling techniques such as ER or UML are often widely accepted but they have not been designed for the purposes of meta modelling. Thus, they occasionally lack the required expressiveness. Figure 13.1 provides an impression of the size and complexity of the meta model for the BWW ontology.

Figure 13.1. The BWW meta model.

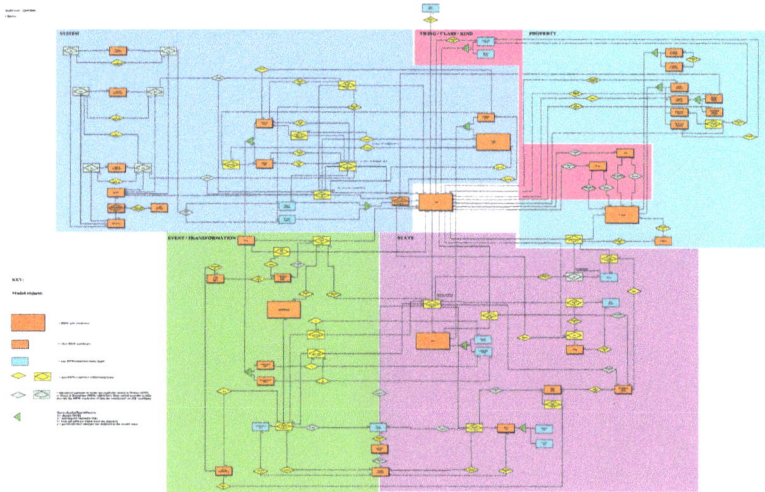

While an ER-based meta model helps to overcome issues related to the understandability of an ontology, a corresponding meta model of the analysed grammar is required to deal with the lack of comparability issue. Many popular modelling techniques (e.g. ARIS or UML, and also interoperability standards such as ebXML) are already specified in meta models using ER-notations or UML Class Diagrams. If the meta models for the ontology and the modelling technique are specified in the same language, the ontological analysis turns into a comparison of two conceptual models. As part of the analysis, it will be required to identify corresponding entity types and relationship types in both models. It also becomes immediately obvious if the paradigm of the analysed grammar differs from the ontology. In the case of ARIS or many Web Services standards, for example, the meta models are centred around *functions* or *activities* instead of being centred around *things*.

Process

The issues related to the process of conducting an ontological analysis have been described as lack of completeness, lack of guidance and lack of objectivity.

Based on the assumption that corresponding meta models for the ontology and the analysed grammar are available, it is possible to clearly specify the scope of an analysis using those meta models. A selection of clusters, entity types and relationship types would define all elements that are perceived of relevance for the analysis. An analysis of an ER-based notation, for example, could be focused on the BWW clusters *thing*, *system* and *property* and could exclude the more behavioural-oriented clusters *event* and *state*. Such boundaries of an analysis could be easily visualised in the meta model and would provide a clear description of the comprehensiveness of the analysis.

The existence of two corresponding meta models and a clear definition of the scope of the analysis are necessary but not sufficient criteria for a well-guided process. Further guidelines are required regarding the starting point of such a process and the actual sequence of activities. Based on our experiences, we recommend starting with the representation mapping; that is, selecting the meta model of the ontology and subsequently identifying corresponding elements in the modelling grammar. The first construct to be analysed should be the most central entity type. For example, in the case of the BWW model, the entity type *thing* is the appropriate starting point. Our previous work provides a strong argument that this analysis should follow a cluster-by-cluster approach. Starting with the core constructs in a cluster allows a more structured and focused analysis of the completeness of a modelling grammar. The analysis of the entity types is followed by the relationships and the cardinalities. Constructs in the meta model that have only been introduced for reasons of correctness of the meta model, but that do not reflect ontological constructs, are excluded from the analysis. The representation mapping is followed by an analysis of the clarity of the target grammar, i.e. the interpretation mapping. In this case the meta model of the grammar under analysis is the starting point. The general procedure is similar. A primary advantage of a cluster-based analysis is that the structure of the two meta models provides valuable input for the ontological analysis. An example is the analysis of generalisation-specialisation relationships in the meta model of the grammar. We propose to ontologically classify the super-type first and then to inherit this ontological classification to all sub-types. This streamlines the process of the analysis and increases consistency.

The lack of objectivity issue, on the other hand, frequently stems from the analysis being performed by a single researcher. This situation results in an analysis that is almost certainly biased by the researcher's background as well as their interpretation of the specification of the grammar. In order to improve the validity of the analysis, a research method can be adopted that involves individual analyses of a particular grammar by at least two members of a research team, followed by discussion and hopefully consensus as to the final analysis by the entire team of researchers. The method consists of three steps:

1. *Step 1:* Using the specification of the grammar in question, at least two researchers separately read the specification and interpret, select and map the ontological constructs to candidate grammatical constructs to create individual first drafts of the analysis.

2. *Step 2:* The researchers involved in Step 1 of the methodology, meet to discuss and defend their interpretations of the representation modelling analysis. This meeting should lead to an agreed second draft version of the analysis that incorporates elements of each of the researchers' first draft analyses. The overlap in the selection of the grammatical constructs and in the actual ontological analysis can be quantified by various figures that are used in content analysis and other more qualitative research.

3. *Step 3:* The second draft version of the analysis for each of the interoperability candidate standards is used as a basis for defence and discussion in a meeting involving the entire research team. The outcome of this meeting forms the final analysis of the grammar in question.

Just such a method was employed in a project that sought to apply the BWW representation model analysis to a number of the leading potential Web Services standards: ebXML, BPML, BPEL4WS and WSCI. The project team was composed of four researchers and the standards were analysed in the order: ebXML à BPML à BPEL4WS à WSCI. Two researchers were involved in Steps 1 and 2 of the method (the individual analysis of a standard followed by a meeting of the two researchers in order to obtain an agreed mapping). This was followed by a meeting of the entire team in order to discuss the mapping and arrive at the final analysis. The process was performed for each of the four standards. Table 13.1 shows the recorded agreement statistics at the second step of the applied method while Table 13.2 shows the recorded agreement statistics at the third step of the method.

Table 13.1. Summary of Step 2 mapping agreement between both researchers

Web Service Language	Construct Mapping agreed upon by both researchers	Total number of specification constructs identified	Mapping conference
ebXML	43	51	84%
BPML	36	46	78%
BPEL4WS	30	47	63%
WSCI	39	49	79%

Table 13.2. Summary of Step 3 mapping agreement

Web Service Language	Construct Mapping agreed upon by the team	Total number of specification constructs identified	Mapping conference
ebXML	49	51	96%
BPML	41	46	89%
BPEL4WS	42	47	89%
WSCI	46	49	94%

The adoption of such a method can be seen to have greatly improved the objectiveness of the carried-out analyses.

Output

The three main shortcomings related to the outcome of an ontological analysis have been characterised as the lack of adequate result representation, lack of result classification and the lack of relevance.

The meta models, which have been used as input for the ontological analyses, are an appropriate medium to visualise the outcomes of the entire analysis process. In our work on the analysis of ARIS, we derived a meta model of the BWW model that highlighted all constructs of the ontology that did not have a corresponding construct in the grammar under analysis. That is, we visualised incompleteness in the model using simple colour coding. In a similar way, we derived three ARIS meta models that highlighted excess, overload and redundancy in ARIS. Such models form a very intuitive way of representing the identified ontological shortcomings. The underlying clustering of the models also helps to quickly comprehend the main areas in which there are shortcomings.

At the present time, the process of an ontological analysis results in the identification of ontological incompleteness and ontological clarity through the identification of missing, overloaded or redundant grammatical constructs. While the end result identifies such problems, it fails to account for their relative importance. For example, *thing* is one of the fundamental constructs of the BWW model. Therefore, a lack of mapping to a modelling grammar for this construct should be considered a more important shortcoming than the lack of mapping for, say, the *well-defined event* construct. There is a need for the development of a scoring model that enables the calculation of the 'goodness' of a grammar with respect to the ontology. In such a scoring model, each of the ontological constructs has a value assigned to it that reflects the relative importance of the construct in the ontology. Core constructs would therefore have high weightings whereas less important constructs would attract lower weightings. Following an ontological analysis of a particular grammar, the weighting of all missing constructs would be calculated to arrive at one value that generally reflects the outcome of the analysis.

An example for such a classification could have the following structure. All core constructs of an ontology (and the modelling grammar) would get the value one. All other constructs represented as an entity type in the meta model of the ontology would receive the value 0.7, and all other constructs get the value 0.3. Such a weighting would then be applied to the outcomes of the ontological analysis. The scores would be aggregated across the ontology and modelling grammar. They could also be calculated separately for completeness, excess, overload and redundancy. Furthermore, they could be aggregated per cluster, which allows a more differentiated view of the particular strengths or weaknesses of a modelling grammar. Though the consolidated score of such an evaluation should not be overrated, it provides better insights into the characteristics of the ontological deficiencies and provides a first rating of the significance and importance of the identified shortcomings.

Apart from the lack of result classification that is addressed by the scoring model, another problem with the outcome of the analyses has been the perceived lack of relevance of the results. Since most modelling grammars focus on modelling a subset of the phenomena that occur in the real world, it would follow that not *all* constructs of an ontology are necessary in order to analyse such a grammar. If the full ontology is used in the analysis, the result may identify potential problems that would not, in reality, occur, because the modelling grammar is not used to model any phenomena described by the missing constructs. Further, there may also be a need for specialisation of some of the ontological constructs in order to enhance analysis of a grammar pertaining to a particular domain.

Figure 13.2. An extension of ontological analysis through the use of focused ontologies.

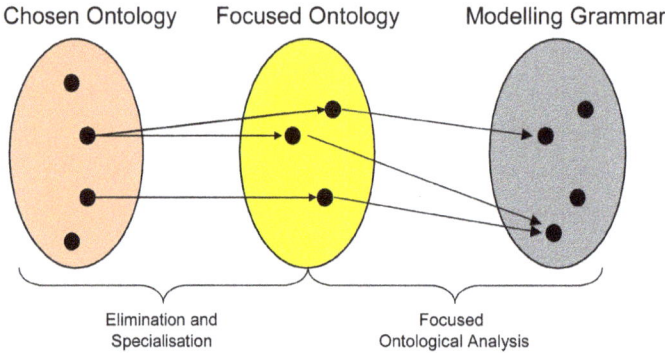

Indeed, the outcomes of the ontological analyses of different modelling grammars to date appear to support the need for a focused ontology, which consists of different subsets of the ontological constructs for different domains. The analyses of the examined grammars consistently show that the constructs *conceivable state space, conceivable event space* and *lawful event space*, for example, have no representative constructs in the grammars. Such missing constructs, if identified as unnecessary for the particular domain, can be ignored, leading to a simpler analysis that does not consider phenomena that are deemed to be outside of the scope of the target grammar.

Summary and future work

There has been a marked increase in the application of ontologies for the purposes of analysing modelling grammars. For example, a literature review identified more than 25 papers that applied the Bunge-Wand-Weber ontology for the analysis of modelling grammars such as ER (e.g. Wand and Weber, 1989; Wand and Weber, 1993; Wand and Weber, 1995), OMT, UML (e.g. Burton-Jones and Meso, 2002; Opdahl and Henderson-Sellers, 2002; Shanks et al., 2002), Petri-Nets, ARIS (e.g. Green and Rosemann, 2000; Green and Rosemann, 2002; Rosemann and Green, 2002) and Web Services standards such as ebXML, BPEL4WS, BPML or WSCI (e.g. van der Aalst et al., 2002; Wohed et al., 2002; Green et al., 2003). In general, selected ontologies and their interpretations, from an information systems viewpoint, are reasonably advanced. However, the actual process of conducting an ontological analysis is still rather immature. At this stage, the process is focused on the identification of the cardinality of the relationships between corresponding elements in the ontology and the modelling grammar under analysis. In our analysis, eight shortcomings of the current ontological analysis process have been identified and categorised into issues related to the input, process and output of the analysis.

This paper has proposed to further enhance the current process of ontological analysis. The objectives of such a method are:

1. to provide guidance for researchers who are interested in conducting ontological analyses;
2. to add rigour to the entire process and reduce the dependence on subjective interpretations of the involved researchers, and
3. to increase the credibility of the ontological analysis and its results.

Examples from our ontological analyses of ARIS and various Web Services standards have been used to exemplify this method. As a consequence, we hope the more rigorous process that has been presented here will increase the overall acceptance of using ontologies for the analysis, comparison and engineering of various modelling grammars.

14. Lessons learned from manual systems: designing information systems based on the situational theory of agency

Simon K. Milton, *Department of Information Systems, The University of Melbourne*
Robert B. Johnston, *Department of Information Systems, The University of Melbourne*
Reeva M. Lederman, *Department of Information Systems, The University of Melbourne*

Abstract

Information systems are part of purposeful socio-technical systems and consequently theories of agency may help in understanding them. Current systems analysis and design methodologies seem to have been influenced only by one particular theory of agency, which asserts that action results from deliberation upon an abstract representation of the world. Many disciplines have, however, discussed an alternative 'situational' theory of agency. There is currently no methodology that fully supports designing systems reflecting the situational theory of agency. The aim of this paper is to develop a first-cut of such a methodology based on concepts from the situational theory of agency, and is supplemented by our exploration of evolved manual situational systems. We intend to iteratively refine this methodology since we believe the situational theory of agency provides a better description of purposeful activity than the deliberative theory and is, therefore, a firmer foundation on which to build successful information systems, especially in pressured routine environments.

Introduction

Theories of agency discuss the possible ways of designing complex systems that display purposeful activity. Theories of agency have been researched in several disciplines (Brooks, 1986; Agre and Chapman, 1987; Suchman, 1987; Hendriks-Jansen, 1996; Johnston and Brennan, 1996; Agre and Horswill, 1997; Clancey, 1997), where two main positions are found – which we will call the 'deliberative' and the 'situational' theories of agency. The two theories have quite different modes of representation and action selection. In previous papers (Johnston and Milton, 2001; Johnston and Milton, 2002a; Lederman et al., 2003; Lederman et al., 2004) we have argued that information systems are purposeful, and that methodologies and tools used to build them should be analysed using theories of agency. However, existing approaches to computerised information system design and development are implicitly informed by the deliberative theory of agency. An approach different from present systems analysis and design methodologies is needed because many information systems fail in pressured routine environments, where we would argue that the situational theory of agency provides a better description of purposeful activity.

Although it is possible to design information systems for pressured routine environments using traditional methodologies, many of these systems are ineffective, inefficient or not accepted by people using them. They work technically but fail, in the context in which they are placed, to support the routine work adequately. We have reason to believe that in order to achieve greater success and acceptance of information systems in routine environments, we need a methodology that explicitly acknowledges the situatedness of socio-technical systems and their components, of which human actors and technical artefacts are examples.

Our long-term aim[1] is to develop a situational information systems analysis and design methodology informed by the situational theory of agency. The first step is to establish an initial methodology to use in later stages of the research, which will employ action research. Consequently, the aim of this paper is to develop a first-cut of such a methodology based on concepts from the situational theory of agency and supplemented by our exploration of evolved manual situational systems. Although the methodology is intended for designing computerised systems, the specific focus of this paper is on learning lessons from existing manual situational systems so that the initial methodology, based on the situational theory of agency, can incorporate and generalise important features of situated systems that are currently in use and known to be effective.

The method we use in the paper is first to extract key concepts from the situational theory of agency as it is understood in robotics and discussed in other disciplines. Based on these concepts, we draw up a skeleton of a methodology for analysing systems. Following this, we examine several manual systems that have been either designed by users or evolved from practice, and that are both discussed in the literature and appear to be situational. We begin by establishing that the systems can be explained using the situational theory of agency. These systems are then used to understand how to apply concepts from the situational theory in practical systems before incorporating our experiences into the tentative methodology. We conclude by showing how we intend to refine the methodology.

Information systems design and theories of agency

We have argued previously (Johnston and Milton, 2002b) that existing information systems implicitly support the deliberative theory of agency. According to this theory (Johnston and Brennan, 1996), purposeful action proceeds by an agent building an abstract model or representation of the external objective world from sense data and then reasoning about this model to determine actions that will achieve goals. For example, in traditional transaction-based information systems, 'transactions' are gathered that represent changes in the world. Data models that correspond to the representation scheme are used to design operational databases that are affected by the transactions. In extreme cases, such as MRPII (Wight, 1981), application programs also deduce goal-attaining actions and human actors are only required to define the goal state, execute the actions in reality by following automatically generated schedules and provide sense data by recording transactions. More typically, applications programs help human actors to make decisions by providing information about objects from reality using data gained through transactions. Decision support systems are good examples of this type of system.

---

[1] This program at The University of Melbourne is supported by an Australian Research Council Discovery Grant DP0451524.

In the past 30 years a number of methodologies have been developed to assist in designing such systems. These are often called information engineering methodologies (IEM), with Structured Systems Analysis and Design Methodology (SSADM), the British government standard, being a typical example. These design methodologies share the ontological assumptions of the deliberative theory, namely, that systems should represent the world in which the system acts in terms of external, independent and objective entities, properties and relations (Wand et al., 1995). Given this focus on symbol/object representation, use of these methodologies encourages designs for socio-technical systems in which the information systems form the representational scheme which mimic the deliberative approach to agency.

On the other hand, disciplines other than information systems have considered an alternative approach called the situational theory of agency. In robotics, specifically, this alternative theory has been motivated by the brittle performance and computation intensity of artefacts based on the deliberative approach. The key to this alternative theory is to provide an agent with largely reactive responses based on sense data obtainable directly from the agent's *ground view* of the world, and to introduce the agent's goals and perspective explicitly in the representation schemes implicit in the theory. In the situational theory, agents respond reactively to 'situations' without deliberation. Situations are descriptions of the world centred on the agent and only include features of the world that relate to the agent's purposes (Agre and Chapman, 1987). These features consist of the *relations of things to the agent given its goals*. Actions are selected from a repertoire used to respond to situations. This approach to action selection leads to goal attainment only if the agent's environment exhibits structure ('affordances') that obviate the need to plan (Agre and Chapman 1987). An affordance is a structural aspect of the environment that makes it possible for an agent to reach a desired situation by merely reacting to its current situation. Analysis and exploitation of environmental structure is an important part of designing situated agents (Agre and Horswill, 1992; Hammond et al., 1995; Horswill, 1995; Agre and Horswill, 1997). An activity in this theory is a grouping of situations and associated actions that together lead to a reliable reaching of a desirable situation.

We can see the differing roles of representation in the situational theory. Situations are agent-centred and intention-laden. Representation of situations on the basis of a symbol/object isomorphism is neither possible nor necessary. An agent responds to being in a situation by taking an action. An agent needs to notice that it is in a situation and does so by sensing aspects of its environment. Consequently, aspects of situations are needed to fire situation-action responses. Agre and Chapman (1987) argue that the representational scheme is 'indexical' and 'functional' in nature. Indexical representations describe things relative to the agent and functional representations select things according to their relevance for the purposes of the agent or concern the activities in which the agent is engaged. Further, Agre and Chapman (1987) argue that to eliminate the computational complexity of action selection inherent in using aerial world models, indexical/functional representations of situation features that are relevant to the agent's goals are rebound 'on the fly'.

The reliance of the situational theory on indexical/functional rather than symbol/object representation shows it is built over different ontological categories: *situations, aspects* of situations, *actions, activities* (groups of situation/action pairs), *environmental structure,* and *environmental affordances.*

To illustrate the situational theory and how it differs from the deliberative theory, consider a rat searching for food in a connected maze without cycles (Figure 14.1 (a)). The rat could:

1. explore and build a mental model by *conceptually* lifting the roof off the maze; or
2. use a left-hand, wall-following rule to reach the food.

The first requires the rat to gather and hold a representation of the maze, as viewed from above and which includes all objects in the maze, before deducing a plan of action that is to be effected by it. The aerial view in Figure 14.1 (a) shows this (deliberative) view. The second is a situational approach, shown in the ground view in Figure 14.1 (b), where the rat notices a limited range of situations relevant to its activity and of which it becomes aware by sensing these aspects – the absence and presence of walls. To act, the rat only needs to be aware of the absence and presence of walls near it, and it is not interested in anything else in its environment. In this way representation is purely indexical (centred on the rat) and functional (for its acting).

Figure 14.1. The two views of 'Rat World'.

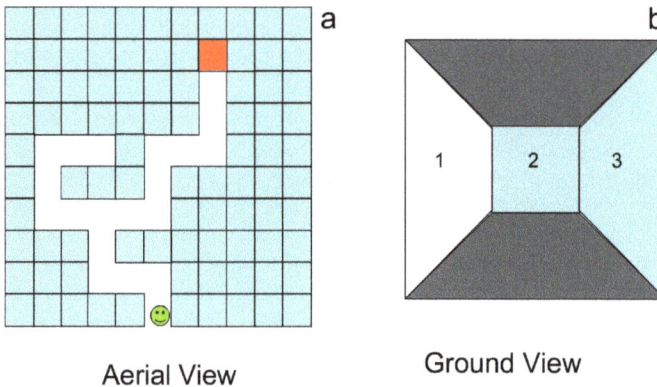

Aerial View   Ground View

In the 'ground view' there are three aspects, numbered 1, 2 and 3. These three aspects completely determine the situation the rat is in, at least in relation to its seeking food. The rat will then select the action appropriate for the situation. All possible situations and their associated responses can be grouped into an activity (called 'seeking food in a maze').

As stated earlier, myopic-situated actions rely on environmental affordances for their efficacy. In this example, the environmental affordance is that the maze is singly connected and does not have cycles. It is the existence of this structural property of the maze that ensures that if the rat invokes the activity it will reliably reach food. This maze-navigating example illustrates the general point made by advocates of the situational theory (Agre and Horswill, 1992) and ecological theories of behaviour (Gibson, 1977; Schoggen, 1989) that environmental structures, or affordances, make a significant contribution to the production of goal-directed behaviour of real agents in real environments. As Agre and Horswill (1992) put it: 'it is almost as if these surroundings were an extension of one's mind'.

There are three ways in which a situational system is brought into being. First, a situational system could *evolve* so that agent actions and the effects of actions knit perfectly with the environment and situations to make activities reliable. Biological organisms are excellent examples of evolved situational systems. In many cases, such as social activities, the activity and its environment may have *co-evolved*. Second, an agent may *learn* an activity by seeing the effect of actions in specific situations. In this case, trial and error is used to find the action rules that best exploit the structures in the environment, but also environments might be chosen because of their particular affordances for action. Third, and this is the approach we propose for information systems, a system can be *designed* so that actions in response to situations have desired effects. Depending on constraints, either or both the action rules and the environment structures will be deliberately designed to ensure the reliability of an activity. It is for this purpose that we propose our methodology, and it is a distinctive feature that 'environmental engineering' is part of it. We assume that some level of iteration may be needed.

When an agent is confronted with an unknown situation, or when an existing activity is not reliable in an environment, there are at least three ways for the agent to respond. The most extreme response is to deliberate from first principles, much like the deliberative theory of agency. According to Heidegger, in his analysis of 'breakdown' (Dreyfus, 1991), an agent will resort to an ascending hierarchy of situated practices of repair before resorting to pure deliberation. For instance, an agent might first engage in another activity that is closely related to the failed routine activity but suited to a slightly different environment. An example of this would be using a different maze-solving routine. Alternatively, the agent could reason about the activities themselves without necessarily building a complete external world-model, which would amount to invoking a routine of problem solving.

We have used the situational theory of agency, as it is discussed in robotics and other disciplines, to determine the concepts central to an agent-centred situational system. Whereas the deliberative theory suggests information systems design should emphasise modelling the world using objects, properties, relations and states, and deduction upon these models to determine action (such as decision support and planning), the situational theory would make central the notions of an activity, situations that comprise activities, actions that are a reaction to situations, and aspects that allow situations to be detected. Also the situational theory would emphasise the importance of proper structuring of environments of action, which is largely ignored in the deliberative approach. Thus, a methodology for designing situational systems must:

1. *Identify the multiple agents and their specific environments that constitute the total situational system.* Situational systems of any complexity will consist of multiple interacting agents (human and technical) each situated in their own unique environment.
2. *Identify the activities that need to be undertaken by the situational systems in pursuit of specific goals.*
3. *Analyse activities of agents into the situations, their aspects, and actions constituting each activity.* Activities can only work if an agent is able to notice when it is in a particular situation and is able to act routinely.
4. *Analyse environmental structures which afford goal attainment for each activity.* Identification of environmental structures is important because they enable an agent to achieve a goal using largely reactive situated actions. Thus, situated systems design is partly 'environmental engineering'.
5. *Check analytically whether the environmental structure identified or engineered, interacting with the situation-action pairs identified for a particular activity, will result in reliable goal achievement.* If not, repeat and refine Steps 3 and 4 until activities within suitably structured environments are found that require a minimum number of deliberative choices on the part of the agents.

6. *Identify choices remaining within the situations within activities that are not accom-modated by environmental affordances. This will define the function of the informational component of the system, which will allow all choices to be resolved by reference to it.* In situated systems the information system component is minimal and remains simply to provide aspects that resolve situations that prevent activities from becoming routine

The final methodology would consist of detailed documented guidelines for performing these steps together with appropriate representational analytical tools.

Thus far, the only experience in analysing situational systems in the literature is for designing robots and software agents. It has not been explicitly applied to socio-technical systems. However, there exist evolved routine work systems involving human actors and we are interested in examining their workings with respect to each of the theories of agency and drawing conclusions about how they work based on the examination. Should they be found to be consistent with the situational theory of agency, we may add depth to our understanding of the characteristics of situational systems. Consequently, in the following section we discuss three cases of evolved manual systems supporting routines. Manual systems are used in this paper because they are examples of effective situational systems. The design methodology for situational information systems assumes that agent environments, sensing mechanisms for situations, and actions may need to be designed from scratch and are thus 'blue sky'. Fine-tuning will be required where any unreliable activities are found: essentially 'tweaking' them to make them more effective. Fine-tuning will involve further moulding of the environment and improvement in sensing situations.

Learning from evolved manual systems

In this section we examine three user-designed routine systems in air traffic control, small-scale manufacturing (the Cash System), and large-scale lean manufacturing (the Kanban System). These systems have all been described in the literature and are interesting because their design does not fit traditional approaches to systems analysis and design. Although these are all manual systems, we do not intend our methodology to be applied purely to manual systems. But despite the fact that the systems we examine are manual, they can nevertheless give us important insights into how situated users view and represent their immediate situation (as opposed to the aerial view of the world used in the deliberative theory). In this section we examine each of the systems by exploring three things: what is being represented, what theory of agency is more likely to be useful in explaining its workings, and what features it has that may be helpful when designing systems to support similar cases.

The structure of the section is as follows: in each subsection, we describe each system, discuss the approach to representation in the system, and classify the system as likely to be either situational or deliberative. We conclude the section with a discussion of what this tells us about designing situational systems.

Air traffic control: landing by the strips system

Airports have traditionally used a largely manual system for landing planes (Mackay et al., 1998). The system is still respected and used in many places, and in this sense is resilient. The system is routine and has an air traffic controller seated in front of a radar screen at an angled table of flight strips. The flight strips can be placed on the table in various configurations in relation to each other. Each airport has several air traffic controllers controlling different parts of the air space around the airport.

The activity of landing a flight begins with a printed-paper flight strip containing basic flight plan information. This strip is generated by computer or can be handwritten in the absence of a working computer system. Figure 14.2 shows a typical flight strip.

Figure 14.2. A flight strip describing Air France Flight 540 (Mackay, 1998, p. 322).

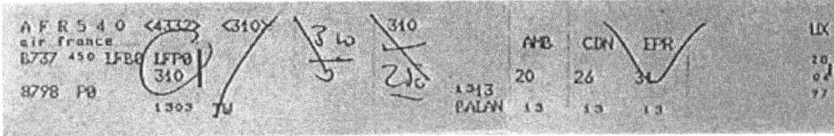

As an aircraft approaches an airport, a flight controller takes over control of its landing. When a new strip is generated, the controller's first task is to remove it from the printer and insert it into a strip holder. Strips are continually picked up and put down, reordered, grouped, offset, moved into columns, arranged and rearranged on the controller's table to denote different traffic conditions. The placement of the strips provides the controllers with information regarding action additional to that written on the strips. As the landing progresses, the flight passes from one controller to another by physical handover of the flight strip that, by its nature, is palpable for both controllers. Often controllers are side by side thus facilitating handover to another sector by structuring the area to help the activity.

Once a controller takes control of a flight strip, he gradually adds information to the typed strip (as seen in Figure 14.3). The markings allow controllers to look at a group of flight strips and quickly select the ones coming under their control and other information about how the activity is progressing. The layout of strips also gives a controller an immediate appreciation of the control environment (involving many flights) thus helping the controller to select the next action.

Figure 14.3. The strips being manipulated by an operator.

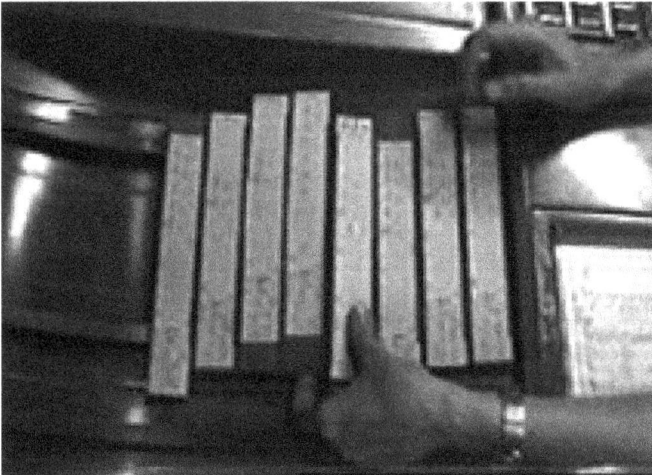

Each strip represents the activity of landing a specific flight and contains information important to landing the plane, not directly relating to the plane itself. In this way, the information on a strip is not tied to any specific object. Neither does each strip contain all of the information required to land the flights that are under control. It is the structuring of the controller's environment using the strips that shows information beyond that which is on the strips themselves. For example, the way the strips are stacked in Figure 14.3 means something specific for the controllers and helps them to remember and reason about the flights they are landing. Handing over control of flights from one controller to another is achieved by passing strips and is facilitated by how the room is laid out, and such handovers seldom include verbal exchanges. The limited space where strips can be placed alerts the controller to busy situations because room for new strips is then hard to find. In these situations controllers will hold new strips in their hands. Controllers sometimes write their own strips when unusual things occur, relying on the convenience and flexibility of paper.

Analysing this system using the deliberative approach is not straightforward. No representation is tied to a specific object. Each strip is about landing a flight rather than the flight itself or the aeroplane. Together, the strips are about the activities of landing that are under the control of the controller. None of them describes a flight enough to say that they represent an object in the sense of the deliberative approach to modelling.

In contrast, this system is easily related to the situational theory of agency. The strips represent the activity of landing a plane and, together with other strips and their relative position, these are sufficient to enable a controller to appreciate the current situation and to select actions. This, in our view, is a more plausible explanation than one based on the deliberative theory of agency.

Small-scale efficient 'cottage' manufacturing: the Cash Compressor System

A small factory (Cash Engineering Research) manufactures air compressors and has built up a system for doing so over several years. The workers in the factory have played an active role in designing the system. Known as the Cash Compressor System, the system is for production control in a small factory of four staff manufacturing about 200 air compressors a year. The system has a whiteboard that represents non-routine aspects of the compressors being made. There are no computers in the factory. What is interesting is how little information is represented on the whiteboard without compromising control or efficiency.

The factory is designed so that the person taking orders on the telephone in the middle of the factory has full view of all available stock hanging on shelves lining the walls. The main components of the system include a whiteboard of open customer orders and the physical parts of the air compressors that, by their construction, implicitly contain information about their own method of manufacture. The information on the whiteboard is job-specific including name of client, and options such as colour, and compressor motor size. The system has been designed deliberately in this way to reduce the need to represent things.

Manufacturing commences when the order is received by phone and a line order is added to the whiteboard. The parts for making the customer's compressor are checked for availability visually, and if need be, ordered on a one-off basis. The machine assembler then takes a machine base and begins construction, referring to the whiteboard only for order-specific information that is not part of the standard assembly routine.

What is interesting in the Cash System is what is not represented. There is no information about how to construct the machine: the machine acts as its own 'jig' through devices for guiding a tool or part to a specific place. Employees have learned the limited number of techniques used with the 'jig'. There is no parts-list or inventory system: the availability and quantity of parts holdings are clearly seen on the shelf. The only recorded re-quirements-related information is in the reference to non-standard choices on the whiteboard.

If this system were to be explained by the deliberative theory of agency, representation would include detailed information about each compressor being manufactured. This is not the case in the Cash System where very minimal information is kept explicitly on the whiteboard. No rules can be found to enable a worker to take the individual parts and assemble a compressor. Instead we see the next action being selected by the partly manufactured machine being presented to the worker. Only a limited range of choice is available to them. The worker knows what happens next because there is very little (often no) choice confronting them. When there is a choice, the whiteboard tells them the option to be selected based on the customer's desires.

The Cash System is a highly situational one where representation is almost absent. Action is selected by routinely acting on the partly manufactured machine based purely on the current status of the machine. In the Cash System, 'the world (is) its own model' (Brooks, 1991) in that the machine 'jigs' itself and parts are visible, obviating the need for stock data. Consequently, the current situation is found in the visible state of the stock on the shelf, the number of jobs on the floor, the condition of the partly manufactured com-pressors that are the jobs on the floor, and the markings on the whiteboard. Due to the careful design of the factory layout, all these are immediately visible to a worker. In addition, the use of a single small whiteboard allows the foreman to grasp the total production situation at a glance. The recorded information on the whiteboard is largely ephemeral (except for a small amount of recorded information for warranty purposes that is kept in a book). When a job is finished it is removed from the whiteboard and the new situation is revealed.

Large-scale lean manufacturing: the Kanban system

The Japanese Kanban system (Schonberger, 1987; Womack et al., 1990) is widely used in the automotive industry for the activity of replenishing parts for production. Kanban is the Japanese word for 'card' and the movement of cards in this system controls stock levels and replenishment activities. For each part there is a fixed size container. A Kanban has printed on it minimal information about the item it is used for, usually product ID, the primary supplier and the workstation where the part is used (see Figure 14.4). There are a fixed number of Kanbans in existence for each item and, except when *desired* manufactured capacity changes, they are neither created nor destroyed.

Figure 14.4. A typical Kanban card.

Imagine a container half-full of parts on a factory floor. The container has a Kanban attached to it. Goods are taken from the container, which is stored at the production workstation, until it is empty. The Kanban in the empty container is then placed on a Kanban board near the goods receiving area where it becomes a signal that the item needs replenishment. The board has hooks in supplier order. When placed on the board the Kanban becomes 'free'. The board has the Kanban system operation rules (Kanban rules) clearly displayed. When a supplier's truck arrives with shipments of items to deliver, the driver checks the Kanban board and takes the Kanbans on the relevant hook back to the supplier's site to authorise replenishment of these items next time around. When the items are subsequently supplied, the Kanbans are returned to the work stations, in the full containers, where they are used.

The deliberative theory of agency cannot relate at all to the Kanban system. The cards do not consistently correspond to anything specific in reality. When they reside with the parts they could be thought of as being a representation of these parts, although they have no system purpose in this state and they will later actually refer to a different group of parts. When they are free, they represent a stock shortage. When they are on the Kanban board they are an authority to re-supply the parts. There are no records of stock levels that we would expect to see in a deliberative approach.

Examining the system using the situational theory, a Kanban card represents part of the activity of maintaining stock of a specific item. All of the Kanbans, together with the rules by which they are used, provide simple ways of reasoning about stock. If many of the same type of Kanban appear at the board then an undersupply may be occurring or there may be trouble with the supplier's transport. An absence over a prolonged period indicates a delayed manufacturing process. In addition to simple, reactive rules for Kanban movement, the affordances of the physical nature of Kanban cards (they can neither be created nor destroyed and they cannot be in more than one place at a time) indirectly enforce all important replenishment business rules, in particular that there can only be a fixed number of parts in the system.

The Kanban is rebound over time from one full container to a different full container some time later. An interesting feature of this system that is the Kanban's meaning changes according to where it is. When it is travelling back to the supplier it functions as a request for an order from the manufacturer. When it is on the board it shows a shortage of a specific item.

Common features of the systems

Each of the systems outlined above has features in common and that mirror the features found described in situational systems literature: activities, situations, aspects of situations, environmental structure, and environmental affordances. We now examine each of these characteristics, highlighting the approaches each system uses. We emphasise interesting features that add practical depth to our understanding of the theoretical constructs.

All systems use tokens to represent activities. Physical strips in landing aircraft represent flights being landed. Rows on the whiteboard represent activities of making a compressor at Cash. Cards in the Kanban system represent the activity of replenishing goods. None of the tokens represent objects and properties in the way advocated in existing data modelling methodologies. An interesting feature of these manual systems is the use of positions of tokens to help actors in reasoning about activities. In the landing system, the relative position of the strips helps the controller to reason about all landings. Kanban cards on the board help operators to reason about goods shortages and priorities. The importance of manipulation of concrete things in the environment for practical reasoning has been emphasised by writers on situated cognition (Lave, 1988; Clancey, 1997).

Tokens representing activities often have information about aspects of situations on them that show the actor the situation they are in. This is best illustrated in the landing system by the markings on strips. However, even in the landing system the position of strips relative to each other also shows aspects of situations. Similarly, in the Kanban system the presence or absence of tokens in various places reveals situations to human actors in the system. The Cash System partly shows aspects of situations on the whiteboard and partly in how much of the compressor has been completed. This is because the stage of manufacture of the compressor shows part of the situation to the worker. This parsimonious use of representation is quite consistent with the situated view, in which a small number of aspects are sufficient to trigger a situated action, but inconsistent with the deliberative approach.

Structuring the environment of systems is critical to situational activity because without it repeated actions would not reliably result in goal attainment. This is achieved in two ways. First, it constrains the possible new situations an actor experiences as a result of action and this reduces the cognitive burden of choosing alternatives. The structure of the maze is an example of this. Second, the environmental structure may help reasoning about activities. Often the palpability of tokens and their physical properties help deliver both benefits. In the landing system, a controller can position the strips relative to each other because of the slope and size of the table, thus enabling situation detection and reasoning about activities. In the Cash System, the partly manufactured machine, by being its own jig, only permits a restricted range of actions. The Kanban system limits the quantity of stock circulating by having only a limited number of cards. Workers can reason about delays in the activity of stock replenishment or in manufacturing by noticing prolonged absence or presence of Kanban cards in particular places. In addition, each of these systems requires considerable structuring of the broader environment of work to make these simple reactive systems work. For instance, the Cash factory is laid out so that the availability of all relevant part options is directly visible to the foreman when adding new records to the whiteboard. The need for work environment structuring, for instance the use of teams and production cells, for the successful implementation of Kanban is also emphasised in the *Just-In-Time* literature (Schonberger, 1987).

Tokens, or other parts of environments, also help actors to hand over situations to others. In the landing system, a controller can hand a strip to another controller because the controllers are often next to each other. In the Cash compressor system, a half-finished machine by its very state facilitates a worker in taking over the activity and situation from another worker.

In the flight landing system not only does the passing of a single strip pass the situation of a particular flight from one operator to another, but the visible arrangement of all strips is used to hand over the total flight situation at the change of shift (Mackay et al., 1998). Similarly, Kanban movements hand over a shortage situation between the multiple participating actors, while the arrangement on the Kanban board allows the total shortage situation to be seen by foremen.

Implications for a situational methodology

By examining the systems described above we can draw two groups of implications for a situational methodology. First, the examples exhibit many characteristics consistent with the situational theory of agency. Second, there are characteristics that emerge from these systems that add to our understanding of the practical application of the situational theory. We discuss each of these below.

Each of the systems confirms activities, situations, actions, environmental structure and environmental affordances as important ontological categories for situational systems. Fundamentally, activities, not objects, are represented in these systems. Situations and aspects of situations are shown to actors so they can select actions or reason about their activities. Environments are structured and use affordances that increase the reliability of the goal of an activity being realised. The relationship between environmental structure and affordance is sometimes complex. This is seen in the Cash System where the machine is its own jig. The jig is designed so that the environment of the worker changes in such a way that precisely one situation is returned.

A characteristic emerging from the study is the extensive use of physical tokens (e.g. strips) to contain information about situations and activities and to facilitate reasoning. Tokens often represent different situations according to their physical relationship to other tokens, and their physicality aids reasoning about situations for human actors. The need for manipulation in situated reasoning is an important feature of these systems and cannot be ignored when designing a methodology for situational systems.

Physical tokens are also used to hand over situations to other actors involved in an activity. This is illustrated in the flight landing system where controllers routinely hand strips to other controllers. Successful handover is helped by the receiving controller having to physically handle the token.

In these systems tokens and other parts of an agent's environment play a critical role in representation. A human agent uses tokens in the environment to reason about activity and to notice situations. Tokens contain some, but not all, information about situations and activities. Often it is the relationship between tokens that completes the picture for an agent. Contrastingly, deliberative systems require a model of the world where objects and their properties are self-contained and correspond with objects in the human agent's environment.

The use of physical tokens requires that careful attention is given to the capabilities of computerised technology such as mobile devices when designing information systems. Poor selection of devices that do not deliver the required palpability, capacity for manipulation, or representational ability may place the success of the whole information system in danger. Further, environments of computerised parts of the information system must be carefully designed with these findings in mind.

Following our examination of manual situational systems, the methodology still consists of six steps. The details of specific steps, however, must be augmented with results from our analysis of the systems. These largely give insights into the implementation of Stage 6 in the method. First, in the manual systems explored, physical tokens are often employed by agents to represent parts of activities and contain information about situations. These are seen to be important for both situation recognition and for reasoning about action. Arguably, they do not reduce simply to the information displayed on them (Mackay et al., 1998). This gives an important insight into the unique character that the informational component of situational systems should possess. Although not all situational systems may need to employ the idea of physically manipulable tokens as the representational component of the system, it seems that it is a prudent approach to consider this possibility in conjunction with information and communication technology as a possible form that part of the information system might take. For instance, in a follow-up study of the manual air traffic control system described above, Mackay et. al. (1998)

trialled a computer-enhanced physical token-based substitute for the flight strips. Clearly new ICT technologies, such as mobile devices and ubiquitous computing can play a role here. Second, where relevant, the environment of the agents must be designed to aid situation handover between agents.

Discussion and conclusions

In this paper we have proposed an initial methodology for designing situational information systems. Using traditional methodologies, designers decompose the world into object correlates for implementation in databases where information about real world objects is held. A situational approach is, by contrast, likely to result in data about activities and situations being recorded so that action can be undertaken. The systems designed are likely to be radically different from those resulting from traditional methodologies. For example, it is highly unlikely that an IS designer trained in existing design methodologies would design a system with the simplicity and elegance of the Kanban system whereas an operator on the shop floor would probably see Kanbans as a logical system for controlling stock. This observation, which is in principle testable, dramatically highlights the gulf between information design theory and operations practice, which our methodology addresses. Furthermore, the use of Kanbans cannot be dismissed as merely a quaint or anachronistic manual system because it is now very widely used in the high-tech automotive manufacturing industry where it often replaces computerised systems based on the deliberative approach. Thus, this methodology has the potential to revolutionise information systems and, we expect, will lead to much more effective information systems in specific contexts.

We built the initial methodology by examining concepts from the situational systems literature and by building a tentative methodology based on these concepts. We then examined some existing (manual) situational systems found in the literature involving human actors to deepen our understanding of the characteristics of situational systems and thereby to strengthen the tentative methodology.

We have found, in examining human actors as part of evolved situational systems, that environmental structuring and the role of physical tokens in an actor's environment are critical to designing situational systems. Representation of situations and activities in an agent's environment helps situated reasoning and enables action with little deliberation. Physical tokens help agents to hand over situations and to solve problems. We also expect that, in computerised information systems, specific physical information and communications technology may be required to support physical tokens for human actors in these systems.

In future work, we intend using three action research cycles (Baskerville and Wood-Harper, 1996; Lau, 1999) to successively refine the methodology from here. In each cycle, an already implemented system in an organisation will be analysed and changed by applying the situational systems methodology. The methodology used in each cycle will be the output methodology of the previous cycle (or that emerging from the pilot cycle, if it is the first). The system selected in a specific cycle will be one that has been implemented using a traditional design and development methodology, involves routine work, and has been deemed to be ineffective.

The methodology being refined in this project is likely to add a much deeper understanding to disparate attempts at designing information systems for difficult contexts involving repetitive routine activity. Soft Systems Methodology, Human-computer Interfaces, and Ubiquitous Computing are all examples of other possible approaches but they lack unifying theory. For the first time, there is prospect of a methodology for building situational information systems based on firm theoretical foundations.

15. Conversations at the electronic frontier: the information systems business language (ISBL)

Douglas Hamilton, *School of Information Management and Systems, Monash University, Victoria*

Abstract

Information systems (IS) capable of acting as autonomous organisational agents are becoming prevalent in contemporary society. This paper proposes that an artificial language, designed to facilitate transactions involving at least one such system as a participant, is emerging in the world of business. The language combines English terminology with IS-style definitions, and is based on a strictly limited lexicon, a rigid syntax, and a controlled context of use. The paper argues that the language can be used as an instrument of social power, and discusses a number of possible developments in this regard.

Introduction

A new language, referred to for the purposes of this paper as the information systems business language or ISBL, is being born in the world of business. It is an artificial language (Lotman, 1990), designed to eliminate possibilities for misunderstandings in the conduct of standardised business transactions. Its primary source language is English but it incorporates information systems (IS) concepts, definitions, symbols and gestures and is therefore not a subset of English. The language has a sphere of operation restricted to interactions involving at least one autonomous IS, and is still in the very early stages of development. The development process is erratic and likely to remain so, in that the language is a by-product of pressures for rationalisation in business interactions, rather than the outcome of a conscious design activity.

Business, like other areas of human activity, is mediated by, and understood through, language. The nature of business has, however, always been such as to impose a premium on the use of literal language and the avoidance of figurative expressions (Yates, 1989). This has led over time to a reliance on strict terminology, a reliance that has been intensified by the emergence of automated systems with zero tolerance for ambiguity. In introducing systems of this type, organisations and system designers have endeavoured to eradicate the problems of meaning that can arise from different presumptions and frames of reference (Fish, 1978) by rigidly defining and controlling the context of interaction. While this has not eliminated all possibilities for misunderstandings to occur, it has for the most part substantially reduced their effects.

Most IS have a purely instrumental character in the sense that they provide support, often very sophisticated support, for a wide range of organisational activities, but cannot be construed as acting independently in a social context. Autonomous systems dealing with other autonomous entities external to an organisation are, in contrast, qualitatively different in that they effectively act as responsible agents of the organisation. These systems, of which an automatic teller machine (ATM) is perhaps the canonical example

(Dos Santos and Peffers, 1995), have been assigned responsibilities for making decisions and taking actions on the basis of information given, received and interpreted in social interactions. While the activities in which they engage are repetitive and mundane, it is the principle involved that is of interest in this paper; there is nothing intrinsic that limits their sphere of operations. If meaningful interactions occur, it seems to follow that such systems must be ascribed a form of social intelligence.

Interactions with autonomous systems take the form of conversations in which progress is achieved through the turn-taking exchange of information, and the proposal in this paper is that such systems and their interlocutors can be conceptualised as speaking a language, the ISBL. While the language is very much in its formative stages, and variations in definitions and usages are still common, there is enormous pressure for standardisation of the terms used. An easily accessible example of this process in action is provided by the progressive routinisation of autonomous payment systems, enabling organisations to use common interfaces and standard payment 'scripts'.

It is perhaps the fact that their operations are mundane that has limited the amount of theoretical interest in autonomous IS. Strategic analysts have not overlooked their competitive significance (Dos Santos and Peffers, 1995), but the systems themselves are generally not particularly complex, and have therefore been of little technical concern. The argument in this paper is, however, that they represent a social development of great potential significance, and that their emerging capacity to 'speak' a common language heralds the realisation of some of that potential.

The development of the ISBL is being fuelled in practice by a range of IS integration initiatives based on enterprise system (ERP) packages, electronic data interchange (EDI), government data-sharing, and business-to-business (B2B) procurement exchanges, all of which rely for their effectiveness on the implementation of standardised IS constructs including data and process definitions. It is these constructs, rather than the perceived interfaces, that enable systems to 'talk' both to people and to other systems. The new language is evolving at an electronic frontier where people and systems are learning how to converse meaningfully with each other, making it a kind of pidgin language (Holm, 2000; Czarniawska, 2003). Pidgin languages are compromise languages that use a restricted lexicon and a rigid syntax to facilitate trade between different cultural groups (Holm, 2000). Continuing development of the ISBL involves a compromise between English usage and the rigid prescriptions of computer systems; while English is the source for much of the terminology, definitional relations are to formal constructs and not to the flexible concepts referenced by natural language.

The general justification for the proposal in this paper resides in the explanatory power of the linguistic perspective. The ISBL concept facilitates the understanding and analysis of a range of IS-related phenomena, particularly organisational issues arising from systems integration initiatives. Several of these relate to social power, and the possibilities for autonomous systems to be used to entrench and extend existing power differentials affecting consumers, and organisations in dependent positions within major supply chains. These aspects are discussed in detail later in the paper.

Language and power

Following the work of theorists including Mead (1962), Goffman (1981), Foucault (1972) and Bourdieu (1991), it has come to be accepted that language plays a number of crucial roles in the establishment and maintenance of social relations. The types of mechanisms involved include the capacity to define a particular language as standard, to vocalise in a certain way, to control the vocabulary in use, and to control turn-taking and the direction of discourse (Bourdieu, 1991). The use of language for control purposes is simultaneously a reflection of existing power relationships, and an exercise in extending and entrenching them (Fairclough, 1989).

There are some qualitative differences between the ISBL and natural languages, and these tend to intensify power effects. The ISBL is essentially an artificial language designed to eliminate the possibility of misconstructions: 'for a total guarantee of adequacy between the transmitted and received message there has to be an artificial (simplified) language … the universalism inherent to natural language is in principle alien to it' (Lotman, 1990, p. 13). The precision of the ISBL enables conversational mechanisms such as turn-taking to be applied as controls rather than to check understandings. This is consistent with the ways in which prescribed turn-taking is used to control the sequence of events and responses that occur during rituals (Wolf, 1999, p. 128).

Issues of efficiency and convenience can be so compelling that questions concerning autonomous IS can naturally reduce to issues of technology adoption, rates of diffusion, and trust (Gefen et al., 2003). The linguistic perspective provides an antidote to this in the form of an analytical platform from which to show that there can be losers as well as winners, and that there is a fine line between encouragement and coercion where technology adoption is concerned.

Conversations at the electronic frontier

The term 'electronic frontier' is used here to refer to the virtual space in which people and automated systems interact as autonomous agents, with the use of 'frontier' justified on the grounds that the two cultural groups (people and autonomous systems) are still in the early stages of meeting, interacting with, and understanding each other (Holm, 2000). The driving force behind development of the ISBL is the problem of finding a vehicle that will enable people, who speak a natural language with all the inbuilt vagaries and inconsistencies of such languages, and systems that speak a conceptually limited but highly precise language of their own, to converse with each other. The emerging language is in this regard English-like, but is not English.

Three types of interaction involving autonomous IS can occur as follows:

1. between an autonomous individual and an organisation represented by an automated system;
2. between an organisation represented by a person and an organisation represented by an automated system;
3. between two organisations each represented by an automated system (in some types of B2B procurement exchanges for instance).

For the purposes of this paper, the focus will continue to be on interactions between a person acting individually and an autonomous system representing an organisation, although it is assumed that the logic is equally applicable to the other two cases. Figure 15.1 shows the basic logic of interactions mediated by the ISBL in schematic form.

Figure 15.1. Business transaction mediated by the ISBL.

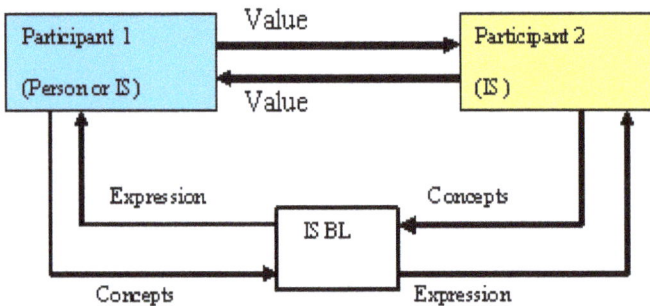

Figure 15.1 shows a standard type of transaction proceeding in parallel at two generic levels. At the action level, it involves an exchange of values, for example the provision of cash in return for the right to debit a bank account. At the second level, the exchange of information supports and enables the completion of first level action. It is axiomatic that genuine communication can only occur on the basis of shared understandings (Gibbs, 1999); in this situation the shared understandings are represented in terminology sourced from the language the participants have in common, conceptualised here as the ISBL.

Permitted interactions are of course tightly scripted by the designers of autonomous systems. An ATM will, for example, work according to a fully defined job description (Dos Santos and Peffers, 1995), but must have the authorisation, the basic intelligence, and the conversational competence to complete transactions on behalf of the organisation(s) represented. That the level of transactional complexity is low is essentially irrelevant to the argument being developed; the practical implication of an effective interaction is that two entities acting autonomously have been able to communicate successfully. The linguistic foundations will in practice usually be sufficiently unproblematic to stay below the threshold of attention, but they can become salient under conditions of breakdown. Thus, for example, the lack of conversational repair mechanisms when dealing with an ATM quickly become apparent when it returns an incorrect amount of money or refuses to recognise a credit card.

Propositions

The following lists twelve theoretical propositions that are discussed as a group in subsequent sections. The propositions are framed in descriptive terms as topics susceptible to empirical research. It is important to note that they were developed on the assumption that a positive perspective on the ISBL is embedded in current thinking about systems and standardisation. The view that autonomous IS provide great benefits of convenience to consumers is not contested, and it is in fact impossible to see how the ever increasing volumes of business transactions could be effectively handled without them (Weizenbaum, 1984, p. 28). The argument is, however, that the increasing spread of ISBL-mediated activity creates possibilities for the exercise of power and the exploitation of consumers that warrant empirical research.

The propositions are as follows:

1. Autonomous IS have been installed as organisational agents.
2. The business behaviour of autonomous IS can be analysed in linguistic terms.

3. To the extent that autonomous IS share basic IS concepts with standardised definitions, they can be conceptualised as speaking a specific language. The language is referred to in this paper as the information systems business language or ISBL.
4. Organisational customers interacting with autonomous IS must use the ISBL for communication purposes.
5. The continuing standardisation of IS definitions in data, process structures and objects, is contributing to the further development of the ISBL.
6. Implementation of the ISBL has social effects on relationships between organisations and their customers; the ISBL can therefore function as an instrument of social power.
7. The emergence of the ISBL as an instrument of social power will tend to encourage its wider adoption.
8. The wider adoption of the ISBL will tend to inhibit possibilities of structural change, by lengthening change management cycles and making change management processes more complex.

The following propositions relate specifically to social power effects:

9. The efficiency gains facilitated by adoption of the ISBL will encourage attempts to impose it as the standard language for conducting some types of business transactions.
10. General adoption of the ISBL will tend to marginalise some people, and create new types of 'outsiders'.
11. Adoption of the ISBL will exacerbate organisations' difficulties in dealing with exceptional cases.
12. Adoption of the ISBL will tend to impede people with unusual or exceptional requirements in the pursuit of their transactional interests.

Information systems with social autonomy

The first computer-based IS were essentially data processing systems designed to assist organisations with the processing and storage of the vast amount of data generated in the course of contemporary business activity (Somogyi and Galliers, 1987). The extension of the scope of IS implementations to encompass the installation of systems capable of acting as autonomous organisational agents has been so gradual as to be almost imperceptible. It has, however, been the case at least since the introduction of ATMs, that some IS directly substitute for, rather than simply support, humans in selected interactive organisational roles. The extent to which this type of substitution has occurred is probably much greater than is obvious on the surface, for it is surely correct to say that there are many organisations in which front-of-house staff are supporting the systems that are actually taking the decisions, rather than the reverse. As might be expected during the early stages of what is in effect a quiet revolution, many situations where systems and humans share the decision-making powers can be somewhat ambiguous. This ambiguity can have awkward consequences, as in the case of Australia's Centrelink, an agency responsible for managing unemployment matters where, during the course of a recent furore over errors, some were blamed on systems taking decisions, and others on systems not taking decisions (McKinnon, 2004).

An autonomous IS is postulated as showing three behavioural characteristics that have traditionally been associated with the possession of intelligence and the capacity to use language effectively; it can understand meaningful input, it can be meaningfully responsive to that input, and it can take socially significant decisions that are responsive to the meanings developed in the interaction. The fact that one party may believe that the other party does not in any sense 'understand' what is going on does not seem to invalidate the perspective taken since the interaction occurs despite this. The effect is the same as if the transaction had involved two people, a meaningful conversation had taken place, and a mutually satisfactory outcome achieved.

The issue of meaning needs to be explicitly addressed, if only because it is difficult to see who or what within the organisation 'knows' what has happened once the transaction has been completed. To argue that the organisation itself is what 'understands' in effect simply shifts the problem up a level. Yet the conclusion that the actions taken have been socially meaningful seems inescapable; value has been exchanged in consequence of entering into the transaction, and the outcomes are fully binding on both parties. Clearly the original system designers would once have understood the process, and it is certain that company accountants and others will understand the nature of the relevant transactions in general terms, but this is not the same as having direct knowledge or an unmediated understanding of actual events. In a contemporary organisation it is in any case quite possible that the original programmers will have left or forgotten the details of the system. In a downsizing world there is no guarantee that anybody still working in the company will know any more about an autonomous system's activities than they would about those of any other colleague carrying out responsible work. The possibility that an autonomous system will carry on doing business on behalf of an organisation long after the last person to leave has turned off the lights is a real one.

It is notable that it is precisely the issue of understanding, or rather what or who understands, that has been at the heart of many an esoteric, acerbic debate in the cognitive science and artificial intelligence (AI) arenas (Rey, 1997). In his now famous 'Chinese Room' thought experiment, the philosopher John Searle postulates a system comprising various entities including people (who cannot speak Chinese) that is able to reliably and instantaneously translate English into Chinese by applying a set of categorical rules; Searle asks who or what it is that understands Chinese (Searle 1980, p. 422). No definitive answer (i.e. satisfactory to both proponents and critics of AI) has been forthcoming (Rey, 1997, p. 271). Alan Turing fell back on a purely behaviourist perspective when proposing the 'Turing test' (Turing, 1950), taking the view that if a system is able to fool its interlocutors about whether or not it is a person, then it should be taken as being able to think, but that was an approach that has caused more debates than it has resolved (Rey, 1997, p. 153).

Autonomous IS are small fry in comparison with the kind of complex and often threatening entity that is usually postulated when AI is discussed (Crevier, 1993). Yet the issue seems to be the same in principle, a view that is strengthened by the clear possibility that the interactional capacities of autonomous systems will continue to increase. With this in mind, the theoretical approach followed here is to adhere to a precedent from cognitive science, and for analytical purposes to ascribe the capacity to understand to the system – '[this] does not say that intentional systems *really* have beliefs and desires, but that one can explain and predict their behaviour by *ascribing* beliefs and desires to them ... the decision to adopt [this] strategy is pragmatic and not intrinsically right or wrong' (Dennett, 1978, p. 7 – emphases in original). The surrounding context makes it quite clear that ATMs were not the type of entity that Dennett had in mind when making his argument, but the logic seems equally applicable.

The information systems business language (ISBL)

It is now generally accepted that a language embeds a world view, or theory of the world (Gadamer, 1989; Pinker 1994), in that the concepts available within it limit what can and cannot be said in that language. The strong form of this idea is the Sapir-Whorf hypothesis, which states it is impossible to conceptualise something in the absence of the appropriate linguistic constructs, and that genuinely new ideas are therefore dependent for their adoption and survival on the progressive extension of the language (Aronoff and Rees-Miller, 2003, p. 99). This extreme view still has support from some philosophers and linguists, but even those who do not accept it in totality concede that the idea contains a critical insight – that possibilities of social interaction are constrained by the language available to the parties concerned (Pinker, 1994).

The ISBL shows this with unusual clarity in that the underlying content reflects both a very specific way of doing business, and a very restricted conceptual universe. It is important to note that a key distinction is drawn between the 'content' and 'expression' planes of a language (Eco, 1997), and that discussion in this paper is limited to the content plane. ISBL expression, which can involve combinations of mouse clicks, key presses, symbols and verbal statements, has some extremely interesting implications, particularly from the perspective of the social disadvantages for people who are unable to 'speak' the language, but these are left for subsequent investigation.

In basic terms, ISBL content is conceptualised as comprising a set of data, process and object definitions that:

1. enable communication between systems and people;
2. enable reference to basic business concepts;
3. enable meanings to be attributed to actions occurring in business transactions;
4. represent the rationalisation and standardisation of business terminology relevant to defined types of business transactions.

In effect, the ISBL is a language that mediates conversations at the electronic frontier; that is to say, at the point of intersection between people and automated systems. The terminology for use is strictly controlled. To take a specific example, the concept 'customer' may be instantiated in the ISBL as an entity characterised by a set of mandatory attributes including a name, address, and telephone number, and associated with a recorded history of one or more purchases from a relevant organisation. In a new transaction entered into by the customer and an IS, both implicitly agree to the use of ISBL terminology and concepts. The system presents itself at a venue at which interactions can occur, the putative customer identifies him- or herself, the system enquires as to the nature and scope of the transaction envisaged, the customer provides this additional information, the system responds, and so on through to an exchange of values and transactional closure. Communication has occurred, and has been mediated through a closely defined language.

Generally speaking the ISBL deals with concepts for which there are approximately equivalent expressions in natural languages. In English, these would include 'customer', 'product', 'service', 'account', 'asset', and 'invoice' among many others. The formality and rigour of ISBL definitions suggest that, while it might be a pidgin language at the moment, it could also be seen as a prototypical 'perfect language' (Eco, 1997) of business. As indicated earlier, there are fundamental differences between the ISBL and English, despite the superficial similarities, and these are summarised in Table 15.1.

Table 15.1. ISBL-English comparison

Language aspect	English	ISBL
Lexicon	Open-ended, additive	Restricted, predefined
Syntax	Enculturated, variable	Prescribed, rigid
Context	Uncontrolled	Controlled
Semantics	Variable in context	Invariant
Pragmatics	Intrinsic to use	None

A reasonable natural language definition of a customer is 'one who currently purchases anywhere; a buyer, purchaser' (Onions, 1973). Within this broad interpretation, the extension of the concept to encompass specific individuals can occur in a variety of ways, which can include personal familiarity, face recognition, showing a receipt from a previous transaction, or a conversation in which the person simply reveals an intention to buy. Both the customer and the vendor have the full resources of natural language to use in their attempt to establish a workable relationship. Such interactions are intrinsically messy, even in a highly structured bureaucracy, where the use of natural language provides a means by which the participants can, if they so choose, step outside any predefined scripts.

The definition of customer in the ISBL is quite different, being in practice something like 'an entity characterised by the following mandatory attributes', where the mandatory attributes might include identification number (valid) + account number (valid) + credit card number (valid) + credit status (valid). More to the point, the adopted definition is designed to leave no room for debate on terminological grounds; a person wishing to be identified as a customer must satisfy the validity requirements no matter what the previous status of his or her relationship with the organisation behind the autonomous system. It may seem redundant to stress the differences in the two conceptions in this way, but the free use of terms like 'customer' or 'client' or 'product' in published literature can help to conceal the full implications of the distinction being drawn here.

A major factor propelling development of the ISBL is that many business activities are supported by information content that tends to be broadly similar across organisations, and it has been recognised that very real gains in efficiency can be made through the general adoption of standardised definitions (Threlkel and Kavan, 1999). Thus, although there may be subtle differences in how different organisations interpret the meaning of the various business concepts involved, the generic assumption is that there should be sufficient commonality of interpretation to make the prospect of coming up with a standard definition feasible as well as economically appealing. It is, in fact, the possibilities for standardisation that have driven a range of systems integration initiatives including B2B procurement exchanges, EDI-based inter-organisational systems, and various types of data sharing arrangements. Progress can be difficult to achieve in practice (Goodhue et al., 1992), but is nevertheless being made on several fronts (Wyzalek, 2000) to the extent that the emergence of a standard or 'authorised' version of the ISBL is becoming probable rather than possible.

Actor network theory

The closest parallel to the ISBL concept is to be found in what is now generally termed actor network theory (or ANT), where both human and non-human entities are assigned roles in the constitution and functioning of a network (Callon and Latour, 1981; Callon, 1989). Callon (1989), for instance, includes the Renault car-making firm, a new kind of fuel cell, consumers and engineers as components of a network concerned with the proposed introduction of an electric car into the French car market. ANT has itself been proposed as a promising theoretical perspective for IS researchers (Underwood, 2002).

There are, however, some basic differences in concept. The proposal in this paper is that autonomous IS be themselves considered as social actors, whereas it is the network that is the actor in ANT. Non-human entities may wholly or partly constitute such a network, but they are held to contribute to the actions of the network by virtue of their position and their associations, not because they act autonomously themselves (Callon, 1989, p. 93). The ANT concept is therefore an important conceptual precedent for the proposal in this paper, but is applicable in a radically different analytical context.

Social impacts of the ISBL

The positive benefits of transaction standardisation have been too well canvassed to need much discussion here. They include streamlined business operations, efficiency gains in dealing with customers, improved data accuracy and reliability, reduced infra-structure, and inter-organisational links for the transmission and sharing of data (Weill and Broadbent, 1998; Parker and Benson, 1988). When standardisation is coupled with the installation of autonomous systems that can be operational around the clock, further benefits come from the reduction or elimination of time dependencies. As the technical problems inhibiting systems integration are progressively solved, there seems no reason to doubt that further efficiency benefits will continue to materialise.

The instrumental impacts of the ISBL on power relations are, however, more problematic and await empirical research. While the range of possibilities is extensive, the linguistic perspective suggests at least two directions for analysis that are likely to be fruitful. These are, first, the consequences of attempts to extend the compass of the ISBL as a standard language of interaction and, second, the implications of limiting the vocabulary available to people wishing to conduct various types of transaction. Each of these appears to have some negative social implications.

A further issue is the possibility that the use of the ISBL as an instrument in support of power-seeking behaviour carries with it some hidden risks to the adopting organisations. These arise essentially from the loss of flexibility that is entailed. The extent of this risk is not easily assessed; what is argued here is that the widespread adoption of the ISBL would represent a commitment to stability tending to inhibit systems change.

Imposing the ISBL

The imposition of a standard version of the ISBL as the language for conducting some types of business transactions is a likely outcome on the basis of existing trends. One approach already in use is to use pricing policies and other strategies to ensure that business partners, including customers and suppliers, find it economically desirable to interact with autonomous systems. Organisations with an interest in imposing the ISBL in this way logically include all those working to an efficiency-oriented business model such as government departments and agencies, banks, utilities, and other organisations with highly routinised modes of doing business.

Examples of the approach can be found with the installation of B2B procurement ex-changes, where purchasers combine to develop a large transaction-processing vehicle based on standard definitions of goods and services (Hammer, 1996). What has quickly become apparent is that large companies can in this way put themselves in a position to dictate to their suppliers on modes of interaction, often at great expense to those other companies. The failure of a number of major B2B projects has somewhat slowed the pace of change in this area, but the innate potential for the exercise of control is evident.

Other examples on a smaller scale can also be found. One such is provided by the organ-isation Tabcorp, one of the major players in the Australian gambling industry. Despite public concern with the level of gambling in Australia, Tabcorp has consistently raised the level of the minimum bets that can be placed by telephone bettors through a human operator. This has been accompanied by an extension of the gambling period and a lowering of the betting minimum for gamblers willing to use online and voice recognition services that interface with autonomous systems. Punters have in effect been forced to decide whether to increase the size of their minimum bets, or use a service that anecdotal evidence suggests is widely disliked.

Vocabulary control

As discussed earlier, the installation and effective operation of an autonomous IS depends in practice on tight vocabulary control through the use of a rigid syntax and restricted lexicon. The effect this has is to very tightly constrain the range of possible directions a conversation can take, and to limit the scope of what a customer can do in the course of any interaction. This is efficient, convenient, and cost-effective.

The power implications are subtle but significant, in that the more people come to depend on the use of ISBL-based modes of interaction, either through economic incentives or the lure of convenience, the more accustomed they become to reduced possibilities for questioning and negotiating with organisations. What happens, in effect, is that the difficulties of dealing with exceptional or unusual issues become greater when the customer has to step outside the normal mode of interaction, use a different language of interaction, and rely on finding an organisational representative able to understand the problem. Given the focus on efficiency that an ISBL installation represents, one of the side effects is that the organisation itself also has a reduced capacity to talk about and understand exceptional circumstances. It seems likely that this type of issue will become increasingly problematic in relation to government agencies, where special cases can in any circumstances be difficult to resolve given the opacity of many rules and regulations (Herzfeld, 1992). A typical example is where a person seeking some form of social support is unable to satisfy an autonomous system that she or he has the attributes required of one of the organisation's clients, and is therefore implicitly defined as an 'outsider'. The challenge, often a discouraging one in practice, is for the person concerned to find another avenue into the organisation through which to change its perception of the situation.

A prediction such as this is not based on any assumption of cynical intent on the part of organisations. What the ISBL perspective suggests, however, is that the very convenience and efficiency of interactions based on a simplified language used in a fully controlled environment creates new possibilities for the exertion of 'bottom-line' pressures by organisational stakeholders (Laverty, 1996). The mere existence of a streamlined mode of operation is a threat to customers or clients who need a larger vocabulary than the one available with which to state or negotiate their requirements. It is also conceivable that some loss of in-depth organisational knowledge will occur. Once the 'understanding' of an interaction is totally devolved to an autonomous IS, the temptation is to adopt the system's interpretation of what can and cannot be done as defining the limits of possibility (Herzfeld, 1992).

The scope of the ISBL

The temptation to widen the use of the ISBL through the further standardisation of IS structures and definitions is great. The efficiency benefits that have effectively fuelled IS developments since the 1950s have derived directly from processes of routinisation and standardisation, and further benefits are clearly to be gained by extending these processes to the societal level. It is in any case generally accepted that it is logical to attempt to impose whatever degree of stability is possible on a favourable set of control relationships (Beniger, 1986), which implies that the more tightly the language of business can be controlled, the better. There is thus a strong argument in favor of standardising the language of interaction as far as possible and to maintain strict controls over the definitions in place. It can be assumed that organisations including government departments and agencies already have the power to achieve a lot in this direction.

If there is an organisational downside to this it must be that some loss of flexibility is entailed in adopting a highly standardised approach. Put another way, the more widely that integrated IS structures are adopted, the more a form of interdependence is created in which agreements on change will become hard to reach. While there are no real precedents for this type of situation, it can be noted that past attempts to 'freeze' a language in the interests of control have tended to create an element of ritual, in which original intentions and meanings have been wholly or partially lost (Crystal, 1987, p. 405).

Overall, the most definite conclusions that can be drawn in this regard stem from the fact that the strong control of vocabulary equates to a rigid formalism of interaction. If there is a practical risk to the adopting organisations, as distinct from the risks to customers and client organisations identified in previous sections, it is one that is difficult to represent in economic terms. The literature on IT economics suggests, for instance, that it is difficult if not impossible to identify any clear loss of organisational flexibility from within the context of a single investment decision (Ryan, 2000; Willcocks and Lester, 1996; Parker and Benson, 1988) and the broader implications of cumulative losses of flexibility are as yet unresearched. What the language perspective suggests is that there must be some loss of flexibility and that this could be problematic if business strategies concerning customers become more volatile.

Conclusion

One of the most complex characteristics of contemporary life has been held to be the simultaneous progress of trends to greater bureaucratisation and rationalisation in some areas, with equally pervasive trends towards greater fragmentation and uncertainty in others (Turner 1996, p. 15). The ISBL is clearly a rationalising concept, and is primarily relevant to those areas of social and business activity already subject to some degree of routinisation. The second trend Turner identifies helps, however, to disguise the potential for the exercise of power based on ISBL implementations for two reasons. The first is that the undoubted convenience of ISBL-based business arrangements is a boon for people under pressure elsewhere in their lives, and second because the volatility evident in other areas of consumption tends to create a sense of drama and excitement likely to counteract any feelings of powerlessness elsewhere.

It has been argued in this paper that the ISBL concept is much more than a 'mere' metaphor, and that it provides an analytically powerful perspective from which to see that the spread of autonomous IS represents some potentially troubling developments in power relations. Autonomous systems and people do, in this formulation, talk to each other, and the way they converse can lead to the creation of a new class of outsiders, as well as possibilities for consumers and organisations to be coerced into arrangements they find undesirable. In a sense, the ISBL represents almost the apotheosis of business rationalisation. It eliminates people as organisational representatives in a range of business dealings, and imposes a linguistic structure that ensures that the vast majority of basic transactions proceed according to a strict formula. Despite the improvements in efficiency this can generate, and despite the convenience it provides to many consumers, not all the implications are positive.

The theoretical propositions listed earlier in the paper could be used as the foundation for a program of empirical research designed to explore these issues. As an outcome of systems integration trends, the ISBL is already in existence, albeit in a limited form. It is the argument in this paper that the impacts of its further development and more widespread adoption are issues that warrant concentrated attention.

References

The struggle towards an understanding of theory in information systems – *Shirley Gregor*

Avison, D. and Fitzgerald, G. 1995, *Information Systems Development: Methodologies, Techniques and Tools,* 2nd ed., McGraw-Hill, London, UK.

Comte, A. 1864, *Cours de Philosophie Positive*, 2nd ed., Bailliere, Paris, France.

Cook, T. D. and Campbell, D. T. 1979, *Quasi-Experimentation Design and Analysis Issues For Field Settings*, Houghton Mifflin, Boston, MA.

Cushing, B. E. 1990, 'Frameworks, Paradigms and Scientific Research in Management Information Systems', *Journal of Information Systems,* Spring, pp. 38-59.

Denzin, N. K. and Lincoln, Y. S. (eds) 1994, *Handbook of Qualitative Research*, Sage, Thousand Oaks, CA.

Dubin, R. 1978, *Theory Building*, (Revised ed.), Free Press, London, UK.

Godfrey-Smith, P. 2003, *Theory and Reality*, University of Chicago Press, Chicago, IL.

Gregor, S. 2002, 'A Theory of Theories in Information Systems', in Gregor, S. and Hart, D. (eds) *Information Systems Foundations: Building the Theoretical Base*, The Australian National University, Canberra, Australia, pp. 1-20.

Gribbin, J. 2002, *Science: a History*, Penguin, Australia.

Guba, E. G. and Lincoln, Y. 1994, 'Competing Paradigms In Qualitative Research', in Denzin, N. K. and Lincoln, Y. S. (eds), *Handbook of Qualitative Research* , Sage, Thousand Oaks, CA, pp. 105-17.

Hevner, A., March, S., Park, J. and Ram, S. 2004, 'Design Science in Information Systems Research', *MIS Quarterly*, vol. 28, no.1, pp. 75-105.

Hospers, J. 1967, *An Introduction to Philosophical Analysis*, 2nd ed, Routledge and Kegan Paul, London, UK.

Hume, D. 1748, 'An Enquiry Concerning Human Understanding' . Reprinted in Perry, J. and Bratman, M. (eds) 1999, *Introduction to Philosophy Classical and Contemporary Readings*, 3rd ed., Oxford University Press, New York, NY.

Iivari, J. 2003, Towards Information Systems as a Science of Meta-Artefacts, *Communications of the Association of Information Systems*, vol. 12, article 37, November.

Jarvinen, P. 2001, *On Research Methods*, Opinpajan Kirja, Tampere, Finland.

Kant, I. 1781, 'Critique of Pure Reason', in McNeill, W. and Feldman, K. S. (eds) *Continental Philosophy*, Blackwell, Malden, MA, pp. 7-23.

Klein, H. and Myers, M. 1999, 'A Set of Principles for Conducting and Evaluating Interpretive Field Studies', *MIS Quarterly*, vol. 23, no. 1, pp. 67-93.

Lee, A. 1989, 'A Scientific Methodology for MIS Case Studies', *MIS Quarterly*, March, pp. 33-50.

— 1991, 'Integrating Positivist and Interpretive Approaches to Organizational Research', *Organization Science*, vol. 2, no. 4, pp. 342-65.

— 2001, Editorial, *MIS Quarterly*, vol. 25, no. 1, iii-vii.

Locke, J. 1689, 'Essay Concerning Human Understanding', Reprinted in Perry, J. and Bratman, M. (eds) 1999, *Introduction to Philosophy Classical and Contemporary Readings*, 3rd ed., Oxford University Press, New York, NY.

Magee, B. 1997, *Confessions of a Philosopher: A journey Through Western Philosophy*, Weidenfeld and Nicolson, London, UK.

March, S. T. and Smith, G. F. 1995, 'Design and Natural Science Research on Information Technology', *Decision Support Systems*, vol. 15, pp. 251-66.

Markus, M., Majchrzak, L. A., and Gasser, L. 2002, 'A Design Theory for Systems That Support Emergent Knowledge Processes', *MIS Quarterly*, vol. 26, pp. 179-212.

Markus, M. L. and Robey, D. 1998, 'Information Technology and Organizational Change: Causal Structure in Theory and Research', *Management Science*, vol. 34, no. 5, pp. 583-98.

Merriam-Webster Online. 2004, http://www.m-w.com , accessed 18 June, 2004.

Mohr, L. B. 1982, *Explaining Organizational Behavior: The Limits and Possibilities of Theory and Research*, Jossey-Bass, San Francisco, CA.

Nagel, E. 1979, *Teleology Revisited and Other Essays in the Philosophy and History of Science*, Columbia University Press, New York, NY.

O'Hear, A. 1989, *Introduction to the Philosophy of Science*, Clarendon Press, Oxford, UK.

Orlikowski, W. 1992, 'The Duality of Technology: Rethinking the Concept of Technology in Organizations', *Organization Science*, vol. 3, no. 3, pp. 398-427.

Orlikowski, W. and Baroudi, J. 1991, 'Studying Information Technology in Organizations: Research Approaches and Assumptions', *Information Systems Research*, vol. 2, no. 1, pp. 1-28.

Passmore, J. 1967, in Edwards, P. (ed.) *Encyclopedia of Philosophy* , vol V, pp. 56, Macmillan, New York, NY.

Popper, K. 1934, *Logik der Forschung*, Julius Springer, Vienna, Austria.

Schwandt, T. A. 1994, '*Constructivist, Interpetivist approaches to Human Inquiry*', in Denzin, N. K and Lincoln, Y. S. (eds), *Handbook of Qualitative Research*, Sage, Thousand Oaks, CA.

Simon, H. A. 1996, *The Sciences of the Artificial*, 3rd ed., The MIT Press, Cambridge, MA.

— 1980, *The Logic of Scientific Discovery*, (Revised ed.), Unwin Hyman, London, UK.

— 1986 *Unended Quest: An Intellectual Autobiography*, Fontana, Glasgow, UK.

Walls, J. G., Widmeyer, G. R., and El Sawy, O. A., 1992, 'Building an Information System Design Theory for Vigilant EIS' , *Information Systems Research*, vol. 3, no. 1, pp. 36-59.

Walsham, G. 1995, 'Interpretative Case Studies in IS Research: Nature and Method', *European Journal of Information Systems*, vol. 4, no. 2 , pp. 74-81.

Weber, R. 1987, 'Toward a Theory of Artefacts: A Paradigmatic Base for Information Systems Research', *Journal of Information Systems*, Spring, pp. 3-19.

— 1997, *Ontological Foundations of Information Systems*, Coopers & Lybrand, Melbourne, Australia.

Information systems theory as cultural capital: an argument for the development of 'grand' theory – *Douglas Hamilton*

Abbott, A. 1988, *The System of Professions: An Essay on the Division of Expert Labor*, University of Chicago Press, Chicago, IL.

Abbott, A. 2001, *Chaos of Disciplines*, University of Chicago Press, Chicago, IL.

Allen, B. R. and Boynton, A. C. 1991, 'Information Architecture: In Search of Efficient Flexibility', *MIS Quarterly*, vol. 15, no. 4, pp. 435-44.

Anon. 1998, 'Apocalypse Cancelled', *The Age*, 22 September.

Aronowitz, S. 2000, *The Knowledge Factory: Dismantling the Corporate University and Creating True Higher Learning*, Beacon Press, Boston, MA.

Avgerou, C. 2000, 'Information Systems: What Sort of Science Is It?', *Omega*, vol. 28, pp. 567-79.

Avgerou, C., Siemer, J. and Bjørn-Andersen, N. 1999, 'The Academic Field of Information Systems in Europe', *European Journal of Information Systems*, vol. 8, pp. 136-53.

Banville, C. and Landry, M. 1989, 'Can The Field Of MIS Be Disciplined?', *Communications of the ACM*, vol. 32, no. 1, pp. 48-60.

Baskerville, R. and Myers, M. 2002, 'Information Systems as a Reference Discipline', *MIS Quarterly*, vol. 26, no. 1, pp. 1-14.

Benbasat, I. and Zmud, R. W. 2003, 'The Identity Crisis Within the IS Discipline: Defining and Communicating the Discipline's Core Properties', *MIS Quarterly*, vol. 27, no. 2, pp. 183-94.

Black, E. 2001, *IBM and the Holocaust*, Little, Brown and Company, London.

Bodanis, D. 2001, $E=mc^2$: *A Biography of the World's Most Famous Equation*, Pan Macmillan, London, UK.

Bogard, W. 1996, *The Simulation of Surveillance: Hypercontrol in Telematic Societies*, Cambridge University Press, Cambridge, UK.

Bourdieu, P. 1980 (trans. 1990), *The Logic of Practice*, Polity Press, Cambridge, UK.

Bourdieu, P. and Wacquant, L. J. 1992, *An Invitation to Reflexive Sociology*, University of Chicago Press, Chicago, IL.

Chomsky, N. 1996, *Powers and Prospects: Reflections on Human Nature and the Social Order*, Allen & Unwin, Australia.

Clemons, E. K. and Row, M. C. 1988, 'Mckesson Drug Company: A Case Study of Economost – A Strategic Information System', *Journal of Management Information Systems*, vol. 5, no. 1, pp. 36-50.

Coleman, J. S. 1990, *Foundations of Social Theory*, The Belknap Press, Cambridge, MA.

Copeland, D. and McKenney, J. 1988, '*Airline Reservation Systems: Lessons from History*', MIS Quarterly, vol. 12, no. 3, pp. 353-370.

Davenport, T. H. 1998, 'Putting the Enterprise Into the Enterprise System', *Harvard Business Review*, July-August, pp. 121-31.

Dos Santos, B. L. and Peffers, K. 1995, 'Rewards To Investors in Innovative Information Technology Applications: First Movers and Early Followers in ATMs', *Organization Science*, vol. 6, no. 36, pp. 241-59.

Earl, M. J. and Feeny, D. F. 1994, 'Is Your CIO Adding Value?', *Sloan Management Review*, Spring, pp. 11-20.

Fish, S. 1999, *The Trouble with Principle*, Harvard University Press, Cambridge, MA.

Foucault, M. 1972, *The Archaeology of Knowledge*, Routledge, London, UK.

Freeman, D. 1997, *Margaret Mead and the Heretic*, Penguin Books, Australia.

Freeman, D. 2000, 'Was Margaret Mead Misled or Did She Mislead on Samoa?', *Current Anthropology*, vol. 41, no. 4, pp. 609-22.

Freud, S. 1938, *The Interpretation of Dreams*, Modern Library, New York, NY.

Giddens, A. 1984, *The Constitution of Society: Outline of the Theory of Structuration*, University of California Press, Berkley, CA.

Goodhue, D. L., Kirsch, L. J., Quillard, J. A. and Wybo, M. D. 1992, 'Strategic Data Planning: Lessons From the Field', *MIS Quarterly*, vol. 16, no. 1, pp. 11-29.

Gosain, S. 2004, 'Enterprise Information Systems as Objects and Carriers of Institutional Forces: The New Iron Cage?', *Journal of the Association for Information Systems*, vol. 5, no. 4, pp. 151-82.

Hamilton, D. G. 1999, *Information Systems Integration in Complex Organizations*. PhD Dissertation, Monash University, Australia.

Hammer, M. and Champy, J. 1993, *Reengineering the Corporation: A Manifesto for Change*, Nicholas Brealey, London, UK.

Harvey, M. and Lusch, R. 1997, 'Protecting the Core Competencies of a Company: Intangible Asset Security', *European Management Journal*, vol. 15, no. 4, pp. 370-80.

Hendry, J. 1995, 'Culture, Community and Networks: The Hidden Cost of Outsourcing', *European Management Journal*, vol. 13, no. 2, pp. 193-200.

Hirschheim, R. and Klein, H. 2003, 'Crisis in the IS field? A Critical Reflection on the State of the Discipline', *Journal of the Association for Information Systems*, vol. 4, no. 5, pp. 237-93.

Horowitz, I. L. 1993, *The Decomposition of Sociology*, Oxford University Press, Oxford, UK.

Introna, L. D. 2003, 'Disciplining Information Systems: Truth and its Regimes', *European Journal of Information Systems*, vol. 12, pp. 235-40.

Kettinger, W. J., Grover, V., and Segars, A. H. 1995, 'Do Strategic Systems Really Pay Off? An Analysis of Classic Strategic IT Cases', *Information Systems Management*, Winter, pp. 35-43.

Khazanchi, D. and Munkvold, B. E. 2000, 'Is Information Systems a Science? An Inquiry into the Nature of the Information Systems Discipline', *The Data Base for Advances in Information Systems*, vol. 31, no. 3, pp. 24-42.

Kline, S. J. 1995, *Conceptual Foundations for Multidisciplinary Thinking*, Stanford University Press, Stanford, CA.

Latour, B. 1987, *Science in Action*, Harvard University Press, Cambridge, MA.

Laverty, K. J. 1996, Economic 'Short-Termism': 'The Debate, the Unresolved Issues, and the Implications for Management Practice and Research', *Academy of Management Review*, vol. 21, no. 3, pp. 825-60.

Lee, S., Koh, S., Yen, D. and Tang, H-L. 2002, 'Perception Gaps Between IS Academics and IS Practitioners: An Exploratory Study', *Information & Management*, vol. 40, pp. 51-61.

Lucas, H. 1999, 'The State of the Information Systems Field', *Communications of the AIS*, vol. 5, No. 1, pp. 1-6.

Luehrman, T. A. 1997, 'What's it worth? A General Manager's Guide to Valuation', *Harvard Business Review*, May-June, pp. 132-42.

Markus, M. L. 1983, 'Power, Politics, and MIS Implementation', *Communications of the ACM*, vol. 26, no. 6, pp. 430-44.

Markus, M. L. 1999, 'Thinking the Unthinkable: What Happens if the IS Field as we Know It Goes Away?', in Currie, W. and Galliers, R. (eds), *Rethinking MIS*. Oxford University Press, Oxford, UK.

Martin, J. 1990, *Information Engineering: Planning and Analysis*, Prentice Hall, PTR Upper Saddle River, NJ, USA.

Marx, K. 1981, *Capital*, Penguin, Australia.

Paton, G. 1997, '"Information System" As Intellectual Construct – Its Only Valid Form', *Behavioral Science*, vol. 14, no. 1, pp. 67-72.

Porter, M. and Millar, V. 1985, 'How Information Gives You Competitive Advantage', *Harvard Business Review*, July-August.

Pratkanis, A. and Aronson, E. 2001, *Age of Propaganda*, Freeman, New York, USA.

Ritzer, G. 1992, *Sociological Theory*, McGraw-Hill, New York, USA.

Segars, A. H. and Grover, V. 1996, 'Designing Company-Wide Information Systems: Risk Factors and Coping Strategies', *Long Range Planning*, vol. 29, no. 3, pp. 381-92.

Slaughter, S. and Leslie, L. L. 1997, *Academic Capitalism: Politics, Policies, and the Entrepreneurial University*, John Hopkins University Press, Baltimore, MD.

Somogyi, E. and Galliers, R. 1987, 'From Data Processing to Strategic Information Systems – A Historical Perspective', in Somogyi, E. K. and Galliers, R. D. *Towards Strategic Information Systems*, Abacus Press, Grand Rapids, Michigan, USA, pp. 5-25.

Stewart, T. A. (ed.) 2003, 'Does IT matter? An HBR Debate', *Harvard Business Review*, vol. 81, no. 4, pp. 1-17.

Sutton, R. I. 1997, 'The Virtues of Closet Qualitative Research', *Organization Science*, vol. 8, no. 1, pp. 97-106.

Swartz, D. 1997, *Culture & Power: the Sociology of Pierre Bourdieu*, University of Chicago Press, Chicago, USA.

Turner, S. (ed.), 2000, *The Cambridge Companion to Weber*, Cambridge University Press, Cambridge, UK.

Vitale, M. R. 1986, 'The Growing Risks of Information Systems Success', *MIS Quarterly*, vol. 10, no. 4, pp. 327-34.

Wand, Y. and Weber, R. 1995, 'On the Deep Structure of Information Systems', *Information Systems Journal*, vol. 5, pp. 203-23.

Weber, R. 2003, 'Still Desperately Seeking the IT Artifact', *MIS Quarterly*, vol. 27, no. 2, pp. iii-xi.

Webster, R. 1996, *Why Freud was Wrong: Sin, Science and Psychoanalysis*, Fontana, London, UK.

Weill, P. and Broadbent, M. 1998, *Leveraging the New Infrastructure*, Harvard Business School Press, Boston, MA.

Wolf, E. R. 1999, *Envisioning Power: Ideologies of Dominance and Crisis*, University of California Press, Berkeley, CA.

Wyzalek, J. (ed.), 2000, *Enterprise Systems Integration*, CRC Press, Boca Raton, FL.

The reality of information systems research – *John Lamp and Simon Milton*

Ackoff, R. L. and Emery, F. E. 1972, *On Purposeful Systems*, Aldine-Atherton, Chicago, IL.

Asimov, I. 1974, 'The Endochronic Properties of Resublimated Thiotimolene', *The Early Asimov 3*, *Astounding Science Fiction*, March, 1948.

Avison, D. E. 1993, 'Research in Information Systems Development and the Discipline of Information Systems', *Proceedings of the 4th Australasian Conference on Information Systems*, Ledington, P. (ed.), University of Queensland, Brisbane, pp. 1-26.

Baskerville, R, Wood-Harper, A. T. 1998, 'Diversity in Information Systems Action Research Methods', *European Journal of Information Systems*, vol. 7, pp. 90-107.

Brentano, F. 1933, *Kategorienlehre* (trans. R. M. Chisholm and N. Guterman, *The Theory of Categories*, Martinus Nijhoff, The Hague) Hamburg, Germany.

Bunge, M. 1977, *Treatise on Basic Philosophy: Vol 3: Ontology I: The Furniture of the World*, Reidel, Boston, MA.

Bunge, M. 1979, *Treatise on Basic Philosophy: Vol 3: Ontology II: A World of Systems*, Reidel, Boston, MA.

Checkland, P. 1981, *Systems Thinking, Systems Practice*. John Wiley & Sons, Chichester, UK.

Chisholm, R. M. 1996, *A Realistic Theory of Categories – An Essay on Ontology*, Cambridge University Press, Cambridge, UK.

Churchman C. W. 1979, *The Systems Approach and Its Enemies*, Basic Books, New York, NY.

DeLone, W. H., McLean, E. R. 1992, 'Information Systems Success: The Quest for the Dependent Variable', *Information Systems Research*, vol. 3, no. 1, pp. 60-99.

Fensel D., Horrocks, I., Van Harmelen, F., Decker, S., Erdmann, M. and Klein, M. 2000, 'OIL in a nutshell', in Dieng, R. and Corby, O. (eds), *Knowledge Acquisition, Modeling, and Management, Proceedings of the 12th European Knowledge Acquisition Conference* (EKAW-2000), Lecture Notes in Artificial Intelligence, Springer-Verlag, pp. 1-16.

Fitzgerald, B. and Howcroft, D. 1998, 'Competing Dichotomies in IS Research and Possible Strategies for Resolution', in Hirschheim, R., Newman, M. and DeGross, J. I. (eds), *Proceedings of the 19th International Conference on Information Systems*, Helsinki, Finland, pp. 155-64.

Galliers, R. D. 2004, 'Trans-disciplinary Research in Information Systems', *International Journal of Information Management*, vol. 24, pp. 99-106.

Gangemi A., Guarino, N., Masolo, C., Oltramari, A. and Schneider, L. 2002, 'Sweetening Ontologies with DOLCE', *Proceedings of the 13th European Knowledge Acquisition Conference (EKAW-2002)*, Siguenza, Spain, pp. 166-181.

Genesereth, M. R. and Fikes, R. E. 1992, *KIF Version 3.0. Reference Manual,* Technical Report Logic-92-1, Stanford University, Stanford, CA.

Gregor, S. 2002, 'A Theory of Theories in Information Systems', in Gregor, S. and Hart, D. (eds) *Information Systems Foundations: Building the Theoretical Base,* The Australian National University, Canberra, Australia, pp. 1-20.

Gruber, T. R. 1992, *Ontolingua: A Mechanism to Support Portable Ontologies,* Stanford Knowledge Systems Laboratory.

Gruber, T. R. 1995, 'Toward Principles for the Design of Ontologies Used for Knowledge Sharing', *International Journal of Human and Computer Studies*, vol. 43, no. 5/6, pp. 907–28.

Guarino, N. 1998, 'Formal Ontology and Information Systems', in Guarino, N. (ed.) *Formal Ontology in Information Systems,* IOS Press, Amsterdam, The Netherlands, pp. 3-15.

Holsapple, C. W., Manakyan, H. and Tanner, J. 1994, Business Computing System Research: Structuring the Field. *Omega: International Journal of Management Science,*vol. 22, no. 1, pp. 69-81.

Honderich, T. (ed.) 1995, *The Oxford Companion to Philosophy*, Oxford University Press, Oxford, UK.

Hurt, M. E., Elam, J. J. and Huber, G. P. 1986, 'The Nature of DSS Literature Presented in Major IS Conference Proceedings (1980-1985)', *Proceedings of the 7th International Conference on Information Systems,* San Diego, CA, pp. 27-45.

IEEE P1600.1 Standard Upper Ontology (SUO) Working Group, http://suo.ieee.org/ , accessed 8 August 2003.

Ingarden, R. 1965, *Das literarische Kunstwerk*, Max Niemeyer Verlag, Tübingen, (trans. G. G. Grabowicz, *The Literary Work of Art: An Investigation of the Borderlines of Ontology, Logic, and Theory of Language*, Northwestern University Press, Evanston, IL., 1973).

Ingarden, R. 1968, *Vom Erkennen des literarischen Kunstwerks*, Max Niemeyer Verlag, Tübingen, (trans. R. A. Crowley and K. R. Olsen, *The Cognition of the Literary Work of Art*, Northwestern University Press, Evanston, IL., 1973).

Ives, B., Hamilton, S. and Davis, G. B. 1980 'A Framework for Research in Computer-Based Management Information Systems', *Management Science*, vol. 26, no. 9, pp. 910-34.

Kant, I. 1787, *Kritik der reinen Vernunft* (trans. J. M. D. Meiklejohn, *Critique of Pure Reason*, J. M. Dent, London, UK, 1991).

Keen, P. G. W. 1991 'Relevance and Rigour in Information Systems Research: Improving Quality, Confidence, Cohesion and Impact', in Nissen H-E., Klein, H. K. and Hirschheim, R. *Information Systems Research: Contemporary Approaches and Emergent Traditions*, Elsevier, North-Holland, Amsterdam, The Netherlands, pp. 27-49.

Kim, J. and Sosa, E. (eds) 1995, *A Companion to Metaphysics*, Blackwell Companions to Philosophy, Blackwell, Oxford, UK.

Lamp, J. 1995, *Index of Information Systems Journals* http://lamp.in-fosys.deakin.edu.au/journals/index.php , accessed 10 January 2004.

Lamp, J. 2002, *IS Journal Categorisation* http://lamp.infosys.deakin.edu.au/journ_cat/ , accessed 18 May 2004.

Lamp, J. and Milton, S. 2003, 'An Exploratory Study of Information Systems Subject Indexing', *Proceedings of the 14th Australasian Conference on Information Systems* (ACIS2003), Edith Cowan University, Perth Australia.

Milton, S. 2000, *An Ontological Comparison and Evaluation of Data Modelling Frameworks*, PhD Thesis, University of Tasmania, Australia.

Milton, S. K. and Kazmierczak, E. 2004 'Using a Common-Sense Realistic Ontology: Making Data Models Better Map the World', in *Ontology and Business Systems Analysis*, Idea Group Publishing, Hershey, USA.

Moore, G. 1925, 'A Defence of Common Sense', in Moore, G. 1959, *Philosophical Papers*, Allen & Unwin, London, UK.

Parker, C. M., Wafula, E. N., Swatman, P. M. C. and Swatman, P. A. 1994, 'Information Systems Research Methods: The Technology Transfer Problem', *Proceedings of the 5th Australasian Conference on Information Systems*, Monash University, Melbourne, pp. 197-208.

Quine, W. V. O. 1953, 'On What There Is', in Quine, W. V. O. *From a Logical Point of View*, Harvard University Press, Cambridge, MA.

Ramakrishnan, R. and Gehrke, J. 2003, *Database Management Systems*, 3rd ed., McGraw Hill, Boston, MA. pp. 928-9.

Rosch, E. 1978, 'Principles of Categorization', in Rosch, E. and Lloyd, B. (eds) *Cognition and Categorization*, Erlbaum, Hillsdale, NJ.

Routledge, 2000, *Concise Routledge Encyclopaedia of Philosophy 2000*, Routledge, London, UK.

Seddon, P. 1991, 'Information Systems: Towards a Definition for the 1990s', *Proceedings of the 2nd Australasian Conference on Information Systems*, University of New South Wales, Sydney, pp. 372-82.

Shanks, G. A., Rouse, A. and Arnott, D. 1993, 'A Review of Approaches to Research and Scholarship in Information Systems', *Proceedings of the 4th Australasian Conference on Information Systems*, University of Queensland, Brisbane, pp. 29-44.

Smith, B. 1978, 'An Essay in Formal Ontology', *Grazer Philosophische Studien*, vol. 6, pp. 39-62.

Smith, B. 1995, 'Formal Ontology, Commonsense and Cognitive Science', *International Journal of Human-Computer Studies*, vol. 43, no. 12, pp. 641-67.

Smith, B. and Mark, D. 1999, 'Ontology with Human Subjects Testing: An Empirical Investigation Of Empirical Categories', *American Journal of Economics and Sociology*, vol. 58, no. 2, pp. 245-72.

Smith, B. and Mulligan, K. 1983, 'Framework for Formal Ontology', *Topoi*, vol. 2, pp. 73-85.

Straub, D. W., Ang, S. and Evaristo, R. 1994, 'Normative Standards for IS Research', *Data Base*, vol. 25, no. 1, pp. 21-33.

Wand, Y. 1996, 'Ontology as a Foundation for Meta-Modelling and Method Engineering' *Information and Software Technology*, vol. 38, pp. 182-287.

Wand, Y., Monarchi, D. E., Parsons, J., and Woo, C. 1995, 'Theoretical Foundations for Conceptual Modelling in Information Systems Development', *Decision Support Systems*, vol. 15, pp. 285-304.

Wand, Y. and Weber, R. 1990, 'An Ontological Model of an Information System', *IEEE Transactions on Software Engineering*, vol. 16, no. 11, pp. 1282-92.

Wand, Y. and Weber, R. 1993, 'On the Ontological Expressiveness of Information Systems Analysis and Design Grammars', *Journal of Information Systems*,vol. 3, no. 4, pp. 217-37.

Wand, Y. and Weber, R. 1995, 'On the Deep Structure of Information Systems', *Information Systems Journal*, vol. 5, pp. 203-23.

Walczak, S. 1999, 'A Re-Evaluation of Information Systems Publication Forums', *Journal of Computer Information Systems*, vol. 40, no. 1, pp. 88-97.

Winch, P. 1958, *The Idea of a Social Science and its Relation to Philosophy*, Routledge and Kegan Paul, London, UK.

Qualitative research in information systems: consideration of selected theories – *M. Gordon Hunter*

Baker, M. 1991, *Research in Marketing*, MacMillan, London, UK.

Bannister, D. and Mair, J. M. M. 1968, *The Evaluation of Personal Constructs*, Academic Press, New York, NY.

Barry, D. and Elmes, M. 1997, 'Strategy Retold: Towards a Narrative View of Strategic Discourse', *Academy of Management Review*, vol. 22, no. 2, pp. 429-52.

Benbasat, I. and Zmud, R. W. 1999, 'Empirical Research in Information Systems: The Importance of Relevance', *MIS Quarterly*, vol. 23, no.1, March, pp. 3-16.

Boland, R. J. Jr. and Day, W. F. 1989, 'The Experience of Systems Design: A Hermeneutic of Organization Action', *Scandinavian Journal of Management*, vol. 5, no. 2, pp. 87-104.

Botten, N., Kusiak, A. and Raz, T. 1989, 'Knowledge Bases: Integration, Verification, and Partitioning', *European Journal of Operations Research*, vol. 42, no. 2, pp. 111-28.

Bruner, J. 1990, *Acts of Meaning*, Harvard University Press, Cambridge, MA.

Chatman, S. 1978, *Story and Discourse: Narrative Structure in Fiction and Film*, Cornell University Press, Ithaca, NY.

Corsini, R. and Marsella, A. J. 1983, *Personality Theories, Research and Assessment*, Peacock Publishers, Itasca, IL.

Czarniawska-Joerges, B. 1995, 'Narration or Science? Collapsing the Division in Organization Studies', *Organization*, vol. 2, no. 1, pp. 11-33.

Dex, S. 1991, *Life and Work History Analyses*, Routledge, London, UK.

Eden, C. and Jones, S. 1984, 'Using Repertory Grids for Problem Construction'. *Journal of Operations Research*, vol. 35, no. 9, pp. 779-98.

Eden, C. and Wheaton, G. 1980, 'In Favour of Structure', Centre for the Study of Organisational Change and Development, *Working Paper 80/06*, University of Bath, UK.

Fransella, F. (ed.) 1981, *Personality – Theory, Measurement and Research*, Methuen & Co., New York, NY.

Galliers, R. D. (ed.) 1992, *Information Systems Research – Issues, Methods, and Practical Guidelines*, Alfred Waller Ltd., Henley-on-Thames, UK.

Girden, E. R. 2001, *Evaluating Research Articles – From Start to Finish*, 2nd ed., Sage, Thousand Oaks, CA.

Glaser, B. G. and Strauss, A. L. 1967, *The Discovery of Grounded Theory: Strategies for Qualitative Research*, Aldine De Gruyter, New York, NY.

Hirschheim, R. 1992, 'Information Systems Epistemology: An Historical Perspective', in Galliers, R. D. (ed.) *Information Systems Research – Issues, Methods, and Practical Guidelines*, Alfred Waller Ltd., Henley-on-Thames, UK, pp. 61-88.

Hirschheim, R. and Newman, M. 1991, 'Symbolism and Information Systems Development: Myth, Metaphor and Magic', *Information Systems Research*, vol. 2, no. 1, pp. 29-62.

Hunter, M. G. 1993, 'A Strategy for Identifying 'Excellent' Systems Analysts', *The Journal of Strategic Information Systems*, vol. 2, no.1, pp.15-26.

— 1994, ''Excellent' Systems Analysts: Key Audience Perceptions', *Computer Personnel*, ACM Press, pp.15-31.

— 1997, 'The Use of RepGrids to Gather Interview Data About Information Systems Analysts', *Information Systems Journal*, vol. 7, no. 1, pp. 67-81.

Hunter, M. G. and Beck, J. E. 1996, 'A Cross-Cultural Comparison of 'Excellent' Systems Analysts', *Information Systems Journal*, vol.6, no. 4, pp. 261-81.

— 2000, 'Using Repertory Grids to Conduct Cross-Cultural Information Systems Research', *Information Systems Research*, vol. 11, no. 1. pp. 93-101.

Hunter, M. G. and Tan, F. 2001, 'Information Systems Professionals in New Zealand: Reflective Career Biographies', *International Conference of the Information Resources Management Association*, May 20-22, Toronto, Canada, pp. 132-3.

Kelly, G. A. 1955, *The Psychology of Personal Constructs*, Norton, New York, NY.

— 1963, *A Theory of Personality*, Norton, New York, NY.

Klein, H. K. and Lyytinen, K. 1985, 'The Poverty of Scientism in Information Systems', in Mumford, E. et al. (eds) *Research Methods in Information Systems*, North-Holland, Amsterdam, Netherlands, pp. 131-61.

Latta, G. F. and Swigger, K. 1992, 'Validation of the Repertory Grid for Use in Modelling Knowledge', *Journal of the American Society of Information Science*, vol. 42, no. 2, pp. 115-29.

Lee, A. S. 1999, 'Rigor and Relevance in MIS Research: Beyond the Approach of Positivism Alone', *MIS Quarterly*, vol. 23, no. 1, pp. 29-33.

— 2001, 'Challenges to Qualitative Researchers in Information Systems', in Trauth, E. M. (ed.) *Qualitative Research in IS: Issues and Trends*, Idea Group Publishing, Hershey, PA, pp. 240-70.

McCracken, G. 1988, *The Long Interview*, Sage Publications, New York, NY.

Mingers, J. 2001, 'Combining IS Research Methods: Towards a Pluralistic Methodology', *Information Systems Research*, vol. 12, no. 3, pp. 240-59.

Nicholls, M., Clarke, G. S. and Lehaney, B. 2001, *Mixed-Mode Modelling: Mixing Methodologies for Organizational Intervention*, Kluwer Academic, Dordrecht, Netherlands.

Phythian, G. J. and King, M.1992, 'Developing an Expert System for Tender Enquiry Evaluation: A Case Study', *European Journal of Operations Research*, vol. 56, no. 1, pp. 15-29.

Rappaport, J. 1993, 'Narrative Studies, Personal Stories and Identity Transformation in the Mutual Help Context', *Journal of Applied Behavioral Science*, vol. 29, no. 2, pp. 239-56.

Reason, P. and Rowan, J. (eds) 1981, *Human Inquiry – A Sourcebook of New Paradigm Research*, John Wiley & Sons, Chichester, UK.

Robey, D. and Markus, M. L. 1998, 'Beyond Rigor and Relevance: Producing Consumable Research About Information Systems', *Information Resources Management Journal*, vol. 11, no. 1, pp. 7-15.

Scholes, R. 1981, 'Language, Narrative, and Anti-Narrative', in Mitchell, W. (ed.), *On Narrativity*, University of Chicago Press, Chicago, IL, pp. 200-8.

Shaw, M. L. G. 1980, *On Becoming a Personal Scientist – Interactive Computer Elicitation of Personal Models of the World*, Academic Press, London, UK.

Stewart, V. and Stewart, A. 1981, *Business Applications of Repertory Grid*, McGraw-Hill, London, UK.

Swap, W., Schields, D. L. M. and Abrams, L. 2001, 'Using Mentoring and Storytelling to Transfer Knowledge in the Workplace', *Journal of Management Information Systems*, vol. 18, no. 1, pp. 95-114.

Trauth, E. M. 2001, *Qualitative Research in IS: Issues and Trends.*, Idea Group Publishing, Hershey, PA.

Tulving, E. 1972, 'Episodic and Semantic Memory', in Tulving, E. and Donaldson, W. (eds) *Organization of Memory*, Academic Press, New York, NY, pp. 381-404.

Vendelo, M. T. 1998, 'Narrating Corporate Reputation: Becoming Legitimate Through Storytelling', *International Journal of Management and Organization*, vol. 28, no. 3, pp. 120-37.

Young, J. 2000, *The Career Paths of Computer Science and Information Systems Major Graduates*, Unpublished PhD Thesis, University of Tasmania, Australia.

The grounded theory method and case study data in IS research: issues and design – *Walter D. Fernández*

Baskerville, R., and Pries-Heje, J. 1999, 'Grounded Action Research: A Method for Understanding IT in Practice', Accounting, Management and Information Technologies, vol. 9, pp. 1-23.

Benbasat, I., Goldstein, D. K., and Mead, M. 1987, 'The Case Research Strategy in Studies of Information Systems', MIS Quarterly, vol. 11, pp. 369-86.

Charmaz, K. 2001, 'Grounded Theory', in Denzin, N. K. and Lincoln, Y. S. (eds), The American Tradition in Qualitative Research, pp. 244-85, Sage, London, UK.

Creswell, J. W. 1998, Qualitative Inquiry and Research Design: Choosing Among Five Traditions, Sage, Thousand Oaks, CA.

Cronholm, S. 2002, 'Grounded Theory in Use – A Review of Experiences', European Conference on Research Methodology for Business and Management Studies, Reading University, Reading, UK.

Dey, I. 1999, Grounding Grounded Theory: Guidelines for Qualitative Inquiry, Academic Press, San Diego, CA.

Eisenhardt, K. M. 1989, 'Building Theories from Case Study Research', Academy of Management Review, vol. 14, pp. 532-50.

Glaser, B. G. 1978, Theoretical Sensitivity: Advances in the Methodology of Grounded Theory, Sociology Press, Mill Valley, CA.

— 1992, Emergence vs. Forcing: Basics of Grounded Theory Analysis, Sociology Press, Mill Valley, CA.

— 1998, Doing Grounded Theory: Issues and Discussions, Sociology Press, Mill Valley, CA.

— 2001, The Grounded Theory Perspective: Conceptualization Contrasted with Description, Sociology Press, Mill Valley, CA.

— 2002, 'Conceptualization: On Theory and Theorizing Using Grounded Theory', International Journal of Qualitative Methods, vol. 1, pp. 1-31.

Glaser, B. G., and Strauss, A. L. 1967, The Discovery of Grounded Theory: Strategies For Qualitative Research, Aldine Publishing Company, New York, NY.

Goleman, D. 1998, Working with Emotional Intelligence, Bloomsbury, London, UK.

Kendall, J. 1999, 'Axial Coding and The Grounded Controversy', Western Journal of Nursing Research, vol. 21, pp. 743-57.

Klein, H. K., and Myers, M. D. 2001, 'A Classification Scheme for Interpretive Research in Information Systems', in Trauth, E. M. (ed.), Qualitative Research in IS: Issues and Trends, pp. 218-39, Idea Group Publishing, Hershey, PA.

Kuhn T, S. 1962, The Structure of Scientific Revolutions, University of Chicago Press, Chicago, IL.

Lehmann, H. P. 2001a, A Grounded Theory of International Information Systems, PhD Thesis, University of Auckland, New Zealand.

— 2001b, 'Using Grounded Theory with Technology Cases: Distilling Critical Theory from a Multinational Information Systems Development', Journal of Global Information Technology Management, vol. 4, pp. 45-60.

Markus, M. L. 1997, 'The Qualitative Difference in Information System Research and Practice', in DeGross, J. I., Liebenau, J. and Lee, A. S. (eds), Information Systems and Qualitative Research, pp. 11-27, Chapman & Hall, London, UK.

Martin, P. Y. and Turner, B. A. 1986, 'Grounded Theory and Organizational Research', The Journal of Applied Behavioral Science, vol. 22, pp. 141-57.

Maznevski, M. L. and Chudoba, K. M. 2000, 'Bridging Space Over Time: Global Virtual Team Dynamics and Effectiveness', Organization Science, vol. 11, pp. 473-92.

Melia, K. M. 1996, 'Rediscovering Glaser', Qualitative Health Research, vol. 6, pp. 368-78.

Miles, M. B. and Huberman, A. M. 1994, Qualitative Data Analysis: An Expanded Sourcebook, Sage, Thousand Oaks, CA.

Orlikowski, W. J. 1993, 'CASE Tools Are Organizational Change: Investigating Incremental and Radical Changes in Systems Development'. MIS Quarterly, vol. 17, pp. 309-40.

Orlikowski, W. J. and Baroudi, J. J. 1991, 'Studying Information Technology in Organizations: Research Approaches and Assumptions', Information Systems Research, vol. 2, pp. 1-28.

Partington, D. 2000, 'Building Grounded Theories of Management Action', British Journal of Management, vol. 11, pp. 91-102.

Pettigrew, A. M. 1988, 'Longitudinal Field Research on Change: Theory and Practice', National Science Foundation Conference on Longitudinal Research Methods in Organizations, Austin, TX.

Sarker, S., Lau, F. and Sahay, S. 2000, 'Building an Inductive Theory of Collaboration in Virtual Teams: An Adapted Grounded Theory Approach', Proceedings of the 33rd Hawaii International Conference on System Sciences, pp. 1-10, IEEE Computer Society, Hawaii.

— 2001, 'Using an Adapted Grounded Theory Approach For Inductive Theory Building About Virtual Team Development'. Database for Advances in Information Systems, vol. 32, pp. 38-56.

Stern, P. N. 1994, 'Eroding Grounded Theory', in Morse, J. (ed.), Critical Issues in Qualitative Research Methods, pp. 212-23, Sage, Thousand Oaks, CA.

Strauss, A. L. 1987, Qualitative Analysis for Social Scientists, Cambridge University Press, Cambridge, UK.

Strauss, A. L. and Corbin, J. M. 1990, Basics of Qualitative Research: Grounded Theory Procedures and Techniques, Sage, Newbury Park, CA.

— 1998, Basics of Qualitative Research: Techniques and Procedures for Developing Grounded Theory, Sage, Thousand Oaks, CA.

Trauth, E. M., and Jessup, L. 2000, 'Understanding Computer-mediated Discussions: Positivist and Interpretive Analyses of Group Support System Use'. MIS Quarterly, Special Issue on Intensive Research, vol. 24, no. 1, pp. 43-79.

Urquhart, C. 1997, 'Exploring Analyst-Client Communication: Using Grounded Theory Techniques to Investigate Interaction in Informal Requirement Gathering', in Lee, A. S., Liebenau, J. and DeGross, J. I. (eds), Information Systems and Qualitative Research, Chapman & Hall, London, UK.

— 1998, 'Analysts And Clients In Conversation: Cases In Early Requirements Gathering', in Hirschheim, R. A., Newman, M. and DeGross, J. I. (eds), Proceedings of the International Conference in Information Systems, pp. 115-27.

— 1999, 'Reflexions On Early Requirement Gathering – Themes From Analyst-Client Conversation', in Larsen, T. J., Levine, L. and DeGross, J. I. (eds), Information Systems: Current Issues and Future Changes, IFIP, Laxemburg, Austria.

— 2001, 'An Encounter with Grounded Theory: Tackling the Practical and Philosophical Issues', in Trauth, E. M. (ed.), Qualitative Research in IS: Issues and Trends, Idea Group Publishing, Hershey, PA.

Van de Ven, A. H. and Poole, M. S. 1989, 'Methods for studying innovation processes', in Van de Ven, A. H., Angle, H. L. and Poole, M. S. (eds), Research on the Management of Innovation: The Minnesota Studies, pp. 31-54, Harper & Row, New York.

Weber, M. 1968, Economy and Society; An Outline of Interpretive Sociology, Bedminster Press, New York, NY.

Yin, R. K. 1994, Case Study Research: Design and Methods, Sage, Thousand Oaks, CA.

A hermeneutic analysis of the Denver International Airport Baggage Handling System – *Stasys Lukaitis and Jacob Cybulski*

Augustine, 427, On Christian Doctrine, Bobbs-Merrill, Indianapolis, IN.

Boland, R. J. 1991, 'Information System Use as a Hermeneutic Process', in Nissen, H.-E., Klein, H. K. and Hirschheim, R. A. (eds), Information Systems Research: Contemporary Approaches and Emergent Traditions, North Holland, Amsterdam, The Netherlands, pp. 439-64.

Butler, T. 1998, 'Towards a Hermeneutic Method for Interpretive Research in Information Systems', Journal of Information Technology, vol. 13, no. 4, pp. 285-300.

Demeterio, F. P. A., III. 2001, 'Introduction to Hermeneutics', Diwatao, vol. 1, no. 1, pp. 1-9.

Dilthey, W. 1990 'The Rise of Hermeneutics', in Ormiston, G. L. and Schrift, A. D. (eds), The Hermeneutic Tradition: From Ast to Ricoeur, State University of New York Press, New York, NY.

Gadamer, H. G. (ed.) 1976, The Historicity of Understanding, Penguin Books, Harmondsworth, UK.

Gadamer, H. G. 1975, Truth and Method, Sheed and Ward, London, UK.

Harvey, L. J., and Myers, M. D. 1995, 'Scholarship and Practice: The Contribution of Ethnographic Research Methods to Bridging the Gap', Information Technology & People, vol. 8, no. 3, pp. 13-27.

Heidegger, M. 1976, Being and Time, Harper and Row, NY.

Kidder, P. 1997, 'The Hermeneutic and Dialectic of Community in Development', International Journal of Social Economics, vol. 24, no. 11, pp. 1191-202.

Klein, H. K. and Myers, M. D. 1999, 'A Set of Principles for Conducting and Evaluating Interpretive Field Studies in Information Systems', MIS Quarterly, vol. 23, no. 1, pp. 67-94.

Lee, A. S. 1994, 'Electronic Mail as a Medium for Rich Communication: An Empirical Investigation using Hermeneutic Interpretation', MIS Quarterly, vol. 18, no. 2, pp. 143-57.

Montealegre, R. and Keil, M. 2000, 'De-escalating Information Technology Projects: Lessons from the Denver International Airport', MIS Quarterly, vol. 24, no. 3, pp. 417-47.

Montealegre, R., Nelson, H. J., Knoop, C. I., and Applegate, L. M. 1999, 'BAE Automated Systems (A): Denver International Airport Baggage-Handling System', in Applegate, L. M., McFarlan, F. W. and McKenny, J. L. (eds), Corporate Information Systems Management: Text and Cases, 5th ed., Irwin McGraw-Hill, Boston, MA, pp. 546-61.

Myers, M. D. 1994a, 'Dialectical Hermeneutics: a Theoretical Framework for the Implementation of Information Systems', Information Systems Journal, vol. 5, pp. 51-70.

Myers, M. D. 1994b, 'A Disaster for Everyone to See: An Interpretive Analysis of a Failed I.S. Project', Accounting, Management & Information Management Technology, vol. 4, no. 4, pp. 185-201.

Ricoeur, P. 1974, The Conflict of Interpretations: Essays in Hermeneutics, Northwestern University Press, Evanston.

Schleiermacher, F. D. E. 1819, 'The Hermeneutics: Outline of the 1819 Lecture', in Ormiston, G. L. and Schrift, A. D. (eds), 1990, The Hermeneutic Tradition: From Ast to Ricoeur, State University of New York Press, New York, NY.

Turner, G. W. (ed.) 1987, The Australian Concise Oxford Dictionary of Current English, 1st ed., Oxford University Press, Melbourne, Australia.

Wolin, R. 2000, 'Nazism and the Complicities of Hans-Georg Gadamer: Untruth and Method', New Republic, vol. 222, no. 20, pp. 36-46.

Information systems technology grounded on institutional facts
– Robert M. Colomb

Berners-Lee, T. and Fischetti, M. 1999, Weaving the Web: The Past, Present and Future of the World Wide Web By Its Inventor, Orion Business, London, UK.

Colomb, R. M. 1997, 'Impact of Semantic Heterogeneity on Federating Databases', The Computer Journal, vol. 40, no. 5, pp. 235-44.

Gregor, S. 2002, 'A Theory of Theories in Information Systems', in Gregor, S. and Hart, D. (eds), Information Systems Foundations: Building the Theoretical Base, The Australian National University, Canberra, Australia, pp. 1-20.

McDonald, C. 2002, 'Karl Popper's Third World – One Foundation for Informatics', in Gregor, S. and Hart, D. (eds), Information Systems Foundations: Building the Theoretical Base, The Australian National University, Canberra, Australia, pp. 73-99.

Popper, K. 1972, *Objective Knowledge: An Evolutionary Approach*, Oxford Clarendon Press, London, UK.

Searle, J. R. 1995, *The Construction of Social Reality*, The Free Press, New York, NY.

Sheth, A. P. and Larsen, J. 1990, 'Federated Database Systems for Managing Distributed, Heterogeneous and Autonomous Databases', *ACM Computing Surveys,*(Special Issue on Heterogeneous Databases), vol. 22, no. 3, pp. 183-236.

Perhaps it's time for a fresh approach to IS/IT gender research? – *Phyl Webb and Judy Young*

Adam, A. 2001, 'Gender, Emancipation and Critical Information Systems', *Proceedings of the 9th European Conference on Information Systems (ECIS)*, Bled, Slovenia.

Adam, A. and Richardson, H. 2001, 'Feminist Philosophy in Information Systems', *Information Systems Frontiers*, vol. 3, no. 2, pp. 143-54.

Adam, A., Howcroft, D. and Richardson, H. 2002, 'Guest Editorial', *Information Technology and People*, vol. 15, no. 2, pp. 94-7.

Ahuja, M. K. 2002, 'Women in the Information Technology Profession: A Literature Review, Synthesis and Research Guide', *European Journal of Information Systems*, vol. 11, pp. 20-34.

Baroudi, J. J. and Igbaria, M. 1994, 'An Examination of Gender Effects on Career Success of Information Systems Employees', *Journal of Management Information Systems*, vol. 11, no. 3, pp. 181-98.

Broido, E. M. and Manning, K. 2002, 'Philosophical Foundations and Current Theoretical Perspectives in Qualitative Research', *Journal of College Student Development*, vol. 43, no. 4, pp. 434-45.

Connell, J., Lynch, C. and Waring, P. 2001, 'Constraints, Compromises and Choice: Comparing Three Qualitative Research Studies', *The Qualitative Report*, vol. 6, no. 4.

Dallimore, E. J. 2000, 'A Feminist Response to Issues of Validity in Research, *Women's Studies in Communications*, vol. 23, no. 2, pp. 157-81.

Frenkel, K. A. 1991, 'Women and Computing', *Communications of the ACM*, vol. 33, no. 11, pp. 34-7.

Grimshaw, J. 1986, *Philosophy and Feminist Thinking*, University of Minnesota, Minneapolis.

Holmes, M. C. 1998, 'Comparison of Gender Differences Among Information Systems Professionals: A Cultural Perspective', *The Journal of Computer Information Systems*, vol. 38, no. 4, pp. 78-86.

Humphries, B. 1997, 'From Critical Thought to Emancipatory Action: Contradictory Research Goals', *Sociological Research Online*, vol. 2, no. 1.

Igbaria, M. and Baroudi, J. J. 1995, 'The Impact of Job Performance Evaluations on Career Advancement', *MIS Quarterly*, vol. 19, no. 1, pp. 107-25.

Khazanchi, D. 1995, 'Unethical Behavior in Information Systems: The Gender Factor', *Journal of Business Ethics,* vol. 14, no.9, pp. 741-52.

Khazanchi, D. and Munkvold, B. D. 2000, 'Is Information Systems a Science? An Inquiry into the Nature of the Information Systems Discipline', *The Data Base for Advances in Information Systems*, vol. 31, no. 3, pp. 24-42.

Marble, R. P. 2000, 'Operationalising the Implementation Puzzle: An Argument for Eclecticism in Research and in Practice', *European Journal of Information Systems*, vol. 9, pp. 132-47.

Maxwell. J. A. 1996, *Qualitative Research Design: An Interactive Approach*, Sage, Thousand Oaks, CA.

Millen, D. 1997, 'Some Methodological and Epistemological Issues Raised by Doing Feminist Research on Non-Feminist Women', *Sociological Research Online*, vol. 2, no. 3.

Nielsen, S. H., von Hellens, L. A. and Wong, S. 2000, 'The Game of Social Constructs', *Proceedings of the International Conference on Information Systems*, Brisbane, Australia.

Neuman, W. L. 2000, *Social Research Methods Qualitative and Quantitative Approaches*, Allyn and Bacon, Boston, MA.

O'Donovan, B. and Roode, D. 2002, 'A Framework for Understanding the Emerging Discipline of Information Systems', *Information Technology and People*, vol. 15, no.1, pp. 26-41.

O'Neill, L. and E. Walker, E. 2001, 'Women in the Information Technology Industry: A Western Australian View', *Proceedings of the 9th European Conference on Information Systems*, Bled, Slovenia.

Panteli, A., Stack, J., Atkinson, M. and Ramsay, H. 1999, 'The Status of Women in the UK IT Industry: An Empirical Study', *European Journal of Information Systems*, vol. 8, pp. 170-82.

Pringle, R., Nielsen, S. H., von Hellens, L., Greenhill, A. and Parfitt, L.2000, 'Net Gains Success Strategies of Professional Women in IT', *Proceedings of the 7th International Conference on Women, Work and Computerization*, Vancouver, British Columbia.

Reinharz, S. 1992, *Feminist Methods in Social Research*, Oakford University Press, New York, NY.

Reynolds, G. 1993, 'Gender, Emotion and a Research Dilemma', in Kennedy, M., Lubelska, C. and V. Walsh, V. (eds.) *Making Connections Women's Studies, Women's Movements, Women's Lives*, Taylor & Francis, London/Washington DC.

Robinson, B. and Richardson, H. 1999, 'The Historical Meaning of Crisis in Information Systems: A Vygotskyan Analysis', *Proceedings of the Critical Management Conference*, Manchester, UK.

Stanley, L. 1990, *Feminist Praxis: Research, Theory and Epistemology in Feminist Sociology*, Routledge, London, UK.

The Women in Science, Engineering and Technology Advisory Group1995, *Women in Science, Engineering and Technology – A Discussion Paper*.

Trauth, E. M. 2002, 'Odd Girl Out: An Individual Differences Perspective on Women in the IT Profession', *Information Technology & People*, vol. 15, no. 2, pp. 98-118.

Trauth, E., Nielsen, S. and von Hellens, L. 2003, 'Explaining the IT Gender Gap: Australian Stories for the New Millennium', *Journal of Research and Practice in Information Technology*, vol. 35, no. 1, pp. 7-19.

Truman, G. E. and Baroudi, J. J. 1994, 'Gender Differences in the Information Systems Managerial Ranks: An Assessment of Potential Discriminatory Practices', *MIS Quarterly*, vol. 18, no. 2, pp. 129-41.

von Hellens, L. A., Nielsen, S. H. and Trauth, E. 2001, 'Breaking and Entering the Male Domain; Women in the IT Industry', *Proceedings of the ACM SIGPR Conference*, San Diego, CA.

Webb, P. 2002, *Gender Imbalance in IS/IT Workplaces a Tasmanian Perspective,* Honours Thesis, University of Tasmania, Australia.

Whittemore, R., Chase, S. K. and Mandle, C. L. 2001, 'Validity in Qualitative Research', *Qualitative Health Research*, vol. 11, no.4, pp. 522-37.

Reflection in self-organised systems – *Maureen Lynch and Carmen Johan*

Alvesson, M. and Skolberg, K. 2000, *Reflexive Methodology*, Sage, London, UK.

Argyris, C. and Schon, D. 1996, *Organizational Learning*, 2nd ed., Addison-Wesley, Reading, MA.

Ayas, K. and Zeniuk, N. 2001, 'Project-based Learning: Building Communities of Reflective Practitioners', Management Learning, vol. 32, no. 1, pp. 61-76.

Brockbank, A. and McGill, I. 1998, *Facilitating Reflective Learning in Higher Education*, Open University Press, Buckingham, UK.

Camazine, S., Deneubourg, J., Franks, N., Sneyd, J., Theraulaz, G. and Bonabeau, E. 2001, *Self-Organization in Biological Systems*, Princeton University Press, Oxford, UK.

Checkland, P. 1981, *Systems Thinking, Systems Practice*, Wiley, London, UK.

Comfort, L. 1994, 'Self-Organization in Complex Systems', *Journal of Public Administration Research & Theory*, vol. 4, no. 3. pp. 393-410.

Courtney, J. F., Croasdell, D. T. and Paradice, D. B. 1998, 'Inquiring Organizations', Australian Journal of Information Systems, vol. 6, no. 1, pp. 3-14.

Dewey, J. 1997, *How We Think*, Dover Publications, New York, NY.

Dooley, J. 1999, 'Problem-Solving as a Double-Loop Learning System', Adaptive Learning Design, http://www.well.com/user/dooley/Problem-solving.pdf, accessed 21 February 2005.

Encyclopedia/Forum, I. E. 2004, 'Chris Argyris: Theories of Action, Double-Loop Learning and Organizational Learning'.

Flood, R. and Romm, N. 1996, *Diversity Management: Triple Loop Learning*, John Wiley & Sons, Chichester, UK.

Fortune, J. and Peters, G. 1997, *Learning from Failure*, John Wiley & Sons, Chichester, UK.

Franks, N. and Deneubourg, J. L. 1997, 'Self-Organising Nest Constructions in Ants: Individual Worker Behaviour and the Nest's Dynamics', *Animal Behaviour*, vol. 54, pp.779-96.

Fuchs, C. 2003, 'Co-Operation and Self-Organization', *tripleC e-Journal for Cognition, Communication and Co-operation*, vol. 1, no. 1, pp. 1-52.

Georgiou, I., 2001, 'The Ontological Status of Critique', Systemic Practice and Action Research, vol. 14, no. 4, pp. 407-49.

Graeff, T. 1997, 'Bringing Reflective Learning to the Marketing Research Course: A Co-operative Learning Project Using Intergroup Critique', Journal of Marketing Education, vol. 19, pp. 53-64.

Holland, O. and Melhuish, C. 1999, 'Stigmergy, Self-Organization, and Sorting in Collective Robotics', *Artificial Life*, vol. 5, no. 2, pp. 173-202.

Hudson, C. 2000, 'From Social Darwinism to Self-Organization: Implications for Social Change Theory', *Social Service Review*, vol. 74, no. 4, pp.533-59.

Humphrey, J. 2000, 'Self-organization and Trade Union Democracy', *The Sociological Review*, vol. 329, no. 330, pp. 262-82.

Kauffman, S. 1993, *The Origins of Order: Self-Organization and Selection in Evolution*, Oxford University Press, Oxford, UK.

Kauffman, S. 1995, *At Home with the Universe: The Search for Laws of Self-Organization and Complexity*, Oxford University Press, Oxford, UK.

Kolb, D. 1984, *Experiential Learning: Experience as the Source of Learning and Development*, Prentice-Hall, Englewood Cliffs, NJ.

Mathiassen, L. 2002, 'Reflective Systems Development', Reflective Systems Development, http://www.cs.auc.dk/~larsm/rsd.html , accessed 31 December 2002.

Mathiassen, L. and Purao, S. 2002, 'Educating Reflective Systems Developers', Information Systems Journal, vol. 12, pp. 81-102.

Merriam-Webster Online http://www.m-w.com/cgi-bin/dictionary, accessed 21 February 2005.

Mingers, J. 1997, 'Systems Typologies in the Light of Autopoeisis: A Reconceptualisation of Boulding's Hierarchy, and a Typology of Self-Referential Systems', *System Research and Behavioral Science*, vol. 14, pp. 303-13.

Molleman, E. 1998, 'Variety and the Requisite of Self-Organization', *International Journal of Organizational Analysis*, vol. 6, no. 2, pp. 109-31.

Morris, M. W. and Moore, P. C. 2000, 'The Lessons We (Don't) Learn: Counterfactual Thinking and Organisational Accountability After a Close Call', Administrative Science Quarterly, vol. 45, pp. 737-65.

Popper, K. 1969, *Conjectures and Refutations*, Routledge & Kegan Paul, London, UK.

Prigogine, I. 1996, *The End of Certainty: Time, Chaos, and the New Laws of Nature*, Free Press, New York, NY.

Raelin, J. 2001, 'Public Reflection as the Basis of Learning', *Management Learning*, vol. 32, no. 1, pp. 11-30.

Rycroft, R. and Kash, D. 2004, 'Self-organizing Innovation Networks: Implications for Globalization, *Technovation*, vol 24, no. 3, pp. 187-97.

Schon, D. 1995, *The Reflective Practitioner*, Ashgate Publishing Limited, Avebury, UK.

Seibert, K. 1999, 'Reflection-in-Action: Tools for Cultivating On-the-job Learning Conditions', *Organizational Dynamics*, vol. 27, no. 3, pp. 54-65.

Vanderstraeten, R. 2000, 'Autopoiesis and Socialization: On Luhmann's reconceptualisation of Communication and Socialization', *British Journal of Sociology,* vol. 51, no. 3, pp. 581-98.

Yates, E., Garfinkel, A. and Walter, D. 1987, *Self-Organizing Systems, The Emergence of Order*, Plenum Press, New York, NY.

Strategic knowledge sharing: a small-worlds perspective – *Mike Metcalfe*

Argyris, C. and Schon, D. A. 1978, Theory In Practice, Jossey-Bass, San Francisco, CA.

Buchanan, M. 2002, Nexus: Small Worlds, W. W. Norton, New York, NY.

Camazine, S., Deneubourg, J.-L., Franks, N. R., Sneyd, J., Theraulaz, G. and Bonabeau, E. 2001, Self-Organization in Biological Systems, Princeton University Press, Princeton, NJ.

Checkland, P. 2000, 'Soft Systems Methodology: A Thirty Year Retrospective'. Systems Research and Behavioural Science, vol 17, no.1, pp. S11-S58.

Comfort L. K. 1994, 'Self-Organization In Complex Systems', Journal of Public Administration Research and Theory, vol. 4, no. 3, pp. 393-410.

Cross, R., Borgatti, S. P. and Parker, A. 2002, 'Making Invisible Work Visible: Using Social Network Analysis to Support Strategic Collaboration', California Management Review, vol. 44, no. 2, pp. 25-46.

Durrington, V. A., Repman, J. and Valente, T. W. 2000, 'Using Social Network Analysis to Examine the Time of Adoption of Computer-Related Services Among University Faculty', Journal of Research on Computing in Education, vol. 33, no. 1, pp. 16-27.

Georges, A. and Romme, L. 1995, 'Self-organizing Processes in Top Management Teams: A Boolean Comparative Approach', Journal of Business Research, vol. 34, no. 1, pp. 11-34.

Hansen, M. T. 1999, 'The Search-Transfer Problem: The Role Of Weak Ties In Sharing Knowledge Across Organization Subunits', Administrative Science Quarterly, vol. 44, no. 1, pp. 82-111.

Hare, A. P. 1976, Handbook of Small Group Research, Free Press, New York, NY.

Keen, P. 1999, *'Middle-Out Ideas'*, http://pwaa002790.psiweb.com/cworld30.htm , accessed July 2004.

Killworth, P. D. and Bernard, H. R. 1979, 'A Pseudomodel Of The Small World Problem'. Social Forces, vol. 58, no. 2, pp. 477-505.

Matsuo, Y., Ohsawa, Y. and Ishizuka, M. 2001, 'A Document As A Small World', http://www.carc.aist.go.jp/~y.matsuo/homepage/papers/sci01.pdf, accessed 21 February 2005.

Milgram, S. 1967, 'The Small World Problem', *Psychology Today*, vol. 67, no. 1, pp. 60-7.

Mingers, J. 1997, 'Systems Typologies in the Light of Autopoiesis: A Reconceptualization of Boulding's Hierarchy, and a Typology of Self-Referential Systems', Systems Research and Behavioral Science, vol. 14, no. 5, pp. 303-13.

Mizruchi, M. S. 1994, 'Social Network Analysis: Recent Achievements and Current Controversies', Acta Sociologica, vol. 37, no. 4, pp. 329-43.

Reagans, R. and McEvily, B. 2003, 'Network Structure and Knowledge Transfer', Administrative Science Quarterly, vol. 48, no. 2, pp. 240-67.

Richardson, K. A. and Lissack, M. R. 2001, 'On the Status of Boundaries Both Natural and Organizational: A Complex Systems Perspective', Emergence, vol. 3, no. 4, pp. 32-49.

Rittel, H. W. J. and Webber, M. M. 1973, 'Dilemmas in a General Theory of Planning', Policy Sciences, vol. 4, pp. 155-69.

Roubelat, F. 2000, 'Scenario Planning as a Networking Process', Technological Forecasting and Social Change, vol. 65, pp. 99-112.

Scott, J. 1996, 'Software Review: A Toolkit for Social Network Analysis', Acta Sociologica, vol. 39, pp. 211-16.

Ulrich, W. 2002, 'Critical Systems Heuristics', in Daellenbach, H. G. and Flood, R. L. (eds.) The Informed Student Guide to Management Science, Thomson Learning, London, UK, pp. 72-3.

Watts, D. J. 1999, 'Networds, Dynamcs and the Small World Phenomenon', American Journal of Sociology, vol. 105, no. 2, pp. 493-527.

Wilson, P. 1983, Second Hand Knowledge, Greenwood Press, Westpost, CN.

A unified open systems model for explaining organizational change – *Doy Sundarasaradula and Helen Hasan*

Allen, P. M. 1981, 'The Evolutionary Paradigm of Dissipative Structures', in Jantsch, E. (ed.) *The Evolutionary Vision: Toward a Unifying Paradigm of Physical, Biological, and Sociocultural Evolution*, Westview Press, Boulder, CO.

Allen, P. M., and Sanglier, M. 1978, 'Dynamic Model of Urban Growth', *Journal of Social and Biological Structures*, vol. 1, pp. 265-80.

_____ 1979a, 'A Dynamic Model of Growth in a Central Place System', *Geographical Analysis*, vol. 11, no. 3, pp. 256-72.

_____ 1979b, 'A Dynamic Model of Urban Growth – II.' *Journal of Social and Biological Structures*, 2: 269-278.

_____ 1981 'Urban Evolution, Self-organization, and Decision-making', *Environment and Planning*, vol. 13, pp. 167-83.

Artigiani, R. 1987a, 'Organizing the Nation: Revolution and the Modern State', *European Journal of Operational Research*, vol. 30, pp. 208-11.

_____ 1987b, 'Revolution and Evolution: Applying Prigogine's Dissipative Structure Model', *Journal of Social and Biological Structures*, vol. 10, pp. 249-64.

Ayres, R. U. 1994, *Information, Entropy, and Progress: A New Evolutionary Paradigm*, American Institute of Physics, NY.

Beetham, D. 1996, *Bureaucracy*, 2nd ed., Open University Press, Buckingham, UK.

Bertalanffy, L. V. 1950, 'The Theory of Open Systems in Physics and Biology', *Science*, vol. 111, pp. 23-9.

_____ 1973, *General System Theory*, George Braziller, NY.

Bertschek, I., and Kaiser, U. 2004, 'Productivity Effects of Organizational Change: Microeconometric Evidence', *Management Science*, vol. 50, no. 3, pp. 394-405.

Boulding, K. E. 1956, 'General System Theory – The Skeleton of Science', in Schoderbek, P. P. (ed.) 1967, *Management Systems*, John Wiley & Sons, New York, NY.

Brown, R. K. 1992, *Understanding Industrial Organisations: Theoretical Perspectives in Industrial Sociology*, Routledge, London, UK.

Byeon, J. H. 1999, 'Non-Equilibrium Thermodynamic Approach to the Change in Political Systems', *Systems Research and Behavioral Science*, vol. 16, pp. 283-91.

Cardon, I. A. S., Schindler, A., Yates, F., and Marsh, D. 1972, *Progress Toward the Application of Systems Science Concepts to Biology*, Army Research Office, Arlington, VA.

Cavaleri, S. and Obloj, K. 1993, *Management Systems: A Global Perspective*. Wadsworth Publishing, Belmont, CA.

Cengel, Y. A. and Boles, M. A. 2002, *Thermodynamics: An Engineering Approach*, 4th ed, McGraw-Hill, New York, NY.

Chase, R. B. and Aquilano, N. J. 1989, *Production and Operations Management: A Life Cycle Approach*, 5th ed., Irwin, Homewood, IL.

Davenport, T. H. 1993, *Process Innovation: Reengineering Work Through Information Technology*, Harvard Business School Press, Boston, MA.

Du Gay, P. 2000, *In Praise of Bureaucracy: Weber, Organization, Ethics*, Sage, Thousand Oaks, CA.

Emery, F. E. and Trist, E. L. 1971, 'The Causal Texture of Organizational Environments', in Maurer, J. G. (ed.) *Readings in Organization Theory: Open-System Approaches*, Random House, New York, NY.

Flood, R. L. and Carson, E. R. 1993, *Dealing with Complexity: An Introduction to the Theory and Application of Systems Science*, 2nd ed, Plenum Press, New York, NY.

Gaither, N. and Frazier, G. 1999, *Production and Operation Management*, 8th ed., International Thomson Publishing, Cincinnati, OH.

Gasco, M. 2003, 'New Technologies and Institutional Change in Public Administration', *Social Science Computer Review*, vol. 21, no. 1, pp. 6-15.

Gemmill, G. and Smith, C. 1985, 'A Dissipative Structure Model of Organization Transformation', *Human Relations*, vol. 38, no. 8, pp. 751-66.

Gersick, C. 1988, 'Time and Transition in Work Teams', *Academy of Management Journal*, vol. 31, pp. 9-41.

_____ 1991, 'Revolutionary Change Theories: A Multilevel Exploration of The Punctuated Equilibrium Paradigm', *Academy of Management Review*, vol. 16, no. 1, pp. 10-36.

Gould, S. and Eldredge, N. 1977, 'Punctuated Equilibria: The Tempo and Mode of Evolution Reconsidered', *Paleobiology*, vol. 3, pp. 115-51.

Greene, J. H. 1997, *Production & Inventory Control Handbook*, 3rd ed, McGraw-Hill, New York, NY.

Greiner, L. E. 1972, 'Evolution and Revolution as Organizations Grow', *Harvard Business Review*, vol. 50, pp. 37-46.

Grey, W. 1974, 'Current Issues in General Systems Theory and Psychiatry', *General Systems*, vol. 19, pp. 97-100.

Guastello, S. J. 1995, *Chaos, Catastrophe, and Human Affairs: Applications of Nonlinear Dynamics to Work, Organizations, and Social Evolutions*, Lawrence Erlbaum Associates, Mahwah, NJ.

_____ 2002, *Managing Emergent Phenomena: Nonlinear Dynamics in Work Organizations*, Lawrence Erlbaum Associates, Mahwah, NJ.

Haken, H. 1980, *Synergetics: A Workshop*, Springer-Verlag, New York, NY.

_____ 1984, 'Can Synergetics Be of Use to Management Theory?', in Ulrich, H. and Probst, G. J. B. (eds) *Self-Organization and Management of Social Systems: Insights, Promises, and Questions*, Springer-Verlag, Berlin, Heidelberg.

_____ 1987, 'Synergetics: An Approach to Self-Organization.' in Yates, F. E. (ed.) *Self-Organizing Systems: The Emergence of Order*, Plenum Press, New York, NY.

Hammer, M. 1990, 'Reengineering Work: Don't Automate, Obliterate', *Harvard Business Review*, vol. 90, no. 4, pp. 104-12.

Hammer, M. and Champy, J. 1993, *Reengineering the Corporation: A Manifesto for Business Revolution*, HarperCollins, New York, NY.

Handy, C. 1995, *Gods of Management: The Changing Work of Organizations*, 4th ed., Oxford University Press, New York, NY.

_____ 1999, *Understanding Organizations*, 4th ed., Penguin Global.

Harvey, D. L. and Reed, M. 1997, 'Social Science as the Study of Complex Systems', in Kiel, L. D. and Elliott, E. (eds), *Chaos Theory in the Social Sciences: Foundations and Applications*, The University of Michigan Press, Ann Arbor, MI.

Hoffman, A. 1989, *Arguments on Evolution: A Paleontologist's Perspective*, Oxford University Press, New York, NY.

Hofstede, G. H. 1997, *Cultures and Organizations*, McGraw-Hill, New York, NY.

Jantsch, E. 1980, *The Self-Organizing Universe: Scientific and Human Implications of the Emerging Paradigm of Evolution*, Pergamon, Oxford, UK.

Johnson, J. D. 1996, *Information Seeking: An Organizational Dilemma*, Quorum, Westport, CT.

Kiel, L. D. 1991, 'Lessons from the Nonlinear Paradigm: Applications of the Theory of Dissipative Structures in Social Sciences', *Social Science Quarterly*, vol. 72, no. 3, pp. 431-42.

Kramer, N. J. T. A. and De Smith, J. 1977, *Systems Thinking*, Martinus Nijhoff Social Science Division, Leiden, The Netherlands.

Leifer, R. 1989, 'Understanding Organizational Transformation Using a Dissipative Structure Model', *Human Relations*, vol. 42, no. 10, pp. 899-916.

Levy, A. 1986, 'Second Order Planned Change: Definition and Conceptualization', *Organization Dynamics*, vol. 15, no. 1, pp. 5-20.

Levy, A. and Merry, U. 1986, *Organizational Transformation*, Praeger, New York, NY.

Mayr, E. 1942, *Systematics and The Origin of Species*, Columbia University Press, New York, NY.

_____ 1982, *The Growth of Biological Thought: Diversity, Evolution, and Inheritance*, Harvard University Press, Cambridge, MA.

Macintosh, R. and Maclean, D. 1999, 'Conditioned Emergence: A Dissipative Structures Approach to Transformation', *Strategic Management Journal*, vol. 20, pp. 297-316.

Miller, D. and Friesen, P. H. 1984, *Organizations: A Quantum View*, Prentice-Hall, Englewood Cliff, NJ.

Miller, J. G. 1978, *Living Systems*, McGraw-Hill, New York, NY.

Morgan, G. 1997, *Images of Organization*, New ed., Sage, Thousand Oaks, CA.

Neumann, Jr., F. X. 1997, 'Organizational Structures to Match the New Information-Rich Environments: Lessons From the Study of Chaos', *Public Productivity & Management Review*, vol. 21, no. 1, pp. 86-100.

Nicolis, G. 1979, 'Conclusions and Perspectives', in Pacault, A. and Vidal, C. (eds) *Synergetics: Far from Equilibrium*, Springer-Verlag, Berlin.

Nicolis, G. and Prigogine, I. 1977, *Self-Organization in Nonequilibrium Systems: From Dissipative Structures to Order through Fluctuation*, John Wiley & Sons, New York, NY.

_____ 1989, *Exploring Complexity: An Introduction*, W. H. Freeman and Company, New York, NY.

Ohmae, K. 1991, *The Borderless World: Power and Strategy in The Interlinked Economy*, HarperCollins, London, UK.

Peters, T. J. and Waterman Jr., R. H. 1982, *In Search of Excellence: Lessons from America's Best-Run Companies*, Harper & Row, New York, NY.

Pfeffer, J. 1981, *Power in Organizations*, Pitman Publishing, Marshfield, MA.

Prigogine, I. 1976, 'Order Through Fluctuation: Self-Organization and Social Systems', in Jantsch, E. and Waddington, C. H. (eds) *Evolution and Consciousness: Human Systems in Transition*, Addison-Wesley, Reading, MA.

Prigogine, I. and Stengers, I. 1984, *Order out of Chaos: Man's Dialogue with Nature*, Bantam Books, New York, NY.

Robbins, S. P. 1990, *Organization Theory: Structure, Design, and Applications*, 3rd ed., Prentice-Hall, Englewood Cliffs, NJ.

Rosenberg, N. 1986, *Inside The Black Box: Technology and Economics*, Cambridge University Press, Cambridge, UK.

Scott, W. R. 1998, *Organizations: Rational, Natural, and Open Systems*, 4th ed., Prentice-Hall, Upper Saddle River, NJ.

Skyttner, L. 2001, *General Systems Theory: Ideas & Applications*, World Scientific Publishing, Singapore.

Smith, C. and Gemmill, G. 1991, 'Change in Small Group: A Dissipative Structure Perspective', *Human Relations*, vol. 44, no. 7, pp. 697-716.

Svyantek, D. J. and DeShon, R. P. 1993, 'Organizational Attractors: A Chaos Theory Explanation of Why Cultural Change Efforts Often Fail', *Public Administration Quarterly*, vol. 17, no. 3, pp. 339-55.

Terreberry, S. 1971, 'The Evolution of Organizational Environments', in Maurer, J. G. (ed.) *Readings in Organization Theory: Open-System Approaches*, Random House, New York, NY.

Tushman, M. L. and Romaneli, E. 1985, 'Organizational Evolution: A Metamorphosis Model of Convergence and Reorientation', *Research in Organizational behavior*, vol. 7, pp. 171-222.

_____ 1994, 'Organizational Transformation as Punctuated Equilibrium: An Empirical Test', *Academy of Management Journal*, vol. 37, no. 5, pp. 1141-66.

Tushman, M. L. and O'Reilly III, C. A. 2002, *Winning Through Innovation: A Practical Guide to Leading Organizational Change and Renewal*, Harvard Business School Press, Boston, MA.

Van Gigch, J. P. 1978, *Applied General Systems Theory*, 2nd ed., Harper & Row, New York, NY.

_____ 1991, *System Design, Modeling, and Metamodeling*, Plenum Press, New York, NY.

Zuboff, S. 1988, *In the Age of the Smart Machine: The Future of Work and Power*, Basic Books, New York, NY.

Research as an information systems domain – *Craig McDonald*

Australian Partnership for Advanced Computing (APAC) http://www.apac.edu.au/

AusGrid http://www.ausgrid.org/ , 21 February 2005.

Batterham, R. 2003, *E-Science: A Frontier Technology For Achieving The National Research Priorities* http://www.glassearth.com/seegrid_pdf/seegrid_batterham.pdf , 21 February 2005

Checkland, P. and Scholes, J. 1990, *Soft Systems Methodology in Action*, John Wiley & Sons, New York, NY.

Cram, L. 2003, *A Roadmap for e-Research* http://conferences.alia.org.au/alia2002/papers/cram_files/v3_document.htm , accessed 21 February 2005.

DSpace Institutional Repository System http://www.dspace.org/ , accessed 21 February 2005

Gibbons, M., Limoges, C., Nowotny, H., Schwartzman, S., Scott, P., and Trow, M. 1995, *The New Production of Knowledge*, Sage, London, UK.

Horton, J. W. 2003, *Changing Research Practices in the Digital Information and Communication Environment* http://www.dest.gov.au/highered/respubs/changing_res_prac/intro.pdf , 21 February 2005.

McDonald, C. 2003, 'eScience and ePractice: Reflections on a KMS development', *Proceedings of the Australian Conference on Knowledge Management and Intelligent Decision Support (ACKMIDS)*, Melbourne, December 2003.

Moody, D. 2000, 'Building Links Between IS Research and Professional Practice: Improving the Relevance and Impact of IS Research' *Proceedings of the 21st International Conference on Information Systems (ICIS)*, pp. 351-60.

National E-Science Center http://www.nesc.ac.uk/ , 21 February 2005.

Rayward, W. B. 1991, 'The Case of Paul Otlet, Pioneer of Information Science, Internationalist, Visionary: Reflections on Biography', *Journal of Librarianship and Information Science*, vol. 23, pp. 135-45.

Ronayne, J. 1997, *Research and the new universities: towards mode 2*, ASTE Focus #98, http://www.atse.org.au/index.php?sectionid=379, accessed 21 February 2005.

UK e-Science Grid http://www.escience-grid.org.uk/docs/pilots/epsrc/mygrid.htm , accessed 30 April 2004.

A procedural model for ontological analyses – *Michael Rosemann, Peter Green and Marta Indulska*

Bansler, J. P. and Bodker, K. 1993, 'A Reappraisal of Structured Analysis: Design in an Organisational Context', *ACM Transactions on Information Systems*, vol. 11, no. 2, pp. 165-93.

Burton-Jones, A. and Meso, P. 2002, 'How Good Are These UML Diagrams?: An Empirical Test of the Wand and Weber Good Decomposition Model', *Proceedings of the 23rd International Conference on Information Systems*, Barcelona, Spain, pp. 15-18.

Gorla, N., Pu, H-C. and Rom, W. O. 1995, 'Evaluation of Process Tools in Systems Analysis', *Information and Software Technology*, vol. 37, no. 2, pp. 119-26.

Green, P. F. 1997, 'Use of Information Systems Analysis and Design (ISAD) Grammars in Combination in Upper CASE Tools – An Ontological Evaluation', *Proceedings of the 2nd CaiSE/IFIP8.1 International Workshop on the Evaluation of Modeling Methods in Systems Analysis and Design*, Barcelona, Spain, pp. 1-12.

Green, P. F. and Rosemann, M. 2000, 'Integrated Process Modelling: An Ontological Evaluation', *Information Systems*, vol. 25, no. 2, pp. 73-87.

_____ 2002, 'Perceived Ontological Weaknesses of Process Modeling Techniques: Further Evidence', *Proceedings of the 10th European Conference on Information Systems*, Gdansk, Poland, pp. 312-21.

Green, P. F., Rosemann, M., Indulska, M. et al. 2003, 'Candidate Interoperability Standards: An Ontological Overlap Analysis', Working Paper, The University of Queensland, Australia.

Gruninger, M. and Lee, J. 2002, 'Ontology: Applications and Design', *Communications of the ACM*, vol. 45, no. 2, pp. 39-41.

Guarino, N. and Welty, C. 2002, 'Evaluating Ontological Decisions with OntoClean', *Communications of the ACM*, vol. 45, no. 2, pp. 61-5.

Karam, G. M. and Casselman, R. S. 1993, 'A Cataloging Framework For Software Development Methods', *IEEE Computer*, February, pp. 34-46.

Olle, T. W., J. Hagelstein, I. G. Macdonald, et al. 1991, *Information Systems Methodologies: A Framework for Understanding*, Addison-Wesley, Wokingham, UK.

Opdahl, A. L. and Henderson-Sellers, B. 2001, 'Grounding the OML Metamodel in Ontology', *Journal of Systems and Software*, vol. 57, no. 2, pp. 119-43.

Opdahl, A. L. and Henderson-Sellers, B. 2002, 'Ontological Evaluation of the UML using the Bunge-Wand-Weber Model', *Software and Systems Modeling*, vol. 1, no. 1, pp. 43-67.

Parsons, J. and Wand, W. 1997, 'Using Objects in Systems Analysis', *Communications of the ACM*, vol. 40, no. 12, pp. 104-10.

Rosemann, M. and Green, P. 2002, 'Developing a Meta Model for the Bunge-Wand-Weber Ontological Constructs', *Information Systems*, vol. 27, no. 2, pp. 75-91.

Scheer, A.-W. 2000, *ARIS – Business Process Modeling*, Springer, Heidelberg, Berlin.

Shanks, G., Tansley, E., Nuredini, J. et al. 2002, 'Representing Part-Whole Relationships in Conceptual Modelling: An Empirical Evaluation', *Proceedings of the 23rd International Conference on Information Systems*, Barcelona, Spain.

van der Aalst, W. M. P., Dumas, M., ter Hofstede, A. H. M. and Wohed, P. 2002, 'Pattern Based Analysis of BPML (and WSCI)', http://xml.coverpages.org/Aalst-BPML.pdf , accessed 21 February 2005, Queensland University of Technology, Brisbane, Australia.

Wand, Y. and Weber, R. 1989, 'An Ontological Evaluation of Systems Analysis and Design Methods', in. Falkenberg, E. D. and Lindgreen, P. (eds), *Information System Concepts: An In-depth Analysis*, North-Holland, Amsterdam, The Netherlands pp. 79-107.

―――― 1990, 'Mario Bunge's Ontology as a Formal Foundation for Information Systems Concepts', in P. Weingartner and Dorn. G. J. W. (eds), *Studies on Mario Bunge's Treatise*, Rodopi, Atlanta, GA, pp. 123-49.

―――― 1990, 'An Ontological Model of an Information System', *IEEE Transactions on Software Engineering*, vol. 16, no. 11, pp. 1281-91.

―――― 1993, 'On the Ontological Expressiveness of Information Systems Analysis and Design Grammars', *Journal of Information Systems*, vol. 3, no. 4, pp. 217-37.

―――― 1995, 'On the Deep Structure of Information Systems', *Information Systems Journal*, vol. 5, pp. 203-23.

Weber, R. 1997, *Ontological Foundations of Information Systems*, Melbourne, Vic., Coopers & Lybrand and the Accounting Association of Australia and New Zealand.

Weber, R. and Zhang, Y. 1996, 'An Analytical Evaluation of NIAM's Grammar for Conceptual Schema Diagrams', *Information Systems Journal*, vol. 6, vol. 2, pp. 147-70.

Wohed, P., van der Aalst, W. M. P., Dumas, M. and ter Hofstede, A. H. M. 2002, 'Pattern Based Analysis of BPEL4WS', *Technical Report FIT-TR-2002-04*, Queensland University of Technology, Brisbane, Australia.

Lessons learned from manual systems: designing information systems based on the situational theory – *Simon K. Milton, Robert B. Johnston and Reeva M. Lederman*

Agre, P. and Chapman, D. 1987, 'Pengi: An Implementation of a Theory of Agency', Proceedings of the Sixth National Conference on Artificial Intelligence, Menlo Park, CA.

Agre, P. and Horswill, I. 1992, 'Cultural Support for Improvisation', Proceedings of the Tenth National Conference on Artificial Intelligence, Menlo Park, CA.

Agre, P. and Horswill, I. 1997, 'Lifeworld Analysis', Journal of Artificial Intelligence Research, vol. 6, pp. 111–45.

Baskerville, R. L. and Wood-Harper, A. T. 1996, 'A Critical Perspective on Action Research as a Method in Information Systems Research', Journal of Information Technology, vol. 11, no. 3, pp. 235-46.

Brooks, R. A. 1986, 'A Robust Layered Control System for a Mobile Robot', IEEE Journal of Robotics and Automation, vol. 2, no. 1, pp. 14-23.

Brooks, R. A. 1991, 'Intelligence Without Representation', Artificial Intelligence, vol. 47, pp. 139-59.

Clancey, W. J. 1997, Situated Cognition: On Human Knowledge and Computer Representations, Cambridge University Press, Cambridge, UK.

Dreyfus, H. L. 1991, Being-In-The-World: A Commentary on Heidegger's Being and Time, Division 1, MIT Press, Cambridge, MA.

Gibson, J. J. 1977, The Ecological Approach to Visual Perception, Houghton Mifflin, Boston, MA.

Hammond, K., Converse, T. and Grass, J. 1995, 'The Stabilisation of Environments', Artifical Intelligence, vol. 72, pp. 305–27.

Hendriks-Jansen, H. 1996, Catching Ourselves in the Act: Situated Activity, Interactive Emergence, Evolution, and Human Thought, MIT Press, Cambridge, MA.

Horswill, I. 1995, 'Analysis of Adaption and Environment', Artifical Intelligence, vol. 73, pp. 1-30.

Johnston, R. B. and Brennan, M. 1996, 'Planning or Organising: The Significance of Theories of Activity for the Management of Operations', OMEGA, International Journal of Management Science, vol. 24, no. 4, pp. 367-84.

Johnston, R. B. and Milton, S. K. 2001, 'The Significance of Intentionality for the Design of Information Systems', Proceedings of the Americas Conference on Information Systems, Boston, MA.

_____ 2002a, 'The Foundational Role for Theories of Agency in Understanding Information Systems Design', Australian Journal of Information Systems, December (Special Issue), pp. 40-9.

_____ 2002b, 'The Foundational Role of Theories of Agency in Understanding Information Systems Design', in Gregor, S. and Hart, D. (eds) Information Systems Foundations Workshop: Building the Theoretical Base, The Australian National University, Canberra, Australia, pp. 165-79.

Lau, F. 1999, 'Toward a Framework for Action Research in Information Systems', Information Technology and People, vol. 12, no. 2, pp. 148-75.

Lave, J. 1988, Cognition in Practice: Mind, Mathematics and Culture in Everyday Life, Cambridge University Press, New York, NY.

Lederman, R., Johnston, R. B. and Milton, S. K. 2003, 'The Significance Of Routines For The Analysis And Design Of Information Systems: A Preliminary Study', Proceedings of the 11th European Conference on Information Systems, Milan, Italy.

Lederman, R., Milton, S. K. and Johnston, R. B. 2004, 'Identifying Theories of Agency in Information Systems', Proceedings of the Americas Conference on Information Systems, New York, (forthcoming).

Mackay, W. E., A.-L. Fayard, Frobert, L. and Mdini, L. 1998, 'Reinventing the Familiar: Exploring and Augmented Reality Design Space for Air Traffic Control', Computer Human Interaction (CHI), Los Angeles, CA.

Schoggen, P. 1989, Behavior Settings : A Revision and Extension of Roger G. Barker's Ecological Psychology. Stanford University Press, Stanford, CA.

Schonberger, R. J. 1987, 'The Kanban System' in Voss, C. A. (ed.) Just-In-Time Manufacture, IFS Ltd., London, UK, pp. 59-71.

Suchman, L. A. 1987, Plans and Situated Action, Cambridge University Press, Cambridge, UK.

Wand, Y., Monarchi, D. E., Parsons, J and Woo, C. 1995, 'Theoretical Foundations for Conceptual Modelling in Information Systems Development', Decision Support Systems, vol. 15, pp. 285–304.

Wight, O. W. 1981, Manufacturing Resource Planning: MRP II, Oliver Wight Publications, Essex Junction, VT.

Womack, J. P., Jones, D. T. and Roos, D. 1990, The Machine That Changed The World, Rawson Associates, New York, NY.

Conversations at the electronic frontier: the information systems business language (ISBL) – *Douglas Hamilton*

Aronoff, M. and Rees-Miller, J. (eds), 2003, *The Handbook of Linguistics*, Blackwell, New York, NY.

Beniger, J. 1986, *The Control Revolution: Technological and Economic Origins of the Information Society*, Harvard University Press, Cambridge, MA.

Bourdieu P. 1991, *Language and Symbolic Power,* Harvard University Press, Cambridge, MA.

Callon, M. 1989, 'Society in the Making: The Study of Technology as a Tool for Sociological Analysis', in Bijker, W., Hughes, T. P., and Pinch, T. (eds) *The Social Construction of Technological Systems*, The MIT Press, Cambridge, MA, pp. 83-103.

Callon, M. and Latour, B. 1981, 'Unscrewing the Big Leviathan: How Actors Macrostructure Reality and How Sociologists Help Them To Do So', in Knorr-Cetina, K. and Cicourel, A. (eds) *Toward an Integration of Micro and Macro Sociologies*, Routledge & Kegan Paul, London, UK, pp. 277-303.

Crevier, D. 1993, *AI: the Tumultuous History of the Search for Artificial Intelligence*, Basic Books, New York, NY.

Crystal, D. 1987, *The Cambridge Encyclopedia of Language,*Cambridge University Press, Cambridge, UK.

Czarniawska, B. 2003, 'This Way to Paradise: On Creole Researchers, Hybrid Disciplines, and Pidgin Writing', *Organization*, vol. 10, no. 3, pp. 430-34.

Dennett, D. 1978, *Brainstorms,*The MIT Press, Cambridge, MA.

Dos Santos, B. L. and Peffers, K. 1995, 'Rewards to Investors in Innovative Information Technology Applications: First Movers and Early Followers in ATMs', *Organization Science*, vol. 6, no. 3, pp. 241-59.

Eco, U. 1997, *The Search for the Perfect Language*,Fontana, London, UK.

Fairclough, N. 1989, *Language and Power*,Longman, London, UK.

Fish, S. E. 1978, 'Normal Circumstances, Literal Language, Direct Speech Acts, The Ordinary, the Everyday, the Obvious, What Goes Without Saying, and Other Special Cases', *Critical Inquiry*, vol. 4, no. 4, pp. 625-44.

Foucault, M. 1972, *The Archaeology of Knowledge*,Tavistock, London, UK.

Gadamer, H. 1989, *Truth and Method*,2nd ed., Sheed & Ward, London, UK.

Gefen, D., Karahanna, E. and Straub, D. W. 2003, 'Trust and TAM in Online Shopping: An Integrated Model', *MIS Quarterly*, vol. 27, no. 1, pp. 51-90.

Gibbs, R.W. 1999, *Intentions in the Experience of Meaning*,Cambridge University Press, Cambridge, UK.

Goffman, E. 1981, *Forms of Talk*,University of Pennsylvania Press, Philadelphia, PN.

Goodhue, D. L., Kirsch, L. J., Quillard, J. A. and Wybo, M. D. 1992, 'Strategic Data Planning: Lessons From The Field', *MIS Quarterly*, vol. 16, no. 1, pp. 11-29.

Hammer, M. 1996, *Beyond Reengineering*, Harper Collins Business, New York, NY.

Herzfeld, M. 1992, *The Social Production of Indifference: Exploring the Symbolic Roots of Western Bureaucracy*,University of Chicago Press, Chicago, IL.

Holm, J. 2000, *An Introduction to Pidgins and Creoles*,Cambridge University Press, Cambridge, UK.

Laverty, K. J. 1996, 'Economic 'Short-Termism': The Debate, the Unresolved Issues, and the Implications for Management Practice and Research', *Academy of Management Review*, vol. 21, no. 3, pp. 825-60.

Lotman, Y. (trans. A. Shukman) 1990, *Universe of the Mind: A Semiotic Theory of Culture*,Indiana University Press, Bloomington, IN.

McKinnon, M. 2004, 'Millions of Mistakes by Centrelink', *The Weekend Australian*, February pp. 14-15.

Mead, G. H. 1962, *Mind, Self and Society*, University of Chicago Press, IL.

Onions, C.T. (ed.) 1973, *The Shorter Oxford English Dictionary (Revised Edition)*, Clarendon Press, Oxford, UK.

Parker, M. M. and Benson, R. J. 1988, *Information Economics: Linking Business Performance to Information Technology*, Prentice-Hall, Englewood Cliffs, NJ.

Pinker, S. 1994, *The Language Instinct: the New Science of Language and Mind*, Allen Lane, London, UK.

Rey, G. 1997, *Contemporary Philosophy of Mind*, Blackwell, Oxford, UK.

Ryan, S. D. 2000, 'Considering Social Subsystem Costs and Benefits in Information Technology Investment Decisions: A View from the Field on Anticipated Payoffs', *Journal of Management Information Systems*, vol. 16, no. 4, pp. 11-40.

Searle, J. 1980, 'Minds, Brains, and Programs', *Behavioral and Brain Sciences*, vol. 3, pp. 417-24.

Somogyi, E. and Galliers, R. 1987, 'From Data Processing to Strategic Information Systems – A Historical Perspective', in Somogyi, E. K. and Galliers, R. D. (eds) *Towards Strategic Information Systems*, Abacus Press, Cambridge, MA, pp. 5-25.

Threlkel, M. S. and Kavan, C. B. 1999, 'From Traditional EDI to Internet-Based EDI: Managerial Considerations', *Journal of Information Technology*, vol. 14, no. 4, pp. 347-60.

Turing, A. M. 1950, 'Computing Machinery and Mind', in Anderson, A. R. (ed.) 1964, *Minds and Machines*, Prentice-Hall, Englewood Cliffs, NJ.

Turner, B. S. (ed.) 1996, *The Blackwell Companion to Social Theory*, Blackwell, New York, NY.

Underwood, J. 2002, 'Stakeholders, Signs and ANT: A Theoretical Basis for IS?' in Gregor, S. and Hart, D. (eds), *Information Systems Foundations: Building the Theoretical Base*, Australian National University, pp. 101-8.

Weill, P. and Broadbent, M. 1998, *Leveraging the New Infrastructure*, Harvard Business School Press, Cambridge, MA.

Weizenbaum, J. 1984, *Computing Power and Human Reason*, Penguin, London, UK.

Willcocks, L. and Lester, S. 1996, 'Beyond the IT Productivity Paradox', *European Management Journal*, vol. 14, no. 3, pp. 279-90.

Yates, J. 1989, *Control through Communication: the Rise of System in American Management*, John Hopkins University Press, Baltimore, MD.

Wolf, E. R. 1999, *Envisioning Power: Ideologies of Dominance and Crisis*, University of California Press, Berkeley, CA.

Wyzalek, J. (ed.) 2000, *Enterprise Systems Integration*, CRC Press, Boca Raton, FL.

www.ingramcontent.com/pod-product-compliance
Lightning Source LLC
Chambersburg PA
CBHW051656210326

41518CB00030B/2595